# Nevada

Deke Castleman
Photography by Jeff Gnass

COMPASS AMERICAN GUIDES
An Imprint of Fodor's Travel Publications

# Nevada

First Edition

Copyright ©2000 Fodor's Travel Publications
Maps Copyright © 2000 Fodor's Travel Publications.
Compass American Guides and colophon are trademarks of Random House, Inc.
Fodor's is a registered trademark of Random House, Inc.

Compass American Guides, Inc., 5332 College Ave., Suite 201, Oakland, CA 94618, USA
ISBN : 0-679-00535-8

Although the Publishers and the Author of this book have made every effort to ensure the information was correct at the time of going to press, the Publishers and the Author do not assume and hereby disclaim any liability to any party for any loss or damage caused by errors, omissions, misleading information, or any potential travel disruption due to labor or financial difficulty, whether such errors or omissions result from negligence, accident, or any other cause.

Editors: Julia Dillon, Jessica Fisher
Creative Director: Christopher Burt
Managing Editor: Kit Duane
Designers: Christopher Burt, Julia Dillon
Cover Design: Siobhan O'Hare

Map Design and Execution: Mark Stroud, Moon
Cartography; illustrated maps by Alex Alford,
Colourfield Cartography
Production House: Twin Age Ltd., Hong Kong
Manufactured in China

10 9 8 7 6 5 4 3 2 1

## PUBLISHER'S ACKNOWLEDGMENTS

All photographs by **Jeff Gnass** unless otherwise noted as follows. **John Brooks, National Park Service** p. 150; **Jean Dixon**, *Reno Gazette-Journal* pp. 169, 190; **Mark Downey** p. 231; **Kerrick James** pp. 13, 31, 38, 40, 41, 42, 43, 46, 47, 49, 50, 51, 52, 53, 54, 56, 57, 64, 66, 74-75, 79, 101; **Pennfield Jensen** p. 252; **Marilyn Newton** p. 230; **Michael Yamashita** p. 81.

Archival images supplied by: **Carson Valley Historical Society, Gardnerville** p. 207; **Central Nevada Museum, Tonopah** p. 160; **Grace Dangberg Foundation, Carson City** p.18; **Library of Congress** p.19, 23, 196, 291, 294; **Nevada Museum of Art, Reno** p. 187; **Nevada Historical Society** pp. 17, 22, 24, 30, 134, 149, 153 (top), 153 (bottom), 157 (top), 157( bottom), 195, 199, 202, 205, 240, 248, 270, 285 (top)288; **Nevada State Museum** p.16; **Northeastern Nevada Museum, Elko** p.251; **Stanley W. Paher Collection, Reno** pp. 142, 161, 198, 234, 254 (bottom); **Underwood Photo Archives, San Francisco** pp. 27, 62, 72, 78, 97, 104, 138, 174, 175, **University of Nevada, Reno Library, Special Collections Dept.** p. 25.

**Michael Kimmelman** piece on Michael Heizer on pp.296-297 © The New York Times Co. Dec. 12, 1999. Reprinted by permission. David Thomson excerpt on p. 33 reprinted by permission from *In Nevada: The Land, the People, God, and Chance,* Alfred A. Knopf, New York 1999.

The publishers would also like to thank **Stanley Paher** for archival research and expert reading; **Ellen Klages** for proofreading; **Jessica Fisher** for the index; **Cheryl Koehler** for editorial assistance; **David Rodrigues** for his piece on Burning Man; **E. Roger Thompson** for his piece on Jarbidge; and **Kevin Mathieu** for source research on Michael Heizer.

*This book is gratefully and lovingly dedicated to my bride, Virginia.*

AUTHOR'S ACKNOWLEDGMENTS
I'd like to thank Vin Suprynowicz, the late Jeanne Suprynowicz, Rick Tompkins, Kathy Harrer, L. Neil Smith, Rick and Chris White, Bill Bonner, and Ian Anderson, and all the small-"l" libertarians in the loop who've helped revive my love of liberty.

As always, I'm much obliged to my editor Julia Dillon, and my old friend and Compass creative director Chris Burt, for taking all the little pieces—messy, over-written, and out of order—and producing a beautiful and useful guidebook. And thanks to Jeff Gnass and Kerrick James for their stunning photography.

I'd also like to give credit where credit is due: to the Silver State itself. For the better part of four decades, I tried to be a New Yorker, Bostonian, Alaskan, and Californian. But I was never really home for good until I became a Nevadan.

# C O N T E N T S

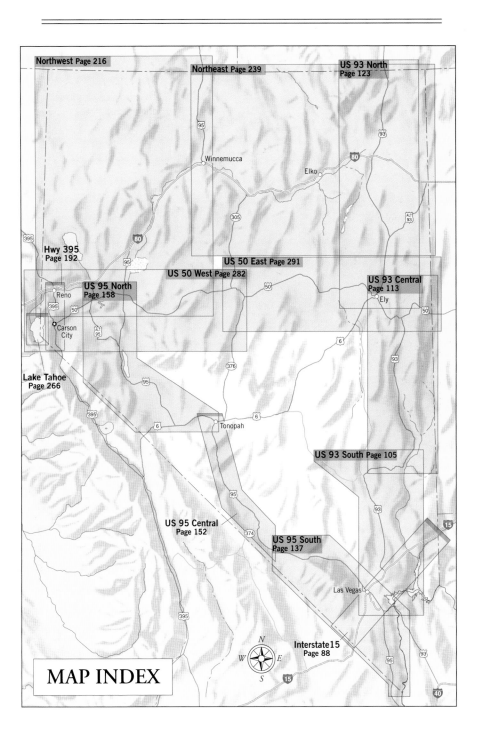

Northwest Page 216

Northeast Page 239

US 93 North
Page 123

Hwy 395
Page 192

US 50 East Page 291

US 50 West Page 282

US 95 North
Page 158

US 93 Central
Page 113

Lake Tahoe
Page 266

US 93 South Page 105

US 95 Central
Page 152

US 95 South
Page 137

Interstate 15
Page 88

MAP INDEX

Winnemucca

Elko

Reno

Carson
City

Tonopah

Las Vegas

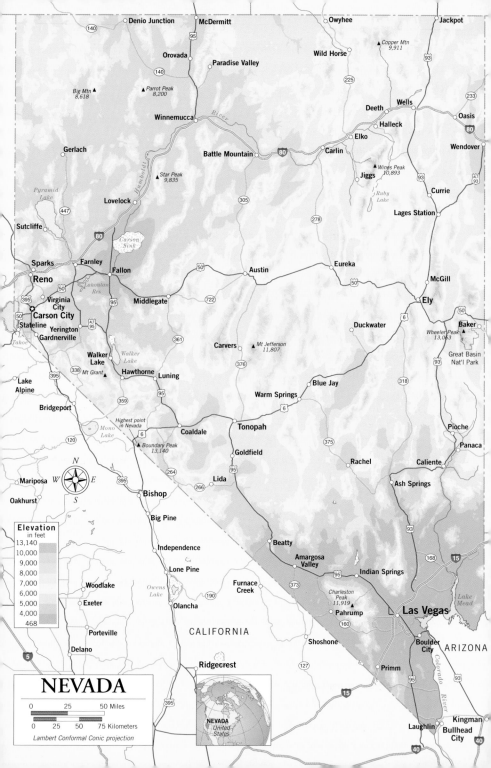

# NEVADA

Elevation
in feet
13,140
10,000
9,000
8,000
7,000
6,000
5,000
4,000
468

0        25        50 Miles

0    25    50    75 Kilometers

Lambert Conformal Conic projection

NEVADA
United States

N
W        E
S

Denio Junction
McDermitt
Owyhee
Jackpot
Copper Mtn 9,911
Orovada
Wild Horse
Paradise Valley
Big Mtn 8,618
Parrot Peak 8,200
Deeth
Wells
Oasis
Halleck
Winnemucca
Elko
Wendover
Gerlach
Battle Mountain
Carlin
Wines Peak 10,893
Jiggs
Star Peak 9,835
Lovelock
Ruby Lake
Pyramid Lake
Currie
Lages Station
Sutcliffe
Carson Sink
Eureka
McGill
Sparks
Farnley
Austin
Ely
Reno
Fallon
Baker
Virginia City
Lahontan Res.
Middlegate
Wheeler Peak 13,063
Carson City
Duckwater
Great Basin Nat'l Park
Stateline
Yerington
Carvers
Mt Jefferson 11,807
Gardnerville
Tahoe
Walker Lake
Walker Lake
Blue Jay
Lake Alpine
Mt Grant
Hawthorne
Luning
Warm Springs
Bridgeport
Pioche
Highest point in Nevada
Coaldale
Tonopah
Panaca
Mono Lake
Boundary Peak 13,140
Goldfield
Rachel
Caliente
Mariposa
Bishop
Lida
Ash Springs
Oakhurst
Big Pine
Beatty
Independence
Amargosa Valley
Indian Springs
Lake Mead
Woodlake
Lone Pine
Charleston Peak 11,919
Exeter
Owens Lake
Furnace Creek
Pahrump
Las Vegas
Olancha
Porteville
Shoshone
Boulder City
Delano
CALIFORNIA
ARIZONA
Ridgecrest
Primm
Colorado River
Laughlin
Kingman
Bullhead City
Humboldt River

# I N T R O D U C T I O N

NEVADA IS A STATE OF ILLUSIONS.

Most people's impressions of Nevada tend to be stereotypical, flimsy, false: that Nevada is a never-ending desert wasteland; or that the great desert has been tamed by oases of infinite water and perpetual growth and streets paved with gold; or that those oases are real, and not just false fronts, mirages.

Perhaps the grandest illusion is that Nevada is a state at all. A little more than 70 million acres comprise the seventh largest of the United States, of which the overlords in Washington, D.C., lay claim to 60 million—a whopping 87.3 percent of the total land area, first out of 50 in federal dominion. (Another nine percent is owned by local governments, railroads, and large mining and ranching corporations. Less than four percent is in the hands of small businesses and private individuals.) A huge chunk of central Nevada real estate, roughly the size of Connecticut and nearly five percent of the state, is off-limits to civilians. This forbidden zone encompasses the Nellis Test Range, which contains a few infamous federal facilities: the Nuclear Test Site, the Yucca Mountain high-level nuclear-waste repository, and Area 51.

Many Nevada legislators, who meet in Carson City for roughly six months every couple of years, believe that the purpose of state government is to implement federal programs, enforce federal mandates, and dispense federal largesse.

The Eastern overseers, for their part, take a somewhat benign-neglect attitude toward the landscape. The Bureau of Land Management "controls" 50 million acres, 83 percent of the federal total. Except for the occasional wild-horse round-up and adoption campaign, grazing-fee increase, wilderness and wetlands quarrel, and land-boundary skirmish, the feds tend to view Nevada the same as people who drive through on long dull stretches of superhighway: a dun monochrome of sand and salt and distant slopes.

Though it's easy to misjudge this place, especially by the view from the road, a little closer look reveals its subtle beauty and great variety. Nevada has a dozen mountain peaks higher than 12,000 feet, another 20 higher than 10,000, and a couple score above 8,000. Most of the mountainsides between 6,000 and 10,000 feet are forested, with piñon pine and Utah juniper at the lower elevations, and a dozen varieties of pine, fir, cedar, and spruce at the higher elevations. Hang out this high in the big ranges and it's no illusion: you *can* see the forest for the trees.

Also of surprise to many is the fact that you don't have to travel far in Nevada to get to water. Eight major rivers flow through the state. Seven are dammed, creating big reservoirs, including Mead, the largest man-made lake in the Western Hemisphere. Upwards of 2,750 miles of waterways course through the state. Nearly 30 Nevada "water holes" are suitable for boating and 125 lakes and reservoirs and 500 streams are suitable for fishing. There's water in them hills; finding and getting to it it can turn into a spiritual quest.

There's gold in them hills, too—the Nevada "wasteland" conceals some of the most concentrated mineral wealth in all the world (Nevada's nickname is the Silver State). The big mining companies have no illusions about what's valuable in the desert. For an urban enviro it's a quasi-religious experience; for the companies it's hard assets.

And where there's gold, there's golf. Talk about trickery! A full 75 duffers' dreamscapes dot the state with lush greenery in the scenery. Three dozen are in southern Nevada, one of the driest locales on the planet. Among the most famous, Shadow Creek is surrounded by the scorched Mojave, while the Desert Inn's links are right on the Strip, adjacent to sizzling megaresorts.

Which brings us to the Nevada economy, one of the boomingest in the country, built on an industry based on castles in the air and coinage of the brain. Though casino gambling is touted as a benign form of indoor recreation, the price of admission is both hidden and high. Still, that's one of the worst-kept secrets around; everyone knows it's a carnival trick, a veritable sleight of hand, but 33 million out-of-towners annually buy the dream, bestowing upon Nevada almost half of the taxes that make up its General Fund. The handling of the hordes accounts for 25 percent of overall employment, up to 50 percent in the southern part of the state.

Yes, Nevada thrives on its make-believe business. The vast majority of state taxes are collected from people who don't live here. Sales, room, gambling, entertainment, rental car, airport—they're all "export" taxes. Nevada has one of the highest taxing capacities in the country, but one of the lowest tax rates for locals. No state income tax is imposed on individuals, businesses, or corporations. Nevada's corporation system is one of the most private and least restrictive in the country. Property taxes are low (especially when compared to California's).

Much of the General Fund is reinvested in the tourist industry, such as never-ending road construction, infrastructure of casino venues, visitor authorities, tourism agencies, advertising, and the like. Nevada ranks low in spending on social services. And Nevada ranks near the bottom of federal spending per capita. Still, it

*Cathedral Gorge was formed hundreds of thousands of years ago: towers of sediment up to 1,500 feet high were left behind when prehistoric Lake Lahontan dried up.*

would be hard to claim that Nevadans' quality of life suffers from the lack of goverment redistribution on any level.

In terms of the gambling itself, the outsiders hold no monopoly on supporting the local economy. The locals do their part to ensure the success of the casino industry. The myth that Nevadans don't gamble is dispelled by the fact that three out of the four world-record slot jackpots have been won by locals—at astronomically long-shot odds, to be sure. One of the oldest gags in the casino joke-ography concerns a down-and-out-looking guy who accosts a stranger on the Strip. "Buddy," he says, "can you lend me a buck to help feed my wife and kids?"

The stranger replies, "How do I know that you won't take the dollar directly to a slot machine and gamble it away on one pull?"

"Oh," the guy shrugs, "I've got plenty of gambling money."

The Wizard of Odds hides behind the curtain, using smoke and mirrors to rake a little jack out of (almost) every bet in the house (a handful of pros eke out a living from tiny edges). If little is as it seems in the Illusion State, then the casino is the perfect symbol of it. Everyone in the gambling hall—tourists, pikers, scufflers, scammers, low rollers, high rollers, comp hustlers, advantage players, dealers, cocktail waitresses, pit bosses, shift bosses, hosts, managers, shareholders—is playing a different game.

The players come in all shapes, sizes, and costumes, but they have one thing in common: They're all fostering the illusion that they can afford to sustain their losses and that it's all in good fun (the compulsive gamblers are all pretending that they're not hooked). But even the winners find out that the dream is not all it's cracked up to be. In the rare event that you get struck by lightning, hit the big jackpot, and win a million, you can expect to clear a mere $35,000 after taxes annually for 20 years. Or when you see a pro win a million-dollar tournament, you can bet the rent that the latest trophy-clutching hero is cut up a dozen different ways and has to duke off more than half the grand prize to people who have pieces of him—including the second-place winner, with whom he may have a side deal going. The next afternoon, he'll be sitting at the tables, looking like everyone else.

And is it any wonder that the most prevalent form of entertainment in the casino centers is based on magic? Siegfried and Roy, Lance Burton, David Copperfield, and scores of lesser illusionists pack 'em in by making things, big and small, disappear, or appear not to be there at all. Meanwhile, Elvis lives, by way of hundreds of impersonators, some of whom (the Asian, African, teenage, and geezer varieties, for example) don't seem concerned by the finer points of impostering. And showgirls? No matter what their shining eyes and brilliant smiles and skimpy G-strings and exposed mammaries might lead you to believe, they're *not* available.

Conversely, the "darlings of the desert" in Nevada's legal "houses of joy" are nothing if not available, though you wouldn't confuse one with a showgirl.

All in all, though, just as the locally preferred brand of show business entertains and astounds by making the real unreal and vice versa, the illusion of Nevada itself is entertaining and astounding. If you come here forewarned that Nevada's surfaces are deceiving, you'll be prepared to dive a little deeper. You'll get out of the city and into the country, where the shimmering mirages resolve into realness. Out here, the culture is substantive, authentic, non-illusory. In the towns and villages and outback, it's a rural culture, a *vaquero* culture, a libertarian culture. Unlike in the city, where physical distances are small and psychic distances are large, in the wilds of Nevada, physical distances are large and psychic distances are small. The people stick together with western music, cowboy poetry, a common live-and-let-live attitude, and a nearly universal distaste for the federal government.

Like an open-pit gold mine, you have to dig deep to get to the bottom of Nevada, to wrest a genuine reality out of the reluctant landscape. And that's the fun of it. After all, as a wise man once said, "An illusion can bring you closer to the truth."

*Las Vegas shimmers like a mirage against a mountainous desert backdrop. (photo by Kerrick James)*

# H  I  S  T  O  R  Y

FOR ROUGHLY 500 MILLION YEARS, most of the North American west coast was covered by a shallow inland sea. Nevada rested underwater. At least twice during the mysterious 340-million-year Paleozoic era, violent and titanic episodes of uplift raised the ocean floor, drained the sea, and left towering mountains, mesas, and alluvial plains.

Over the next 160 million years, cataclysmic extinctions, megashears, volcanism, and climatic crises, punctuated by long stoic periods of erosion, continually altered Nevada, several times obliterating its life and landscape. Seventeen million years ago, today's familiar basins and ranges were created by the colossal jostle of tectonic forces. More than 250 separate ranges have been named in Nevada. Ninety percent of them are oriented northeast-southwest, and on a map they look like a herd of earthworms marching toward Mexico.

Beginning nearly two million years ago, four great ice ages advanced into and retreated from history. Nevada's Basin and Range Physiographic Province, which had been shuffled by earthquakes, tilted by crustal adjustments, and whittled by erosion, was now alternately drowned, drained, and ground down by glaciers.

About 11,000 years ago, Paleo-Indians appeared on the scene. Evidence suggests they lived in caves along the shorelines of vast glacial lakes (such as mighty Lake Lahontan in northwest Nevada, but also great Lake Las Vegas in southern Nevada) and hunted large mammals—woolly mammoth, bison, mastodon, giant sloth. Four thousand years ago, the last remnants of the cold and wet ice-age climate ended, taking the lakes, lush vegetation, and meaty creatures with them. The land began its transformation into the arid environment that it is today, and the shore-dwelling Indians adapted a desert culture, both in the northern and southern portions of what would become Nevada. Their lifestyle remained fairly consistent over the millennia.

In the north, the Lovelock Indians hunted small mammals and fished with rock and bone hooks. They made baskets and decoys from reeds, tules, and willows; gathered duck eggs, cattails, swamp cane, wild onions, and squaw cabbage; and harvested pine nuts.

*Nevada's landscape bears witness to its cataclysmic geologic past. Here, volcanic boulders litter the rim of Lunar Crater Volcanic Field, just east of Warm Springs in Nye County. While the crater resembles the imprint of a meteorite, it is actually a cinder cone which collapsed a few thousand years ago.*

*This basket was woven by renowned Washoe basketmaker Dat So La Lee, circa 1910. (Courtesy Nevada State Museum, Carson City)*

In the south, the Archaic Indians lived in pit houses, traveled in small bands, used the *atlatl* (an arrow launcher), hunted big-horn sheep and desert tortoise, and harvested screwbean mesquite and cholla fruit. The Archaic Indians evolved into the Anasazi, a highly civilized culture that featured large settlements made up of 100-room pueblos, bean and corn agriculture in irrigated fields, the inclusion of artistic elements in their baskets and pottery, and even salt and turquoise mining.

The transitions are vague at best, and whether the succeeding people expelled, annihilated, merged with, or evolved from the previous people is academic, but 600 or 700 years ago, Paiute and Shoshone settled the desert. The Washoe had long been ensconced in the western mountains.

■ CONTACT

They came from the west: hardy Russian *promyshleniki,* explorers with fur-fever roaming the far southern edge of their great northern empire. Though there's no record of contact between the Russians and the desert or mountain Indians, surely late 17th-century trappers and traders stationed along the California coast, from Fort Ross in the north to Catalina Island in the south, would have wandered a few hundred miles inland—if only to stretch their land legs between long ocean voyages.

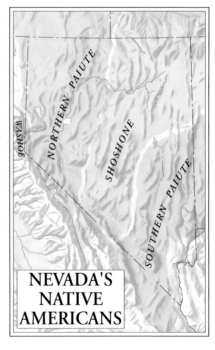

NEVADA'S NATIVE AMERICANS

They also came from the south: Spanish conquistadors and their Toltec slaves, explorers with gold fever wandering the far northern edges of their vast western empire. In the late 1700s, Franciscan missionaries traveled through what's now southern Nevada on their way from New Mexico to southern California, encountering the Paiute people along the way.

And they came from the north: refugees from civilization, fugitives from an encroaching future. Anonymous Anglo mountain men, though mavericks and pariahs, were nonetheless welcomed by the Indians at the lakes and rivers and hunting grounds according to long inviolable tradition. These early trappers and travelers shared the Indians' lifestyles, more or less, and certainly knew how to conduct

*Paiute chief Wah-Quadzy was a young man when Jedediah Smith first set foot in present-day Nevada. (Nevada Historical Society)*

themselves appropriately to the local cultures—or they didn't survive for long. Although they left no footprints, their passing remained as imprints in the imagination of the indigenous inhabitants.

And they came from the east: the strangest of visitors, less a curiosity than a curse. The records of their reconnaisances are copious. In 1826, Jedediah Smith led a party of fur hunters on the Spanish Trail through southern Nevada. Peter Skene Ogden, legendary trapper for the Canadian Hudson's Bay Company, discovered the Humboldt River in 1829 and followed it almost all the way to its sink. Though the Paiute welcomed him with customary hospitality and he treated them with respect, his party's "saturation trapping" of Humboldt beaver, plus its consumption of grasses and other foods, strained the local resources.

In 1830, Mexican trader Antonio Armijo stumbled upon a shortcut on the Spanish Trail via Big Spring; he named it Las Vegas, Spanish for "The Meadows." In 1831, Joseph Walker blazed a trail through northern and western Nevada that, a decade later, was followed by the Bidwell-Bartleson party, the first pioneers to emigrate from Missouri to California. Three years later, John C. Frémont, the famous Army explorer, mapped large sections of Nevada, naming almost every topographic feature he saw.

Technically, all these Anglos from the east were trespassing on land claimed by the Spanish Crown. In 1848, however, the United States emerged victorious from the Mexican-American War. In the Treaty of Guadeloupe-Hidalgo, Spain ceded the Southwest, including the area that would become Nevada, to the United States.

## ■ THE COMSTOCK LODE

Beginning in 1849, the Far West was being eyed by Easterners with manifest destiny in their veins and gold fever in their brains. Not surprisingly, most fortune seekers and pioneers passed through Nevada without noticing it, but a handful of hardy prospectors drifted back across the Sierra Nevada to look for gold in the creeks on the eastern flanks.

A year later, a crude settlement of miners formed in Johntown (now Dayton) at the confluence of the Carson River and Gold Canyon. Also in 1851, Latter-day Saints from five-year-old Salt Lake City built a trading post at Mormon Station (now Genoa) at the west edge of broad Carson Valley. In 1855, missionaries were also dispatched from Salt Lake City to civilize southern Nevada at the watering hole along the Spanish Trail known as Las Vegas.

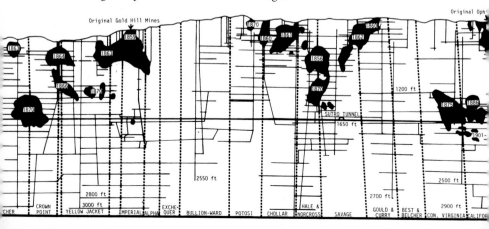

By that time, attracted by the bountiful and scenic valleys at the base of the eastern scarp of the Sierra Nevada, traders, prospectors, and homesteaders had settled into this far western corner of Utah Territory. And in 1855, the western half of Utah was designated Carson County, administered by local Mormon officials and colonists at Genoa, the first county seat.

Meanwhile, in Gold Canyon, miners followed placer gold along Gold Creek to its source below Sun Mountain in the Virginia Range, setting up a settlement that they named, appropriately, Gold Hill. In May 1859, on the outskirts of Gold Hill, one intuitive prospector sunk his shovel into the mountain itself—and struck the richest ore body ever discovered in the Lower 48.

The original locators of the Comstock Lode—named after one Henry Comstock, a ne'er-do-well blowhard who claimed the entire hillside as his "ranch" and the whole mining district as "his"—were initially unaware of what they'd found. A heavy blue-gray mud interfered with the recovery of the gold, bringing the mining to a near standstill. Piles of blue mud began to grow; thought worthless, pieces were given away as souvenirs. One chunk made its way to a California assayer's office, where, in July 1859, the mud was found to contain $875 to the ton in gold—and $3,000 in pure sulphuret of silver. Silver fever spread far and wide, and the rush to the Comstock was on.

*(above) Miners prepare to descend a shaft in the Savage Mine in the Comstock Lode. (left) This "Vertical Section of the Comstock Lode" indicates the ownership of each cross-section and the date discovered; note the location of the Savage Mine along the Sutro Tunnel. The solid lines represent mine shafts and tunnels. (graphic courtesy of Grace Dangberg Foundation, Reno)*

Within a year, 10,000 stampeders had carved the boomtown of Virginia City into the mountainside and dug the Comstock out of the mountain. By late 1860, the lack of a consensus on duly constituted judicial authorities began to take its toll. There were Mormon justices, federal district judges, and mining district arbitrators. The legal discord over the Comstock, however, was but a micro-chaos of a much grander incoherence. At least three or four provisional governments were still in contention for control of the population centers east of the Sierra: Genoa, Dayton, Gold Hill, Virginia City, and the new settlement in the middle of the four, Carson City.

The "oldtimers" in Genoa, for example, were by now on their fifth or sixth provisional government. The Carson Valley Settler's Government, formed in 1851, had met in Genoa once a year to legislate land, water, and timber rights, until the Carson County Government arrived from the capital of Utah Territory in Salt Lake City in 1855. That was replaced by the Sierra Nevada Territory, which held meetings in Genoa in 1857. Meanwhile, a group of miners formed the Gold Hill Mining District to oversee the Comstock mobocracy, and the Sierra Nevada group attempted to become the Provisional Territorial Government to compete with, and eventually secede from, the Utah jurisdiction!

The Sierra dissonance was itself merely a stanza in the national score. In November 1860, Abraham Lincoln was elected President of a nation in crisis, and true to its threat, South Carolina seceded, taking 10 Southern states with it. This actually ensured Nevada's admittance into the Union as a free territory: Lincoln needed all the support he could muster. In March 1861, though the population was only an estimated 6,000, a bill naming the Territory of "Nevada" (which means "Snowy Ridge," shortened from Sierra Nevada), was passed by Congress.

The year-old settlement of Carson City prevailed over Genoa, Dayton, and Virginia City to become the territorial capital. Lincoln named James Nye, a former New York City police commissioner, as the territorial governor. Orion Clemens traveled west with Nye as his personal secretary. Clemens's 20-year-old brother, Sam, followed a few months later. He spent the next year adventuring around the western part of the territory.

## ■ THE BOOM SPREADS EAST

The rush to a silver strike in Unionville, in the Humboldt Range 100 miles northeast of Virginia City, swept Sam Clemens along with it in December 1861.

It took Clemens and some companions 15 days to haul all their gear to the Humboldts. They found a handful of prospectors, a dozen hovels, plenty of ground to prospect, and even some indications. They tried their hands at mining, but never uncovered any silver. More prospectors, miners, and boomtowners arrived in the meantime, and Clemens and his partners found it easier to speculate in "feet," the instant currency of mining claims, than to actually dig out the ore and mill it into metal. In all, the Unionville district produced $5 million in silver over a decade, but Clemens had long since rushed to the new find in Aurora, 80 miles south of Carson City near the California border. From there, it was off to Virginia City for Sam Clemens, where he took a job as a reporter for one of the daily newspapers and adopted the pen name Mark Twain *(see page 195)*.

More silver was discovered in May 1862 in steep Pony Canyon in the Toiyabe Range in central Nevada. Being so remote (180 miles from Virginia City), the assays weren't conducted until the fall, and the news didn't spread until early 1863, when the rush to the Toiyabes got underway in force. By spring 1863, a thousand claims had been staked in the canyon and on nearby hills. The settlement was named Austin, after the Texas hometown of one of the original locators.

By fall 1863, Austin was booming. It was named the seat of vast Lander County, which occupied nearly one third of the entire Nevada Territory. The Recorder's Office listed 1,300 mining companies in the district. Three quartz mills were operating. And prospectors fanned out into the far northern, northeastern, eastern, and central reaches of the territory, returning only for supplies. Austin quickly turned into a thriving, clamoring hub for all of vast and sparsely populated central Nevada.

In 1864, silver was discovered 70 miles east of Austin in Eureka, then again in 1867, 70 miles east of Eureka in Hamilton. Silver was unearthed at Belmont in the Toquima Mountains, across Great Smoky Valley from Austin and the Toiyabes, in 1865; in 1867, Belmont became the seat of Nye County, which encompassed all of southern Nevada at the time. Also in the mid-1860s, homesteaders were settling Las Vegas Valley; one in particular, O. D. Gass, rebuilt the fort abandoned by the Mormon missionaries 10 years earlier, which grew over the next 35 years into the Las Vegas Ranch. And in 1869, silver and gold were found in southeast Nevada in the Highland Range; Pioche, the town that grew on its eastern slope, was the roughest and most lawless boomtown in Nevada history, on a par with Bodie, California, and Tombstone, Arizona.

# ■ THE RAILROADS

The Territorial Legislature met in 1862 and 1863, agitating for statehood. Constitutional conventions were held in 1863 and 1864. On October 31, 1864, Lincoln, the most powerful and, some believe, tyrannical of all the U.S. Presidents, proclaimed Nevada the nation's 36th state. It was a mere three years after becoming a territory, and there were still barely enough residents to qualify for statehood, but Lincoln was anxious for additional Union representatives from the West, as well as the use of Nevada silver and gold to help finance his various federal campaigns, including the Civil War.

In 1863, the Central Pacific Railroad began laying track eastward from Sacramento, claiming as much easement property as it could before meeting up with the Union Pacific, marching west out of Omaha. It took four years for the rail line to reach the state line of Nevada; it wasn't until 1868 that the track pushed through the Sierra to the Truckee Meadows, site of a growing settlement centered on a bridge across the Truckee River and the wagon roads out of California that connected with the important route to Virginia City.

*A Nevada Central shortline delivers wood to Austin in this photograph circa 1880.*
*(Nevada Historical Society)*

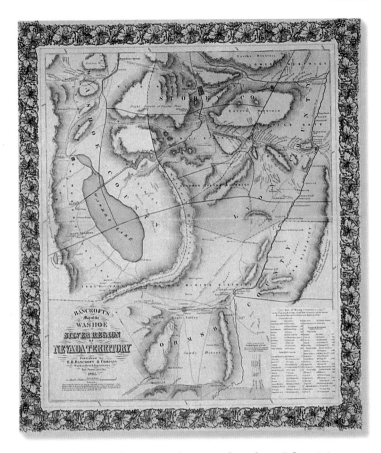

*This 1862 map of the Nevada Territory's silver region shows the area's first mining towns and various mining claims. (Library of Congress)*

Most of the Truckee Meadows land and water rights were owned by Myron Lake. Lake ceded 60 acres of his holdings to the Central Pacific in exchange for a passenger depot and warehouse facilities near his land, turning Lake's Crossing into the distribution center for the Comstock Lode. In May 1868, 400 lots were auctioned; within a month more than 100 homes and businesses had been constructed. Railroad officials renamed Lake's Crossing for Jesse L. Reno, a Union general who'd been killed in the Civil War.

From there, the Central Pacific marched eastward across Nevada, founding the towns of Wadsworth, Lovelock, Winnemucca, Battle Mountain, Carlin, Elko, and Wells along its route. It met up with the Union Pacific at Promontory Point, Utah, in May 1869, completing the nation's first transcontinental railroad.

*A Chinese miner in Nevada carries a rocker to his gold dig in this photo from the 1860s. (Nevada Historical Society)*

Thousands of Chinese laborers were laid off and abandoned by the Central Pacific after it was completed; many settled and worked in the railroad and mining towns. Others headed back to Virginia City to help build the Virginia & Truckee Railroad, connecting the mines of the Comstock to the mills along the Carson River. The 21-mile track from the mountain to the valley dropped 1,600 feet in 13 miles, necessitating tortuous curves and switchbacks and numerous trestles and tunnels. Though it took a mere six weeks to complete, it cost $50,000 per mile of track. Three years later, in 1872, the V&T was extended from Carson City to Reno, directly connecting Virginia City to San Francisco and the rest of the country. In its 81 years of operation, the V&T ranked among the most profitable shortline railroads in the country.

Other shortlines were laid in quick succession between the mining districts and the main line: the Nevada Central between Austin and Battle Mountain; the Eureka-Palisade between Eureka and Palisade (near Elko); the Carson & Colorado, from Dayton to Hawthorne; and even the *short* shortline, Pioche & Bullionville, which ran 30 miles from the mines to the mill.

# ■ THE BIG BONANZA

In 1873, 1,200 feet directly below Virginia City, a group of miners struck the richest orebody on the Comstock, known as the Big Bonanza. This was the high point in all of the mining, in all of Nevada, in all of the early years of the state's history. Of the half-billion dollars in precious metals produced by the Comstock, the Big Bonanza alone accounted for more than a quarter. So much silver was unearthed from the Big Bonanza that a U.S. Mint opened that same year in Carson City, flooding the country with good cheap silver (and gold) coins, creating an enormous flood of wealth. There was so much wealth that even the Great Fire of 1875, which destroyed 33 blocks of Virginia City, including most of the 10-square-block downtown, barely made a dent. Big Bonanza capital financed the rebuilding of the town, far beyond its previous splendor, in less than a year. For a time, Virginia City rivaled San Francisco; indeed, Comstock precious metals inaugurated the Golden Age of the City by the Bay.

The Comstock reached its peak in 1878. By then, more than 20,000 residents were in on the greatest mining miracle the country had ever seen. All of the other important mining districts—Austin, Aurora, Eureka, Unionville, Hamilton, and Pioche—had generally played out. All the other boomtowns were in decline. The first Lode had outlasted the rest.

*It often took teams of more than 16 horses to haul the ore wagons from the Comstock mines. (Special Collections Department, University of Nevada, Reno Library)*

It took 18 years from start to finish, but the heyday of the Comstock boom finally quieted and the inevitable bust began. A few more years, however, were required for the news to sink in. The boomers still had a couple of years' worth of money to gamble in the saloons and trade in the mining stock market, but by the beginning of the 1880s, Virginia City had fallen into the same long, slow decline as the rest of the state.

The Big Bonanza had been a five-year high, but the Big Bust continued unabated for 20 years, into the new century.

## ■ SILVER TO GOLD

It started out with silver. In May 1900, a winter farmer/summer prospector from Belmont (then the seat of Nye County) located a promising vein of silver ore in the San Antonio Range a half-day's horse-ride south. When word got out, it unleashed two decades' worth of pent-up energies of the die-hard Nevada boomers, who'd hunkered down during the Comstock bust and were ready to rock and roll. Within a year, Tonopah was a bona fide boomtown. Two years later, the Tonopah Mining Company had bought out all the claims and had introduced corporate efficiency to the district.

Meanwhile, a couple of prospectors were working a mineralized ledge near Columbia Mountain, 25 miles south of Tonopah, and discovered, to their amazement, that the metal wasn't silver. It was gold. The mere word infected the whole state with the most ferocious fever since the California Mother Lode, and the rush to the new town of Goldfield was on. What's more, it was high-grade gold, so rich that hard-rock miners could pocket chunks of it and turn them into lots and lots of Carson City coins.

It also meant, however, that the forces vying to control the gold were enormously powerful. The owners—represented by George Wingfield, a Reno power broker—attempted to curtail the smuggling of nuggets by imposing strict uniform requirements on the miners, who didn't like the idea. The miners organized. The owners hired private security. Goldfield was taken over by territorial tension. The large contemporary international labor union, the Wobblies, showed up to represent the workers. Wingfield countered by calling for federal troops, who wasted no time in breaking the back of the union, allowing non-union workers into the mines. Next, Wingfield pulled strings to turn his security force into duly deputized officers of the state. (This group evolved into the state police: in fact, many

*Vigilante justice—often used to counter organized labor—claims a long history in Nevada. This 1938 photo shows a motorist near the Nevada border being stopped by a posse after hearing a group of California CIO members were organizing to picket a highway project near Reno. (Underwood Photo Archives, San Francisco)*

state police forces evolved out of men "keeping the peace"—that is, containing the labor violence of the early 1900s.)

Prospectors again fanned out across Nevada. Mining districts, all of them gold, erupted at Round Mountain and Manhattan, on the other side of the Toquima Range from Belmont; at Rhyolite, 75 miles south of Goldfield; and at Searchlight, in the southern tip of the state. The waste dumps around the long-abandoned silver mines were reworked for their mineral content. And a huge deposit of copper was discovered near Ely in eastern Nevada.

Railroad activity picked up as well. The Northern Nevada connected Ely's copper mines and smelter with the main line north of Wells. The Southern Pacific, which had replaced the Union Pacific as owners of the main line, founded the town of Sparks, east of Reno, to house the maintenance shops and serve as a division point.

Most importantly, another interstate railroad line was being laid across Nevada, on its way from Salt Lake City to Los Angeles, serving the southern tip of the state. Two new railroad towns were created in the process, both locations chosen for their surface water: Caliente and Las Vegas. The Las Vegas & Tonopah Railroad connected Las Vegas with Rhyolite, 110 miles northwest; another shortline ran from Rhyolite up to Goldfield and Tonopah. But the town that benefitted most from the new Nevada mining and railroad boom was Reno.

## ■ SIN CITY

Reno was a whistlestop on the transcontinental in 1905, but also a crossroads town. By this time the Carson & Colorado and Virginia & Truckee lines connected Reno to many settlements in central Nevada. George Wingfield, the main power broker in the state, held court in Reno, giving it a certain aura of glamour and prestige. Also that year, Reno launched its checkered career as a divorce colony.

When Nevada was granted statehood, the new legislators simply copied statutes that prevailed in other western states. One of the codes called for a six-month requirement to establish residency in the state. The relatively short residency requirement swelled the census with citizens and provided voters for elections and taxes for revenues. As a matter of expedience, the legislature deemed the same six months as the minimum waiting period for the dissolution of residents' marriages.

Even though divorces were as good as illegal at the time, Nevada's highly liberal six-month residency requirement raised few eyebrows in the late 19th century in or outside the state. Between 1867 and 1886, only 1,128 divorces were granted in Nevada, slightly more than 55 a year. But in the 1890s, South Dakota made a little reputation for itself as a "divorce colony," actively offering quickie (for the time) divorces.

Meanwhile, Nevada was a divorce capital waiting to happen: splitting up a marriage in Nevada was practically automatic. Couples strolled into a county courthouse with the proper legal papers, appeared before a judge to answer the appropriate questions, and walked out single men and women. A judge could grant a decree for a divorce—uncontested, with the private property already divided and no children—in a matter of minutes. And both parties were free to remarry immediately.

Between 1900 and 1905, 300 divorces were granted in Reno alone, as lawyers around the country, with miserable couples on one hand and local divorce prohibitions on the other, discovered Nevada's short six-month residency requirement.

Then, in 1905, one of Reno's divorces hit the society pages in all the nation's newspapers, and the harsh spotlight hit Reno. William B. Corey was the most famous rags-to-riches success story at the turn of the 20th century. He started out as a shoeshine boy, and before he turned forty, he was the president of U.S. Steel, the world's first billion-dollar corporation. He'd been married to his wife Laura for 20 years, and had a strapping teenage son Allan, when he initiated a highly public affair with actress and chorus girl Maybelle Gillman. Public opinion weighed in heavily on the side of the jilted wife and virtuous mother, who was eventually discovered in Reno with her sister-in-law (William's own sister) and her manly son providing emotional and moral support during her six-month divorce residency.

Then in 1907, a New York attorney moved to Reno, opened a law office, and proceeded to advertise his divorce services from coast to coast. In 1909, William H. Schnitzer, the New York attorney, published a 24-page booklet titled *Divorce Practice and Procedure,* which summarized Nevada's divorce law. Its 50-year-old six-month residency requirement was the shortest in the nation. It provided seven grounds for divorce, including the ambiguous and omnibus "cruelty" clause. And Nevada's remoteness provided privacy. Schnitzer's advertising of his booklet landed him in deep doodoo with the Nevada Bar Association, which considered advertising unethical, and compelled the Supreme Court to suspend his license for eight months in 1911.

By 1910, about 300 divorces were granted in Reno annually, nearly one every working day. The divorce business grew slowly and steadily, until 1926, when the Reno Courthouse was granting 1,000 divorces a year. Other states, predictably, started taking notice and making noise about lowering their residency requirements to compete with Nevada's lucrative divorce trade. With this whiff of competition in the air, the powers in Reno, primarily George Wingfield, decided that reducing the residency requirement even further would be good for business. It didn't hurt that Wingfield had just remodeled the Riverside Hotel, fanciest lodging in Reno, directly across the river from the courthouse.

In March 1927, Wingfield engineered the secret passage of a bill through the legislature, at 3 A.M.; the governor, Fred Balzar, signed it into law at 8 A.M. the same morning. Literally overnight, Nevada had cut its residency requirement in half, to a mere 90 days. The number of divorces quickly doubled until Reno, a town of 15,000, was handling 2,000 divorces a year. One judge, on his way to issuing a record 27,150 "liberty bonds," dozed through most of the proceedings, each of which lasted no more than five minutes flat.

Meanwhile, the mining boom at Tonopah had played out by 1915, after a good 15 years during which $150 million in silver had been produced. Goldfield peaked in 1910, with a population even larger than Reno's. But by 1919, most of Nevada's 20th-century mines were closed. Tonopah, Goldfield, Rhyolite, Manhattan, Round Mountain—all busted. Only the huge open-pit copper mine in Ely survived this second statewide bust (it kept producing well into the 1970s).

By 1930, the stock market crash and the subsequent Great Depression, along with a rising divorce rate, prompted officials from several other states to lower their residency requirements in order to attract the divorce trade. To protect its position, in March 1931, Nevada reduced its residency requirement for a third and final time, to six weeks. One-and-a-half months. A mere 42 days. The vote was 34-0 in the Assembly, 13-1 in the Senate.

Reno's big year for divorces was 1931, by which time it had gained the reputation as the naughtiest town in the country. Within a few years, however, competition from Idaho, Arkansas, Mexico, and Florida began to cut into Reno's monopoly. In addition, Las Vegas had grown and, now boasting 5,000 residents, was getting in on the action. That same year, construction began on Hoover Dam, giving the dusty railroad town of Las Vegas so much electricity and water that it's been growing brighter and wetter ever since.

Also in March 1931, the legislature legalized wide-open casino gambling.

## ■ NEVADA TAKES A GAMBLE

Gambling began changing the focus and the image of Nevada almost immediately. In 1935, Raymond "Pappy" Smith opened Harold's Club in Reno and commenced to popularize gambling for the masses. Smith invented and implemented procedures that remain standard in the casino industry today: free drinks to players,

*Las Vegas skyline circa 1906. (Nevada Historical Society)*

comped meals, junkets, the eye-in-the-sky, casino promotions, even walking money to bust-outs. William Harrah, meanwhile, dressed up his casino in carpet and drapes, upscale decorative elements that appealed to the middle class.

Gambling spread to all of the large towns in the state, where hotels and saloons installed faro, poker, blackjack, and crap tables, keno boards, and mechanical slot machines. But it was Las Vegas that embraced gambling with a fiery passion that's never cooled off. By the late '30s, casinos lined both sides of Fremont Street, a block from one of the last surviving official red-light districts in the country. In 1941, a carpet joint called the El Cortez opened at Fremont and Sixth at the far end of downtown. Also that year, the luxury resort, El Rancho Vegas, opened two miles south of downtown on the Los Angeles Highway, soon to be known as the Las Vegas Strip.

The Last Frontier, Flamingo, Thunderbird, Desert Inn, Sahara, Sands, Riviera, Tropicana—the 1940s and '50s were Las Vegas's wildcat years. Mob money and management built and manned the joints, attracted the gamblers, and expanded the town. The U.S. Senate Committee to Investigate Organized Crime had already held hearings in Las Vegas. The Atomic Energy Commission was conducting above-ground testing of nuclear weapons within view of the rooftops. The Las Vegas News Bureau was established to provide positive PR for the otherwise naughty resort destination. By 1958, when the Stardust opened as the largest hotel in the world, Las Vegas had a dozen world-class hotel-casinos, 60,000 residents, chuckwagon buffets, and a convention center; 8,000 divorces were granted and 25,000 weddings were conducted annually.

When the power of the federal government began to be felt in Las Vegas in the early 1960s, the writing appeared on the wall for Las Vegas's freewheeling days. Most of the mob was ready and willing to sell out or go into deep cover, and

*Las Vegas skyline circa 2000. (photo by Kerrick James)*

Howard Hughes showed up in 1966 to buy out the old gangsters. In a little less than four years, Hughes owned six major hotel-casinos, paving the way for the entrance of the new, more socially acceptable masters of the game, the corporations. Still, federal, state, and local heat didn't roust the last hidden mob interest in the casinos until the early '80s.

## ■ LAS VEGAS KEEPS COMING ON

Reno, which had legislated a 25-year casino-containment policy in the early '50s, broke that chain in the late 1970s; in 1979 alone, eight casinos opened around the Truckee Meadows. Still, Reno to this day remains deeply ambivalent about its gambling product, especially by comparison with Las Vegas's headlong rush for supremacy; fortunately, Reno diversified into warehousing and light industry, and doesn't depend on gambling revenues as much as its sister city to the south does.

In the rural counties, gold mining experienced a major boom in the late '80s and early '90s. Even factoring in the big bust of the late '90s, Nevada remains the third largest gold-producing region in the world and number one in production in the nation.

Nevada has also come into its own as a relocation and retirement destination, especially for Californians, but also for snowbirds from the Northeast and Midwest. Southern Nevada in particular, but also western Nevada, are being developed at a breakneck pace. Nevada has been the fastest-growing state in the country for more than a decade.

Still, Las Vegas has been the main story hereabouts for years. In 1989, the Mirage opened, launching a boom that's now a dozen years old and counting. Since then, nearly 30 major hotel-casinos, half of them megaresorts, have been added to the Vegas skyline. The stock market boom of the '90s fueled the growth of the gambling corporations to an extreme: Bellagio, which opened in October 1998, is the most expensive hotel ever built. In 1999, Mandalay Bay, the Venetian, the Regent Las Vegas, Paris, and the Hyatt at Lake Las Vegas increased the room inventory by another 10,500 rooms. Nearly $4 billion was spent on these five hotel-casinos.

Las Vegas claims the top 18 of the world's 21 largest hotels; 33 million visitors left behind 20 billion dollars in 1999. That's a lot. There's no place on Earth like the Las Vegas Strip, God's own miniature golf course. Las Vegas is one of the world's truly singular cities. It's even setting itself up to be a prototype city of the future, in that the kind of imagination and money invested in developing "virtual" attractions is one key to the future of travel destinations—or at least the entertainment found there.

## THE "STEWARDSHIP" OF NEVADA

*W*ell, "stewardship" is a convenient word. It seems to stand for decent, judicious respect toward all things. But stewardship failed wherever great amounts of gold and silver were taken out of Nevada's ground; witness the vast, spectacular gougings that mark the copper mines of Ruth, outside Ely. Stewardship may be assailed for insisting on the great Hoover Dam on the Colorado River. It surely abandoned purity, prior existence, silence, and desolation in letting Las Vegas grow up as it has. And stewardship itself now admits the torturous, nearly eternal problems in all things nuclear. There are still guardians to our welfare, or moral stewards, who would berate Nevada, and America, for its laxity in being so ready to experiment with divorce, prostitution, and gambling....

On the other hand, it's not too remote an argument to say that the bullion made the residential splendor of San Francisco, or that the bombs, the testing, and the dogged strafing of Bravo 20 helped bring something like liberty (with all its scars, excesses, and errors) to Prague, to Budapest, to Warsaw, and even to Saint Petersburg.

There is a vanity and a righteousness in the "stewardship" of the Earth that defies all the natural forces of alteration—the drift of continents, the upheaval of earthquake, the rage of fire and rain—that would go on whether or not the Earth was inhabited. For myself, I feel that sense of history in Nevada as much as the sensible need to preserve things.

In other words, I believe that the instincts that lead toward gambling, the overthrow of marriage, the desperate tearing at the ground for wealth, the putting on of martial airs, and playing the saxophone are natural and human. They merit their own stewardship, or at least they had their chance at the larger gaming table and they may be the number we choose to play. For things do grow in the desert, and in the very end of it all, I am against nothing—except to be moribund, to be dead in advance. We have no right or reason in nature, and no evidence in history, to think that living is safe. Or was ever meant to be.

—David Thomson, *In Nevada: The Land, the People, God, and Chance*, 1999

*(following pages) Rye Patch Reservoir, when full, provides irrigation water for 40,000 acres of reclaimed Humboldt River bottomland.*

# L A S   V E G A S

## ■ HIGHLIGHTS

## ■ TRAVEL BASICS

Las Vegas. If you haven't been there for a couple of weeks, you won't recognize the place. This city changes faster than oil filters at a Q Lube. Between October 1998 and September 1999, four megaresorts and two miniresorts—including 13,000 rooms, 50 restaurants, five showrooms, and an events arena, and nearly $6 billion in capital investment—arrived on the scene. And between November 1989 and September 1999, the building of 30 major hotel-casinos helped make Las Vegas one of the most popular vacation destinations in the world.

Most people think Las Vegas *is* Nevada (though most northern Nevadans would like to think Las Vegas is south of the border). And in many ways, they're not far from wrong. The sprawling metropolitan area claims upwards of 75 percent of: the state population, out-of-state visitors, casinos, revenues, and attractions. If you're looking for action, sweaty and sexy and non-stop and cheap, this is your kind of town.

And the amazing thing is, Las Vegas is set in one of the most remote, inhospitable, and homely places in the country.

An hour's run up (northeast) Interstate 15 puts you in Mesquite, the fastest growing border town in Nevada, with its casinos, country clubs, and gorgeous basin and range scenery. A half-hour's run down (southwest) the interstate delivers you to Primm, a casino-resort destination, complete with thrill rides, golf course, and factory outlet mall, on the California state line.

### Information

Las Vegas Chamber of Commerce, 3720 Howard Hughes Pkwy., 89109; 702/735-1616; www.lvchamber.com. Las Vegas Convention and Visitors Authority, 3150 Paradise Rd., 89109; 702/892-0711 or 800/332-5333. www.lasvegas24hours.com.

## Getting Around

Las Vegas is the place where most people begin a visit to—well—Las Vegas, although a handful head into the state from there. The city is served by McCarran International Airport, one of the busiest in the world. Interstate 15 cuts a wide swath through town; it crosses US 95/93 at the Spaghetti Bowl intersection just west of downtown. A large percentage of visitors drive in from southern California on I-15, creating 250-mile traffic jams northbound on Friday evenings and southbound on Sunday afternoons.

People who fly in, take a limo to their Strip hotel, and make short excursions probably don't need a rental car. You can get up and down the Strip by foot, cab, the Strip Trolley, free casino shuttles, and CAT—the Las Vegas public bus system, which also runs downtown. However, if you want to tool around and take in the locals casinos and attractions near and far, you'll have to rent a car, which is as easy as calling your favorite agency and booking your trusty steed of choice.

## Food and Lodging

Almost overnight, Las Vegas has become a dining mecca. These days, casinos don't open restaurants unless they're owned or sponsored by celebrity chefs or movie stars, and the rooms are as much of an attraction as the food. Keep in mind, however, that while a star chef may headline the menu, he or she is probably still running a restaurant kitchen in New York, Boston, Los Angeles, or Santa Fe. Just the same, it's more than likely that the deputy chef will be no slouch.

Should you prefer simpler fare, you'll find that the bargain scene is alive and well, and 50-cent hot dogs, 99-cent shrimp cocktails, and $10 "superbuffets" abound.

Las Vegas now has more than 120,000 hotel rooms, as many as New York and Chicago combined. That's a quarter of a million beds. Yet, finding one on a weekend, or when a big convention is in town, can be challenging. This town fills up fast—especially the top megaresorts, the best-value hotels, and the cheapest motels. Book a room as soon as you know your dates.

### *STRIP HOTELS*

| | | | |
|---|---|---|---|
| Bally's | 800-634-3434 | Mandalay Bay | 877-632-7700 |
| Bellagio | 888-987-6667 | MGM Grand | 800-929-1111 |
| Caesars Palace | 800-634-6661 | Mirage | 800-627-6667 |
| Circus Circus | 800-634-3450 | Monte Carlo | 800-311-8999 |
| Excalibur | 800-937-7777 | New York–New York | 800-693-6763 |
| Flamingo Hilton | 800-732-2111 | Paris | 877-796-2096 |
| Imperial Palace | 800-634-6441 | Rio | 800-888-1808 |
| Las Vegas Hilton | 800-732-7117 | Treasure Island | 800-944-7444 |
| Luxor | 800-288-1000 | Venetian | 877-857-1861 |

# ■ THE NEWEST WAVE  *map page 44–45*

If Nevada is a state of illusions, then Las Vegas, the "City of Hidden Agendas," is its capital. No other city on Earth performs more hocus-pocus, possesses more juju, or casts more spells than this Merlin of the Mojave. The trickery, the smoke and mirrors, is most evident in the casino, controlled by the men behind the curtain, the Wizards of Odds. Of course, Las Vegas has nearly 70 major gambling halls, and some have better wizards (more convincing illusions) than others.

## ◆ THE VENETIAN

The Venetian has, perhaps, the best illusions (of the optical sort) in town. It has the requisite "themescape," the fantastic façade that propels visitors into a total pre-packaged simulation. The exterior includes detailed replicas of the Rialto Bridge, the Clock and Campanile towers, the Doge's Palace, and other landmarks. Inside, hanging behind the front desk, is a giant pictorial overview of historical Venice. Costumed characters straight out of a Titian painting roam the lobby and public areas, singing opera, playing flute, juggling, even kissing hands.

Overhead, reproductions of famous frescoes adorn the 65-foot-high domed ceiling, rimmed by 24-karat gilded frames. But the centerpiece of the themescape is the quarter-mile Grand Canal, meandering along the storefronts of the 70-store Grand Canal Shoppes, enclosed by brick walls and iron fencing. Gondolas ply the waterway, steered and powered by gondoliers who serenade the passengers. The canal ends at an authentic reproduction of St. Marks Square.

The Venetian is big, with 3,000 suites, each a third larger than the average Las Vegas hotel room. It has a sprawling casino, more than a dozen restaurants, a lounge, a showroom-nightclub, and an ultra-upscale health spa. The attached **Sands Convention and Expo Center,** all 1.3 million square feet of it, makes the Venetian the largest single hotel-and-convention facility in the world.

There are two other impressive *trompes l'oeil,* too. The first is an eye-popping geometric design on the flat-marble lobby floor that gives an M.C. Escher–like optical illusion of climbing stairs. The floor design continues throughout the Grand Canal Shoppes, with different colors and shapes to vary the theme.

The second is the Venetian's coolest attraction for the sheer squealing merriment of it: **Madame Tussaud's Wax Museum.** Getting to the museum is a minor sensation in itself. A conveyor belt—a unique cross between a people mover and

*Gondoliers on the Grand Canal at the Venetian. (photo by Kerrick James)*

an escalator—climbs up and over the steep-pitched Rialto Bridge to the entrance. Once there, Tussaud's nearly 100 statues of movie, pop, and rock stars, athletes, and Las Vegas legends are so true-to-life that you do double-takes from start to finish. Tussaud's sculptors take more than 150 measurements of each subject to imbue their facsimiles with as much authenticity as possible, and it works; *3355 Las Vegas Blvd. South; 800-494-3556.*

◆ BELLAGIO

A lot of local observers disagree, but in my opinion, the Venetian outguns its $1.8 billion down-the-Strip counterpart, Bellagio. The main difference is that the Venetian has distinguished itself with an effectively unified theme, while Bellagio only pretends to have one, relying instead on the same old "contemporary mob chic" that's been trying to pass itself off as classy since 1946.

Oh, Bellagio has some exquisite details, sure. The dome above the shopping wing is a 50-foot-tall ceiling of glass and oxidized copper, which bathes the shops in glorious natural light throughout the day. In addition, all the horticultural

*Original Picassos adorn the walls at the Picasso restaurant at Bellagio. (photo by Kerrick James)*

ornamentation throughout the hotel is alive, supplied by a two-acre greenhouse and managed by a 115-employee garden department. Bellagio's **Picasso** has not only been recognized by fancy-food critics as one of the great restaurants in the country, but original Picassos adorn the room. The pool area is lush and luxurious to a tee. *3600 Las Vegas Blvd. South; 888-987-6667.*

**The Gallery of Fine Arts,** as well, is pretty impressive. For its size, this is one of the most expensive collections of classic paintings and sculpture on display anywhere in the world: Cézanne, Degas, Gauguin, Giacometti, de Kooning, Leger, Manet, Matisse, Van Gogh, Renoir,

*Dale Chihuly's* Fiori di Como *hangs above the lobby at Bellagio. (photo by Kerrick James)*

Pollock, and Warhol, to name a few. Las Vegas is fortunate to feature a collection of art with more star power than most museums, let alone mere hotels, can boast. (Be prepared to wait and to pay for admission.)

On the other hand, the lobby centerpiece, Dale Chihuly's $10 million glass-flower chandelier—sort of an upside-down petunia garden of colored glass—is a bit over the top. And the **Conservatory,** a 12,500-square-foot botanical garden displaying flowers, shrubs, and trees, is a little overpowering—especially the floral scents sprayed into the air. And the dancing-waters spectacle out front is, compared to the volcano and pirate shows down the Strip *(see pp. 58–59),* a bore.

Though Bellagio is supposedly modeled after an actual northern Italian town, the real theme is exclusivity. Expensive art, live flowers, credit-card-maxing menu prices, super-upscale shops, one of the highest rack rates and costliest show tickets in town, and beautiful people all combine to make us homely working folk feel inferior and unwanted.

But most explicitly unwanted are children. Parents who defy the strong discouragement from reservations agents and book the family into Bellagio can bring kids, but they're not exactly welcome—some say they're even harassed—by security guards. If you're not a Bellagio guest, you must have reservations for dinner or a show to bring minors in with you. It's perhaps typical of a town that's so intent on manufacturing gaiety that Bellagio takes a distinctly unfriendly stance toward children in order to maintain the image of adult *bonhomie*.

### ◆ MANDALAY BAY

Another 1999 megaresort, the $1 billion Mandalay Bay, shares with Bellagio the lack of a bona fide unifying theme. Mandalay Bay, first, is a misnomer: The real Mandalay is an ancient temple town in central Myanmar (Burma), which has no bay. The lush Polynesian decor stands in stark contrast to the dusty Burmese plains. In a circumstance that's twisted even for Vegas, Mandalay Bay is a façade on top of a façade. *3950 Las Vegas Blvd. South; 877-632-7700.*

Further confounding matters, there's an *underlying* theme that has nothing to do with a misnamed and imaginary South Seas casino-resort. Mandalay Bay

*Aureole is MBay's signature eatery.*
*(photo by Kerrick James)*

(affectionately known as "MBay") is infused with a special vitality, hipness, and whimsy—the most contemporary, even futuristic, of the latest megajoints. If the Venetian is the crowning achievement of 20th-century resort development, then MBay presents a door into the 21st. To see the future on parade, visit the restaurants.

At the signature eatery, **Aureole** (with celebrity chef Charlie Palmer at the helm), there's an amazing centerpiece: a four-story stainless steel and plexiglas "wine tower" storing nearly 10,000 bottles. Athletic women in black unitards and hard hats work motorized cables with a bright yellow hand control that allows them to ride

*The water park at Mandalay Bay. (photo by Kerrick James)*

up and down the tower to retrieve ordered bottles.

**China Grill Cafe** has a novel approach to food delivery: a conveyor belt circles the Cafe's bar to and from the open kitchen, carrying plates of appetizers, primarily sushi, on color-coded (for the different priced) dishes. In the more upscale restaurant portion, the bathrooms, reached through bead curtains, are individual stalls in turquoise plastic—sort of an iMac-meets-Porta-Potty design aesthetic.

Then there's **Red Square,** an ostensible Russian restaurant specializing in caviar and vodka. The restaurant bartop is a solid block of ice, to keep your drink cold (though it's better for leaving your fingerprints on). If vodka tasting is your thing, this is the place—but if symbols of fascism aren't your thing, then give Red Square a wide berth. The theme here is a paean to the Soviet '30s, when Stalin was slaughtering millions of innocent Russian citizens. Inside, huge heroic posters of Russian intellectuals and professionals carrying shovels and automatic weapons fill the walls. Red Square wins the award for the Most Tasteless Las Vegas Theme.

Otherwise, Mandalay Bay possesses major megaresortitude, boasting eight other eateries, 3,000-plus rooms, an arena, an 1,800-seat theater, showroom, and an 11-acre waterpark with one of the biggest wave pools around.

MBay also hosts a 400-room **Four Seasons** hotel-within-a-hotel. The rooms occupy the 35th through 39th floors, reached via express elevators; the front desk, lobby, restaurants, pool area, and banquet rooms are in a separate wing.

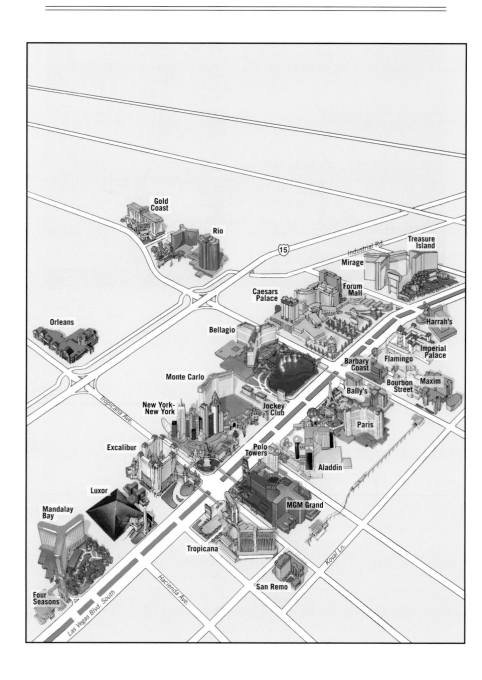

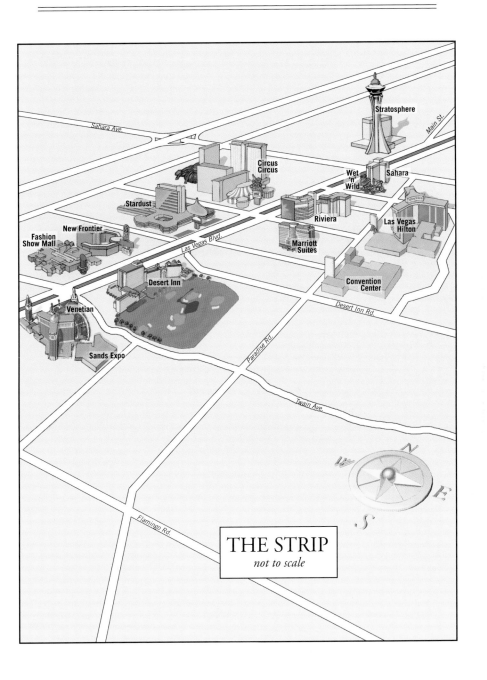

THE STRIP
*not to scale*

*The Eiffel Tower at Paris rises 460 feet above street level. (photo by Kerrick James)*

◆ PARIS

The last megaresort of the four that opened in 1999 is Paris. There's nothing illusory or even ambiguous about this joint: this is the 1930s in the City of Light. Employees greet you with a smattering of *française* (but don't embarrass them by speaking French: *monsieur* and *madame* pretty much sum up their vocabulary). The security guards wear gendarme get-ups; the cocktail waitresses are straight out of *Gigi;* even the porters wear fitted jackets and berets.

The exterior façade sports minutely detailed replicas of the Arc de Triomphe (built to two-third scale), the Paris Opera House, the Louvre, and an *Around the World in Eighty Days* balloon marquee. Also out front is the **Mon Ami Gabi** sidewalk cafe, the only al fresco dining right on the Strip. And, of course, the 540-foot **Eiffel Tower** towers above it all, the half-scale replica dwarfing even the most mega of the megaresorts nearby. A glass elevator takes you to the observation cage on the 460-foot level; the view is of the center Strip in the foreground and out over the rest of the Las Vegas landscape. It's an inspiring crow's nest.

Inside, the casino is all decked out in Gallic regalia, right down to the French Impressionistic floral carpeting. Among the many shops on **Le Boulevard** is the Re Galeria/Atelier, where a lithographer runs a one-of-a-kind 100-year-old eight-ton press to reproduce vintage posters. The restroom sinks are made of (what looks like) French porcelain. *3655 Las Vegas Blvd. South; 877-796-2096.*

# ■ THE FOURTH WAVE

Recent histories and conventional guidebooks refer to the "waves" of Las Vegas resort-casino openings, as in ocean waves rolling in on southern Nevada shores or even sound waves emanating from the great Las Vegas building boom. By my count, the Bellagio, Mandalay Bay, Venetian, and Paris quartet comprises the fifth Las Vegas wave. It's certainly the greatest, a veritable tsunami, awash in $5 billion worth of capital investment on the Las Vegas Strip alone. The previous, fourth, wave was a $1.3 billion ripple by comparison: the $450 million New York–New York, opened in January 1997; the $350 million Monte Carlo in June 1996; and the $500 million Stratosphere in April 1996.

But in this book the waves are neither tidal nor sonic. They're waves of a magic wand. These megaresorts materialized as if out of thin air, one minute a vacant lot or a derelict casino, the next a mini-skyline of New York, a replica of Europe's great gambling principality, and the tallest building west of the Mississippi.

*The Statue of Liberty in front of New York–New York is reputedly half the height of the original, the 151-foot-tall statue on Liberty Island in Manhattan's Upper Bay. (photo by Kerrick James)*

### ◆ MONTE CARLO

Consider this: the Monte Carlo, modeled after the Place du Casino in Monaco, complete with 3,000 rooms, an elegant European-style casino, an opera-house showroom, and a lush pool area, took only 14 months to pop into place. That's a little more than a year from groundbreaking to grand opening of a $350 million megacomplex. Fourteen months does not a must-see make; admittedly, there's not much magic in the Monte Carlo theme. For that, you have to walk next door to New York–New York; *3770 Las Vegas Blvd. South; 800-311-8999.*

### ◆ NEW YORK–NEW YORK

This joint is the superstar impersonator of the Big Apple on a Las Vegas stage. A facsimile of the famous skyline, with reproductions of the Empire State Building, Brooklyn Bridge, Statue of Liberty, and a Coney Island–like roller coaster, has cemented New York–New York's place in the pantheon of the world's great buildings and is, fittingly, a colossal piece of pop art.

Inside, there's the New York Racetrack, the New York Stock Exchange, Times Square, and Central Park. The hotel lobby and Empire Bar (with its giant red-apple disco ball rotating overhead) are a Vegas brand of art deco. But the crowning touch of the interior design is the stunning simulation of the backstreets of Greenwich Village, which frames the Village Eatery area, with its storefront pizzerias, burger joints, and sushi counters. This corner of the casino could be called virtual reality, only instead of head-mounted displays and 3-D video, it's achieved with concrete and neon and paint.

New York–New York has 2,000 rooms, a 2,000-car parking garage, a big casino, a dozen eateries, a huge arcade, a roller coaster, and more, all crammed into 18 acres. (By contrast, the 3,000-room Monte Carlo next door occupies 54 acres.) One of Las Vegas's greatest megaresorts jammed onto a postage-stamp parcel perhaps best recreates the way one of the world's greatest cities is jammed onto a tiny island: New York–New York *and* New York are cramped and crowded, and always will be. *3790 Las Vegas Blvd. South; 800-693-6763.*

### ◆ STRATOSPHERE

Finally, there's Stratosphere, saddest megaresort story in town. The magic here was of the dark variety, encompassing a rough location, a failed IPO, a towering inferno, a stock fiasco, a marketing plan based on the if-you-build-it-they-will-come illusion, a bankruptcy, and a hostile takeover. The whole sordid story is well told

*The High Roller roller coaster spins you around the summit of the Stratosphere some 1,000 feet above the ground. (photo by Kerrick James)*

in *No Limit: The Rise and Fall of Bob Stupak and Las Vegas' Stratosphere Tower*, by Las Vegas's favorite newspaper columnist, John L. Smith. And the ending, happy or otherwise, is yet to be written: open since 1996, this joint is still unfinished, with the concrete skeleton of a 1,000-room tower brooding in the rear.

Still, Stratosphere today is a (mostly) successful and popular property. It ought to be: it boasts the tallest observation tower in the country (also the tallest building west of the Mississippi), the two highest thrill rides in the world, and a revolving restaurant with a spectacular view. In addition, because the tower attraction doesn't quite overcome the not-so-hot location, Stratosphere has to try a little harder to attract players into its profit center, the casino. Unlike almost all Strip casinos, which cater to out-of-towners and aren't known for their attractive odds, Stratosphere has by far the best video poker schedules; the slot machines, likewise, are "certified loose"—though don't go spending your sure-thing jackpots before you hit them. *2000 Las Vegas Blvd. South; 800-998-6937.*

Comprising this fourth, or second newest, wave, the three 1996 megaresorts still have a little of the original magnetism left.

# ■ THE THIRD WAVE

The third-wave megaresorts, on the other hand, are so "old" that the term "megaresort" was coined to describe them, and they've all been altered significantly since. This wave was a $2 billion breaker, a monster swell way back when, in 1993. To make it even more dramatic, all three came to fruition in three consecutive months: Luxor in October, Treasure Island in November, and MGM Grand in December.

Actually, this whitecap picked up its initial momentum with two grand openings that didn't involve casinos, but did establish major Las Vegas trends—one that has flooded the town ever since, the other that backfired and turned into a nasty sucking vortex, fluxus interruptus.

## ◆ THE FORUM SHOPS AT CAESARS PALACE

In May 1992, the $250 million Forum Shops at Caesars debuted, and shopping Las Vegas–style has never been the same. The unparalleled success of this mall, the most successful in the country (with astronomical average sales of $1,200 per square foot, compared to the $300 mall-industry average) helped transform Las Vegas into a shopping mecca. Indeed, for most megaresorts planned and built

after May 1992, having a unique shopping experience in the mix has become as vital as a detailed theme and celebrity chefs.

Most people are aware that Las Vegas has always been about building better mousetraps. Here, new has never been just new. Hotel-casinos have always had to be bigger, bolder, brighter. They've always had to have more theme, more panache, more spectacle. This trend started to gel with these third-wave megaresorts. But the Forum Shops tied the rest of the

*The Forum Shops at Caesars Palace.*
*(photo by Kerrick James)*

Vegas experience into the "nouveau new" trend with a pretty pink bow. Post-Forum, the shopping has had to be infused with entertainment value. And the entertainment has had to be infused with brand value. The restaurants have had to be owned by celebrity chefs or movie stars and the rooms themselves have had to be as much of an attraction as the food.

*The roller coaster at Circus Circus. (photo by Kerrick James)*

### ◆ THE AMUSEMENT PARK AT CIRCUS CIRCUS

The second non-casino grand opening of the third wave introduced a trend that sputtered and fizzled, then died aborning. Or did it? In August 1993, Circus Circus Enterprises (now called Mandalay Resort Group) unveiled Grand Slam Canyon (now called Adventuredome) behind Circus Circus. This five-acre amusement park, enclosed by a big pink boob and offering the world's largest indoor roller coaster, among other rides and attractions, marked the transformation of Las Vegas from Sin City to the Babysitting Capital of the World, as the traditionally "X"-rated town strove for the "G" of general admittance in an attempt to attract the big "F," as in families.

As everyone now knows, of course, Las Vegas wasn't really trying to turn itself into the Disney World of the West with its new amusement parks and thrill rides and video arcades and pirate shows and dolphins and bowling alleys and movie theaters. Nosirree Bob. Why, if casinos started catering to nuclear foursomes or fivesomes, the adults would spend less time (that is, less money) in the casinos, and the good grown-up customers would complain bitterly about baby carriages and dirty diapers and rugrats underfoot. Las Vegas isn't into kids (and never was, by god!). A new family attraction hasn't opened up since, jeez, who can remember when? The bambino backlash killed the brief "bring-the-kids" trend.

*Luxor soon after its construction in 1993. (photo by Kerrick James)*

## ◆ LUXOR

But none of this had transpired when Luxor erupted from the desert in fall 1993. It started out as a 2,500-room pyramid, one of the world's greatest architectural wonders. (The design was sorely compromised in 1996 when two 1,000-room ziggurat towers were added onto the north side, but it rendered Luxor the third largest hotel in the world.)

Inside, the soaring 30-story atrium encompasses 29 million square feet of open space and "inclinators" rise up the sides at a 39-degree angle. There's a motion-simulator attraction, a 3-D IMAX theater, and a high-tech video arcade. With a King Tut museum, a popular subterranean buffet, and a tram that connects to Excalibur and Mandalay Bay, Luxor is eminently kid-friendly (but don't tell anyone).

## ◆ TREASURE ISLAND

A month after the debut of Luxor, Treasure Island flung open its doors, at the same moment that the Dunes was imploded down the Strip. In this respect, Treasure Island appears always overshadowed by Bellagio, which replaced the Dunes. It

*(opposite) The pirate ship* Hispañola *under attack from the* HMS Brittania *in front of Treasure Island resort. (photo by Kerrick James)*

also plays second fiddle to the virtuoso Mirage next door. None of this is a coincidence. The TI hotel tower was built plain and small to enhance the beauty and bigness of the Mirage, like a Holiday Inn next to a Hyatt Regency.

That's not to say that the TI isn't an attraction of its own. It's recently completed a $60-million renovation of all 2,900 rooms. It has the large-as-life pirate show out front, framed by a Polynesian pirate village that's one of the great false fronts in a town full of great false fronts. The gold-plated skull-and-crossbones lobby chandelier, the talking-skeleton arcade greeters, and other touches endear the theme to kids of all ages. In addition, *Mystère,* the Cirque du Soleil showroom extravaganza, is as pure as performance gets, the essence of timeless and ageless entertainment.

## ◆ MGM GRAND

Lastly, the MGM Grand burst onto the scene, all billion dollars worth of it—an unheard-of sum at the time. But Kirk Kerkorian, majority owner and developer of three of the world's largest hotels over the years, got what he paid for. This joint

*With over 5,000 guest rooms, the MGM Grand was, as of 1999, the largest hotel in the world. (photo by Kerrick James)*

isn't just big. It's gigantic, titanic, epic. There are three other hotels in the world with between 4,000 and 4,500 rooms, but there's only one hotel in the world with 5,035 rooms. Only the Grand, it seems, can manage the critical mass of 10,000 guests, 5,000 employees, and perhaps another 5,000 casino gamblers, restaurant diners, conventioneers, amusement-park patrons, and showgoers at any given time.

And lest you suspect that no hotel can regularly book, fill, and clean 5,000 rooms, dig this: the MGM Grand reported a 99.8% occupancy rate in a recent SEC third-quarter filing, meaning that the largest hotel in the world had an average of 10 unoccupied rooms per night July through September, one of the slower times of year at that.

On an average day, the MGM has a larger "population" than every rural town in Nevada except Elko; when there's a rock concert or heavyweight prizefight in the MGM Garden Arena, it *is* as if every man, woman, and child in Elko were stuffed into this property.

Yep, it's colossal, prodigious, elephantine, all right, but that doesn't mean it's not resilient, that it can't change with the times. This megaresort, of all the 1990s' Las Vegas megaresorts, has been a work-in-progress. A staggering $750 million has been spent in the past couple of years, renovating, upgrading, and—believe it or not—expanding. A mile-long monorail was built to connect with Bally's at the corner of Flamingo and the Strip. The entire pool area was rebuilt; its original space was taken by a separate convention center, which also encroached on the amusement park, where SkyScreamer, a monster thrill ride, was built. The Mansion was added: ultra-exclusive suites for the wealthiest gamblers in the world, a veritable private island in a vast sea of hospitality.

The interior, as well, has changed qualitatively. A shopping mall between the parking garage and the lobby, a decent lion habitat, an expanded buffet, restaurant upgrades—all have altered the shape and style of this gargantuan gambler gobbler.

The downside? The same things. The size of it: you need a meal or a nap after making the trek from one side to the other. Hell, I'm all tuckered out just writing about it. And the people. Hordes of them, all waiting. Waiting to check in, waiting for an elevator, waiting to get into the buffet, waiting on ticket lines, waiting for a urinal.

You can't exactly escape to a quieter corner around here, either. New York–New York (which MGM owns) is even more crowded. And Excalibur, across from New York–New York, is a—well, let's take a look at Excalibur.

*Excalibur has positioned itself as a family-friendly resort hotel. (photo by Kerrick James)*

## ■ THE SECOND AND FIRST WAVES

### ◆ EXCALIBUR

The second wave, the one that foretold and catalyzed the three waves that followed, was a two-casino, billion-dollar splash. Excalibur was the second casino in that wave. It opened in June 1990 at a bargain $375 million. Especially for what it bought: one of the world's great castles, possessing four 1,000-room towers, the world's largest hotel at the time. It also had the world's biggest casino, a medieval carnival complete with the first motion simulator in the country, Las Vegas' biggest buffet (still is), and a subterranean showroom encompassing a jousting arena.

The second wave also triggered the two opposing trends of family-friendly and adult-oriented. Guess which one lined up with Excalibur! In 10 years, the popularity of Excalibur with families hasn't faded a fraction. Don't try to escape the MGM crowds here either. This joint is overrun with, shall we say, youthful exuberance.

The midway on the lower level has neat medieval carnival games. *Tournament of Kings* is by far Las Vegas's best show for children older than five or so. Upstairs on the mezzanine, strolling Renaissance performers are a perennial favorite with

Mom, Dad, Buddy, and Sis. The buffet, though it seats 1,400, often has a 20-minute wait in line. The restaurants serve decent and reasonably priced family fare; the **Nitro Grill,** a professional-wrestling-themed eatery, is a huge crowd pleaser. And the **Canterbury Wedding Chapel** is, surprisingly, the most beautiful casino chapel in Las Vegas.

## ◆ THE MIRAGE

Which brings us, finally, to the first joint of this wave, the one that still sits at the center of both the Strip and every subsequent wave. The Mirage. This is where it all started, the opening salvo of the greatest boom in the greatest boomtown in the history of the world, which inspired upwards of $10 billion worth of southern Nevada megaresort action.

At the time, however, the Mirage was a gamble of monumental proportions. It was built at the tail end of a 16-year lull in the fortunes of Las Vegas, especially in terms of new hotel-casino construction. It was budgeted to cost more than $600 million, requiring a daily million-dollar net, *every* day, just to stay afloat—triple

*The volcano erupts at the Mirage. (photo by Kerrick James)*

# FREE SPECTACLES

## ◆ THE CIRCUS CIRCUS CIRCUS

Spectacles—extravagant free shows that casinos have rolled out as loss leaders to get the people through the doors—can be traced to the feverish imagination of Jay Sarno, the promoter and mad genius who, it's been said, "threw off a shower of sparks wherever he went." After dreaming up the toga-clad and statue-strewn Roman theme for Caesars Palace in the mid-1960s, Sarno went on to open a bizarre casino that featured circus acts performed over the crap tables and slot machines. For the past 33 years, Circus Circus has presented its clowns, trapeze artists, jugglers, stiltwalkers, unicyclists, trained poodles, and the like—free of charge, all day, every day.

## ◆ THE MIRAGE VOLCANO

The free spectacle as gambler bait, however, lay dormant until 1989, when the feverish imagination of another promoter and mad genius, Steve Wynn, dreamed up an automated free show: an erupting volcano. Nightly after dark, a 54-foot manmade mountain fronting the Mirage—with just a sidewalk separating it from the Strip—roars to life, spewing steam with a serpentine hiss, shooting gas-fed tongues of flame to lick the night sky, and roiling the reflecting-pool waters with red-light lava.

## ◆ THE TREASURE ISLAND PIRATE BATTLE

When Wynn opened Treasure Island next door four years later, he outdid himself in the free-spectacle department with Buccaneer Bay, again between the casino and the Strip. Every night a Navy frigate sails around the corner from Spring Mountain Avenue into the bay, there to engage a parked privateer's schooner in eight minutes of swashbuckling, cannon-firing, powder-keg-exploding "pirate-technics." Twenty stuntmen wind up in the drink and the Navy ship sinks all the way up to its sails; the British commander goes down, then comes back up, with the ship.

## ◆ CAESARS PALACE OLYMPIADS

In 1992, Caesars Palace opened a high-tech indoor spectacle, the **Festival Fountain,** to entertain the estimated 20,000 people (19,900 window shoppers) who walk through the Forum Shops each day. Laser lightning and stereo thunder awaken Bacchus, Roman god of free spectacles and animatronic MC for the show. Bacchus introduces Pluto, Venus, and Apollo, who do their little acts. The whole thing strikes Bacchus as hilarious, and he laughs and laughs from deep in his belly, invites the audience to empty their pockets in the shops, then bows out with a burp.

The **Atlantis spectacle** in the new wing of the Forum Shops, opened in 1998, goes to show how far the technology has advanced in five years. The Atlantis fountain sits in the center, quite benignly, of the Great Hall rotunda, with a 50,000-gallon horse-shoe-shaped saltwater aquarium and statues that stand high overhead and preside over flowing fountains. But then, at the top of every hour, the lights dim, thunder rumbles, and the statues descend through the floor and disappear. Up through the fountains, amidst fire, smoke, and steam, rise three animatronic characters: Atlas; Alia, his daughter the princess; and Gadrius, his son the prince. For the next eight minutes, the royal family struggles for control of the mythical kingdom. As they threaten, taunt, argue with, and laugh at each other, the polyurethane figures seem so real that you start thinking they're human.

◆ FOUR BLOCKS OF DAZZLING LIGHTS ON FREMONT STREET
The Fremont Street Experience, launched in 1996, is a colossal graphic display system that delivers state-of-the-art animation and acoustic effects on the curved underside of a 90-foot-high four-block-long canopy covering Fremont Street downtown. More than 2.1 million polychromatic lightbulbs and 208 concert-quality speakers combine for six-minute high-fidelity kaleidoscopic light shows with country, spacey, and Vegasy themes. Each show is a one-of-a-kind free spectacle, but perhaps the greatest moment in the Experience is when someone somewhere flicks a switch and Glitter Gulch's whole flamboyant neon facade simply shuts down. For a moment, it's dark on Fremont Street, and that's something to see (or not to see).

◆ FOUNTAIN SHOW AT BELLAGIO
Dancing waters are an old attraction in Las Vegas, dating back to the '50s. Today, the big one is at center Strip, a water-fountain ballet performed in Lago di Bellagio. "Choreographed" to orchestral music (and some Sinatra), the spectacle stretches 900 feet across the lake, employs 1,200 fountain nozzles, 4,500 lights, and 27 million gallons of water. Each show runs three to five minutes (one song long). The powerful jets can thrust the streams of water 200 feet high. The best view is 460 feet above it, at the top of the Eiffel Tower directly across the street.

◆ A CARNAVAL EVERY DAY AT THE RIO
The "Show in the Sky" is the Rio's own Strip-style free spectacle. Performed every two hours, the show consists of dancers, jugglers, singers, stiltwalkers, and bungee bouncers, all in outrageous costumes and masks, plus parade floats that inch along a 950-foot track suspended from the ceiling. You can actually dress up and ride in the floats for a nominal fee. This ceiling parade is actually the modern-day equivalent of Jay Sarno's circus acts; the wildness goes on right over the slot machines and blackjack tables every couple of hours.

the normal numbers. It was financed primarily by high-interest junk bonds. And it was being built by a cocky, spotlight-hogging, 47-year-old casino wunderkind who many not-impartial observers were hoping and betting would go down in highly visible flames.

Well, the rest is highrise history. The fire-spewing volcano rising from the Strip's first lake stopped pedestrians and traffic dead in their tracks. The lush Polynesian rainforest theme (grown ever more lush and verdant over the years), including the 100-foot glass dome, 20,000-gallon aquarium, and sensational pool area, wowed even the naysayers. The white-tiger habitat was a master stroke of advertising for *Siegfried & Roy*, a stage extravaganza that was lavish even by Las Vegas standards. For years the Mirage was *the* place to see, stay, eat, and play. And not only did it crack its daily nut, but it surpassed it with ease; debt was quickly retired, shareholders made small fortunes, new megaresorts were financed—and competitors were challenged.

Fitting that the forerunner of the frenzy of this city's future was inaugurated by a Mirage.

## ■ PARALLEL UNIVERSE: LOCALS CASINOS

A by-product of the great Las Vegas building boom of the '90s has been an overwhelming in-migration of boomtowners. Las Vegas and vicinity have expanded ferociously over the past 10 years, as 25 or so major hotel-casinos, accounting for 50,000 rooms, have opened and a half-million people have moved to the city. Has anyone not heard that Las Vegas has been the fastest-growing metropolitan area in the country for more than a decade?

Construction workers, hotel employees, dealers, casino managers, truck drivers, doctors, franchise owners, teachers, gamblers, service tradesmen, retail salespeople, lawyers, butchers, bakers, candlestick makers have all resettled in the City of Second Chances. Retirees, too, have flocked to southern Nevada, and why not? Restaurant and buffet meals can actually be less expensive than cooking at home. Entertainment is abundant and reasonably priced. Personal visitors are frequent: as soon as you move to Las Vegas, everyone you know and everyone they know commence to darken your doorstep.

Even if you just frequent the casinos for the food, drink, and entertainment, you can take advantage of all the loss leaders without having to risk a plug nickel. But if you're a player, then the whole town's your huckleberry. By playing beatable

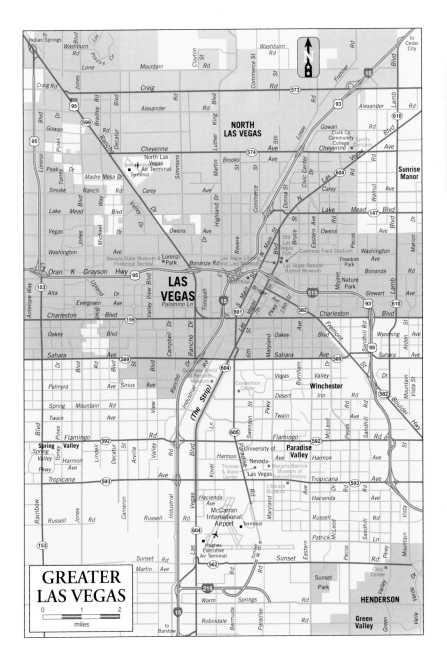

GREATER
LAS VEGAS

0     1     2
miles

games such as blackjack and video poker, combined with casino promotions, paycheck-cashing bonuses, and the never-ending drawings, you qualify to get almost everything at no charge at all. Thanks to newfangled electronic player tracking at the slots and tables, comped rooms (for all your visitors), meals, shows, parties, tournaments, and special events become an integral part of your existence. In gambling lingo, if you're willing to fade the risk of action and the bankroll swings, you can live large on the house.

As people move to Las Vegas in droves, new neighborhoods erupt from the desert like there's no tomorrow. Las Vegas is growing so fast that as soon as the new maps are printed, they're already out of date. As neighborhoods appear and expand, locals casinos are built to service them.

## ◆ WHERE THE LOCALS GAMBLE

You've probably heard that Las Vegas residents don't gamble. Don't believe it; it's a crock. "Locals casinos" are among the most popular and successful of all. Why? Several reasons. They have a regular and lucrative customer base nearby, to which

*Pit bosses at locals casinos pay close attention to their customers.*
*(Underwood Photo Archives, San Francisco)*

they market continuously and creatively through promotions and loss leaders, thus enjoying tremendous return business. What's more, they compete ferociously by one-upping each other with their products, which are similar, and that works to the ultimate benefit of the consumer.

Locals casinos have the best buffets; the restaurants are top-shelf; and the fast food is good, cheap, and convenient. Neighborhood joints offer hot lounges and dance clubs, cool movie theaters and bowling alleys, even child care. Mostly, though, they try to attract the local players with the best gambling odds and the best slot club benefits and the best casino coupons that they can.

Ten locals casinos have arrived on the Las Vegas scene within the past decade. The newest is also the farthest out, on the edge of the

*Charlie Fey, one of the first slot-machine manufacturers, designed this "draw poker" machine in 1901.*

metropolitan area in southeastern Henderson, though the city is quickly catching up and overtaking it. **The Reserve** opened in February 1998. It has killer video poker, a generous slot club, tons of promotions, and a fantastic buffet.

A bit closer in is **Sunset Station**, in the heart of Henderson, dubbed by some the San Fernando Valley of southern Nevada. Miles from any other locals joint (except for the Reserve), it's the most wildly successful branch of the Station Casino group, itself the most wildly successful of the locals casino companies. Sunset Station shares the same formula with its sister casinos: **Texas Station,** in North Las Vegas; **Boulder Station,** on Boulder Highway in the east part of town; and **Palace Station,** a mile west of the Strip on Sahara Avenue, generally credited with catalyzing the locals casino movement in the late 1980s. The formula? Great bargain buffets and restaurants, food-and-drink loss leaders such as potent 99-cent margaritas, movie theaters, sizzling lounges, kid care, and bingo.

In the northwest suburbs, at the intersection of Rancho and Lake Mead Boulevards, the **Fiesta** faces off against **Texas Station** in a sort of friendly Coke-Pepsi rivalry. **The Santa Fe** is a couple of miles farther north of the Fiesta along what's become the Rancho Strip. It has the best video poker, a big bingo hall, a bowling alley, and, unique to a Nevada casino, a professional-level ice-skating rink.

Then there's the **Orleans** on West Tropicana, a couple of miles from the Strip. It starts to sound like a broken record: super video poker, super buffet, super slot club, super bowling alley, super bingo, super lounge entertainment. The Orleans is a sister property to the **Gold Coast,** a couple blocks over on West Flamingo, with video poker, bingo, and bowling. Points in the Gold Coast's slot club are good for a catalog full of gifts and discounts at local department stores.

Also on the west side, at West Charleston and Decatur, is **Arizona Charlie's.** Here, you'll find the cheapest buffet in town, cheap food, and bingo. Charlie's is promotion crazy; three or four cash and prize drawings a day aren't unusual. Also

*An original Pullman car in a restaurant at Main Street Station. (photo by Kerrick James)*

noteworthy for promotions is **Silverton,** on the far south side of Las Vegas. And **Sam's Town,** on Boulder Highway between Boulder Station and Sunset Station, holds what could be the most participated-in promotion of all: they give away a new *house* every year. Sam's Town is the second oldest locals casino, opened in 1979. It's also the second largest, boasting 650 rooms.

The largest locals casino is also the oldest. **The Showboat** opened in 1954 on East Fremont about two miles from downtown. It was inconvenient to out-of-town visitors, but Las Vegas residents flocked there in droves. The Showboat had bingo, bowling, 49-cent breakfasts, and a good cheap buffet. Though it took another 40 years and a population boom for the concept to catch on, the 'Boat as a place for Las Vegans to gamble, eat, and relax was envisioned by bosses who came up from the trenches of illegal casinos, and therefore well understood what would attract local people into casinos.

◆ FOR LOCALS *AND* SAVVY VISITORS

Don't be misled by the moniker "locals casinos" or get the notion that none of these properties offers anything of interest to non–Las Vegas residents. Far from it. A sizable cadre of out-of-town visitors-in-the-know take full advantage of their potent tandem of quality and value. In fact, it's the casino that skims the cream off the top of both the tourist and resident trade that wins the fierce Las Vegas marketing war.

Two joints have connected with just such a one-two punch. The first is the **Hard Rock,** on Paradise Road. The Hard Rock is a haj for the hip, and that's not just hype. The implementation of its rock 'n' roll theme is creative and clever: table-game layouts festooned with Grateful Dead and Sex Pistols lyrics, slot machine handles shaped like guitar necks, custom gambling chips, rock memorabilia displayed throughout, the 1,400-seat Joint concert hall, and, of course, the best music of any public address system anywhere. The Hard Rock has been so successful that it recently doubled in size, adding 300 rooms, three restaurants, and casino space, plus expanding the pool area with Las Vegas's second swim-up blackjack table.

Only one Las Vegas resort-casino does it even better than the Hard Rock. And that's the **Rio.** The Rio opened in January 1990, a few weeks after the Mirage. The original Rio was comparatively small and out of the way, about a mile west of the Strip over the interstate and railroad tracks. But it distinguished itself with its all-suite configuration, stunning neon sign, sandy beach by the pool, and skimpy cocktail-waitress uniforms.

The Rio quickly lured locals by the lorry load, enticed by fabulous food, lots of promotions, and an all-around Mardi Gras party flavor. The Rio also introduced the "superbuffet," a sort of mini food city defined by separate serving stations for different ethnic fare. Soon new towers were added, and out-of-towners began discovering the suites. Everything about the casino, as well, grew and got more elaborately themed.

In 1997, the Rio opened a 41-story 1,000-room tower, bringing the room count to a respectable 2,500. A second casino wing houses a half-dozen more restaurants, a handful of upscale retail shops (including the $6 million 65,000-bottle **Wine Cellar Tasting Room,** one of the foremost oenological collections in the world and the only public wine cellar in Nevada), and a casino called Masquerade Village, home to the Show in the Sky ceiling parade *(see pages 58–59)*.

In short, the Rio rules. On the downside, the Rio knows it, and there's a distinct arrogance to the place, especially if you're trying to get something out of them—information, service, comps. Still, this will hardly be noticeable to the average guest or player. And if it is, well, it's still the Rio, perhaps the quintessential "locals megaresort."

■ FAST REVERSE    *map pages 44–45, page 69*

Times were tight in Las Vegas for a decade and a half before the Mirage and the Rio opened. That's not to say that nothing happened, but progress was spotty.

◆ THE 1980s

In 1989, the **San Remo** opened; this 800-room hotel-casino next door to the Tropicana caters to a large Japanese tour crowd and serves excellent 24-hour prime rib and steak-and-eggs meal deals in the coffee shop.

A year earlier, the **Boardwalk** debuted. This Atlantic City–themed casino, on the Strip between Monte Carlo and Bellagio, had been a small Holiday Inn previously; it was bought by Mirage Resorts in 1997 for a cool $80 million and will probably be torn down to make way for wave six.

When it debuted in 1980, **Fitzgeralds** downtown was the tallest building in Nevada at 400 feet; it's still the second tallest, behind Stratosphere. Fitz has the highest-tech slot club in town and Fremont Street's only second-floor outdoor balcony, complete with patio furniture.

*The Fremont Street Experience, launched in 1996, consists of a four-block long canopy of computerized lights set to music. (photo by Kerrick James)*

◆ THE 1970S

The '70s saw intermittent development similar to the '80s. In 1979, the **Imperial Palace** towers rose from center Strip, replacing a low-rise motel; today, this 2,700-room hotel-casino is known for the long-running *Legends in Concert* superstar-impersonator show and the Imperial Palace Auto Collection.

In 1977, the **Golden Nugget,** which had been a Fremont Street grind joint for 30 years, opened the first of what would eventually add up to 1,900 rooms—the largest and classiest hotel-casino downtown.

**The California** was completed in 1975, on Ogden Street downtown, one block north of Fremont Street. Despite the implication of the name, today the California caters almost exclusively to a Hawaiian clientele.

In 1973, Kirk Kerkorian completed the original MGM Grand, now **Bally's,** his second world's-largest hotel. Bally's is still known for its size, though now it's a giant among giants; it has a good workmanlike buffet, a monorail to the new MGM Grand, and *Jubilee!,* the long-running old-time Las Vegas extravaganza.

The Holiday Inn opened in 1972 at center Strip. It later became **Harrah's** and is now the flagship of the extensive Harrah's fleet, which encompasses a couple dozen hotel-casinos—megaresorts, riverboats, tribal casinos—in nearly every gambling jurisdiction in the country.

And in 1971, the **Plaza** (née Union Plaza) arrived to anchor Fremont Street at Main. The Plaza could be the most photographed joint in town; it's also low-roller heaven, with penny slots, quarter craps, $2 blackjack, and full-pay nickel video poker.

◆ THE 1960S

Three major hotel-casinos, along with trends they introduced, survive from the '60s. In 1969, Kirk Kerkorian built the International, his first world's-largest hotel. A year later, Kerkorian got into financial trouble and had to sell his edifice to Hilton. Next door to the Las Vegas Convention Center, the **Las Vegas Hilton** caters mostly to conventioneers and trade-show goers, though fans of Star Trek also make frequent pilgrimages here to take in the **Star Trek: The Experience** attraction.

In 1968, Jay Sarno, the man who thought up the idea of infusing Las Vegas casinos with detailed themes, launched **Circus Circus.** The world, however, wasn't ready for three-ring acts and carnival midways to go with their gambling, and it wasn't until William Bennett, the man credited with melding casinos and families, took over Circus a few years later that it became a success. Circus ever since has

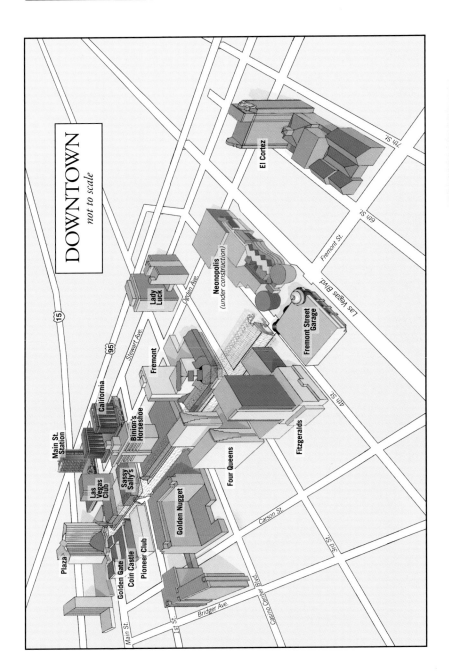

# DOWNTOWN
*not to scale*

El Cortez

7th St.

6th St.

Fremont St.

Las Vegas Blvd.

Neonopolis
*(under construction)*

Lady Luck

Ogden Ave.

Fremont

Fremont Street Garage

Stewart Ave.

California

Binion's Horseshoe

4th St.

Main St. Station

Sassy Sally's

Four Queens

Fitzgeralds

Las Vegas Club

Golden Nugget

Carson St.

3rd St.

Plaza

Golden Gate

Coin Castle

Pioneer Club

Main St.

1st St.

Bridger Ave.

Casino Center Blvd.

been a family madhouse, with Big Top performances, the midway, the **Adventure-dome** indoor amusement park, and a buffet that claims to serve the most meals (four million a year) of any restaurant in the world.

Two years earlier, Sarno had insured that his name would live in Las Vegas legend when he introduced **Caesars Palace** to a stunned and gaping public. Today, the Roman Coliseum theme is a bit passé, though the rest of the place more than makes up for it. The Caesars complex, which includes the Forum Shops, has 2,500 rooms, four-score stores, 20 restaurants, two sprawling casinos, a huge sports book, a big showroom, and so on. Though Caesars is only the 16th largest hotel in town, it more approaches the MGM Grand in grandness than any other.

## ◆ THE 1950s

Which brings us to the '50s. A dozen major hotels were built in the heady years when the old-time illegal gamblers ran the casinos. (Nine are left; the other three were imploded.) The '50s were the glory years, the glamour years, the first wave. These were the years when: everyone dressed in formal wear to go out in the evening—to the dinner show, the casino, or even just the chuckwagon buffet or 24-hour coffee shop; casinos held roof parties to watch aboveground testing of atomic bombs 70 miles away; Jakie Friedman owned the Sands and shot craps there with a wad of 500 hundred-dollar bills, and Nick the Greek held court at the poker tables, going from millionaire to bust-out back to millionaire in the course of a weekend; huge parcels of Strip frontage sold for a few grand and the Strip had one traffic light; Joe E. Lewis, Liberace, and 12-year-old Wayne Newton performed in the lounges; and Sheriff Ralph Lamb ran the town with an iron fist. Back then, Las Vegas was about high rollers, not roller coasters.

**The Stardust** was the last of the dirty-dozen hotels to go up in the '50s. It cost roughly $10 million to build what, at the time, was the largest hotel in the world, with 1,000 rooms. (Today, $10 million will buy you a small addition to the buffet.) A lot of crooked deals were cut here over a span of nearly 20 years, well-dramatized by the movie *Casino*. But little remains of that joint. Today, the Stardust is a typical first-wave property: expanded a half-dozen times, themeless, nondescript casino and restaurants, bargain rooms—and a candidate for future implosion.

A year earlier, the **Tropicana** debuted, at $15 million the toniest of the bunch, immediately earning the sobriquet "Tiffany of the Strip." A lot of crooked deals were cut here over a span of nearly *30* years. It's a typical first-wave property, though it retains the original several hundred two-story bungalow rooms; they actually have outdoor patios, the only such amenity on the Strip. The Trop is also renowned for the old-growth lushocity of its pool area and the original swim-up blackjack game. And *Folies Bergère* is the longest-running old-fashioned revue in town, the last gasp of '50s Las Vegas stage entertainment.

The Riviera, Hacienda, and Dunes all vied for grand-opening attention in 1955; only the Riv remains. **The Riviera** was the first high-rise on the Strip, a whole nine stories. The original wing is still there, at the heart of the requisite half-dozen expansions of a first-wave joint; these are the oldest original rooms for rent on the Strip. The Riv these days tries to distinguish itself with a choice of four stage shows, including *Crazy Girls*, for years the sexiest (soft-core) show in town. It also has Nickel Town, a low-roller casino annex with a snack bar popular for its fill-'er-uppers at rock-bottom prices, such as 50-cent draft beers.

The Sands and the Sahara were both unveiled in 1952; they cost in the neighborhood of $2-3 million each. The Sands was imploded in 1997 to make way for the Venetian. **The Sahara** managed to hang on to a few first-wave assets till a couple of years ago when William Bennett, after being forcibly retired at Circus Circus, bought it and began an extensive renovation. Incongruously, the Sahara has a Moroccan porte cochère and a race-car theme. Speedworld is a virtual racing attraction; there are also a NASCAR Cafe and a roller coaster. And the Sahara is the last casino in Las Vegas where you can play $1 blackjack at nearly every table.

Meanwhile, downtown, the **Fremont** became the tallest building in the state, at 15 stories, when it was built in 1955. Like the Stardust, it's a standard first-wave hotel (expanded a few times, bargain rooms, no themes). The one standout is the **Second Street Grille,** a fine restaurant for fresh fish Pacific Rim–style.

Run by legendary Texan Benny Binion, **Binion's Horseshoe** began its fascinating life in 1952. Binion was a cowboy, an independent; he owed no allegiance to any of the mob bosses—rare at the time and one indication of how powerful he was. Binion was a gambler who took everyone as they came, fading any action. He was a promoter (his official title at the Horseshoe was Director of Public Relations). He set an enduring standard for food comps ("Play and we'll feed ya'") and loss leaders (he served a $2 steak for 40 years). He displayed a hundred $10,000 bills and took people's pictures by it, best free souvenir in town; the bills were recently sold for upwards of $6 million. He instituted the World Series of Poker, the most prestigious gambling tournament in the world. And he was a father who trained his children to manage the family business. Two of them still do.

*Wilbur Clark's Desert Inn, circa 1950. (Underwood Photo Archives, San Francisco)*

Binion's Strip counterpart in power was Moe Dalitz of the **Desert Inn**, opened in 1950. (The DI was dreamed up and begun by Wilbur Clark; he later sold out to Dalitz, who finished building and opened the joint. But Clark remained the casino's front man.) Dalitz was the first underworld boss to follow in Benjamin Siegel's footsteps by building a fabulous resort-casino in the southern Nevada desert. Dalitz was already 50 when he moved to Las Vegas, and he knew what he was doing. He paved the way for all the bosses who followed him into the façade of legitimacy, while keeping a lot of the old ways alive. No less than Howard Hughes bought him out when the old ways stopped working; no less than Kirk Kerkorian bought out Hughes Corporation when they wisely bailed out of the casino business. Since then, a succession of owners has spent hundreds of millions on restoring the DI to its former glory. It's the smallest major hotel-casino in town, on the largest plot of property; the 160-acre golf course, the last of three on the Strip, sees to that. The casino is elegant and quiet, and the restaurants are non-pareil. It'll cost you, though, to eat, sleep, gamble, or golf there.

♦ THE 1940s

Five casinos—El Cortez, El Rancho Vegas, the Last Frontier, the Flamingo, and the Thunderbird—were built in the '40s; incredibly, three survive. **The Flamingo** looks nothing like it did 55 years ago. The Oregon Building, the last vestige of Ben Siegel's handiwork, was torn down in 1993. Since 1969, the Flamingo has been a Hilton, the first corporation to buy into the gambling business after the Nevada Legislature allowed publicly owned companies to do so. Hilton expanded the place continuously over two decades, finally finishing the Flamingo a few years ago. It now has 3,600 rooms, a 400-room timeshare tower, a top-notch pool area, and the Rockettes in the showroom.

**The New Frontier** has been through four incarnations and name changes since opening in 1942. Back then it was the first themed resort-casino, sporting Wild West accouterments that included an entire village of frontier artifacts collected from around the west. The story from then to now is a book in itself. Today, it

*"Bugsy" Siegel's penthouse used to rise above the rest of his Fabulous Flamingo (to the right, in the background), providing him an excellent view of the pool and of current swimwear fashions.*

boasts the Atrium Tower (all two-room suites), the only bingo on the Strip, and a country-and-western nightclub, Gilley's—a club that, in a roundabout way, is a return-to-roots for the New Frontier.

**The El Cortez** opened in 1941 and if you want to see what it looked like back then, just drop by: the original wing still stands. It has been minimally altered over the past 60 years, though a major expansion added a new casino wing and hotel tower in the '80s. **Roberta's** restaurant here is an institution—Las Vegas's original "bargain-gourmet" room.

## ◆ AND BEFORE...

One casino from the '30s is still around. **The Las Vegas Club,** on the corner of Fremont and Main, was one of the first joints to be granted a license after wide-open gambling was legalized in Nevada in 1931. About all that's the same as 1931, of course, is the location.

Gambling was technically illegal in the 1910s and '20s. It went on in back rooms and saloons, but no tangible evidence of it remains to be seen today.

Though the name **Golden Gate** didn't appear till the mid-1950s, its building has been in the same spot, across Fremont Street from the Las Vegas Club, since 1906, a year after Las Vegas was founded. Several years ago the exterior was restored to its original condition; the two floors of hotel rooms upstairs, through remodeled, are also original. The Golden Gate is known far and wide for its 99-cent shrimp cocktail; more than 30 million of them have been sold over the past 40-odd years.

Prior to 1905, when the town was founded by the San Pedro, Los Angeles & Salt Lake Railroad, Las Vegas Valley consisted of a few ranches, small truck farms, a handful of residents, and the Big Springs. Las Vegas owes its existence to the Big Springs, which watered the ranches, the railroad, and the town itself, from 1905 until Lake Mead filled up in the late '30s. The railroad had purchased the big Las Vegas Ranch, which comprised 1,800 acres of valley centered on the Springs, for $55,000 from seller Helen Stewart. Stewart and her second husband had doubled the size of the ranch from the time that her first husband bought it in 1874 for $6,500.

*The $6,500 that Archibald and Helen Stewart paid for Las Vegas in 1874 might now just cover the bill for a high roller's dinner at Picasso... before tip. (photo by Kerrick James)*

# Las Vegas Timeline

11000 B.C.E. Paleo Indians living at Tule Springs in northwest Las Vegas Valley

4500 B.C.E. Archaic Indians hunting and gathering throughout southern Nevada

300 A.D. Basketmaker Indians appear near what's now Las Vegas

700      Anasazi, Southwestern Pueblo Indians, settle permanently in fertile southern Nevada river valleys

1000      Peak of Anasazi civilization: the Lost City Period

1200      Lost City colony suddenly abandoned for unknown reasons

1300      Nomadic Paiute tribe settles southern Nevada

1776      Two Spanish missionaries blaze a trail through Southwest, between New Mexico and southern California, entering southern Nevada

1826      Jedediah Smith leads a party of fur trappers on the missionaries' Spanish Trail

1830      Antonio Armijo, a Mexican trader, discovers a shortcut on the Spanish Trail via Big Springs; he names it Las Vegas, "the Meadows"

1844      John C. Frémont explores, maps, and names large sections of Nevada, including Las Vegas Valley

1848      Treaty of Guadeloupe-Hidalgo ends Mexican-American War, and cedes the Southwest, including Nevada, to the United States.

1855      Latter-day Saints (Mormons) from Salt Lake City establish a colony at Las Vegas

1858      Mormon colony disbanded

1864      Nevada becomes the nation's 36th state

1865      O. D. Gass homesteads Las Vegas Valley, appropriating the Mormon fort

1881      Gass's Las Vegas Ranch taken over by Archibald and Helen Stewart

1884      Archibald Stewart murdered; ranch expanded by Helen over the next 20 years

1902      Helen Stewart sells 1,800 acres to the San Pedro, Los Angeles & Salt Lake railroad for $55,000; deeds 10 acres to Las Vegas Paiute

1904      J. T. McWilliams lays out first Las Vegas town site, known as Ragtown

1905      *January* San Pedro, Los Angeles & Salt Lake line completed through Southern Nevada

            *May* Las Vegas founded as a railroad division point and company town

            *September* Ragtown abandoned

1906      Las Vegas & Tonopah Railroad line built northwest to Beatty

1909      Las Vegas becomes seat of new Clark County, population 1,500

1915      Round-the-clock electricity supplied to residents

1929      Bureau of Reclamation selects Boulder Canyon for site of Hoover Dam

| | |
|---|---|
| 1930 | Bureau of Reclamations starts building Hoover Dam, and Boulder City, 40 miles from Las Vegas, population 5,000 |
| 1931 | Wide-open casino gambling legalized in Nevada |
| 1935 | Hoover Dam completed; first convention held in Las Vegas, population 8,400 |
| 1940 | Army Air Corps opens Las Vegas Aerial Gunnery School |
| 1941 | El Rancho Vegas, the first resort-motor inn, built on Los Angeles Highway |
| 1942 | Basic Magnesium founds Henderson; Last Frontier opens on LA Highway |
| 1945 | Soldiers start returning to Las Vegas to live, population 20,000 |
| 1945 | Nevada Tax Commission formed to oversee state casinos |
| 1946 | Ben Siegel opens Fabulous Flamingo on road now called the Las Vegas Strip |
| 1947 | Ben Siegel gunned down in Beverly Hills |
| 1950 | Atomic Energy Commission conducts first nuclear test at the old Gunnery School; Desert Inn opens. Las Vegas population 24,000. |
| 1952 | Sahara, Sands, and Binion's Horseshoe open |
| 1955 | Riviera, Dunes, Hacienda, and Fremont open |
| 1957 | Tropicana opens |
| 1958 | Stardust opens; Las Vegas becomes the largest city in Nevada |
| 1963 | Aboveground nuclear tests banned, forced underground |
| 1966 | Howard Hughes moves to Las Vegas, "buys out the mob"; Caesars Palace opens |
| 1968 | Circus Circus opens |
| 1969 | Barbra Streisand performs at opening of Las Vegas International |
| 1970 | Hilton buys International, inaugurating new corporate era |
| 1976 | Skimming scandal uncovered at the Stardust |
| 1980 | Deadly fire at old MGM Grand (now Bally's) claims 84 lives |
| 1983 | Last of old-time mob bosses hounded out of town |
| 1989 | Mirage opens, launching current boom |
| 1990 | Rio, Excalibur open; Las Vegas population 600,000 |
| 1993 | Luxor, Treasure Island, MGM Grand open |
| 1995 | Hard Rock opens |
| 1996 | Stratosphere, Monte Carlo, Orleans open; Las Vegas population exceeds one million |
| 1997 | New York–New York opens |
| 1998 | Bellagio opens |
| 1999 | Mandalay Bay, Venetian, Paris open |

*The third annual World Series of Poker, played for a week at the Horseshoe on May 18, 1972, featured (left to right): finalists "Amarillo Slim" Preston, from Texas; the casino dealer; Doyle Bronson; and W. C. "Puggy" Pearson, from Tennessee. (Underwood Photo Archives, San Francisco)*

## ■ A STORY OF GAMBLING: FROM DICE TO DIGITAL

Near the smaller of the two dice pits at **Binion's Horseshoe** downtown, on the front wall, is a gun exhibit. To my knowledge they're the only guns on display in a casino south of Ely, where the Hotel Nevada has a few firearms on the walls. The Horseshoe itself is one of the few casinos south of Ely that's still family-owned; these are Grandpa Benny's fancy pieces. And the family, the Binions, is unique among Nevadans in that it continues to live out some disreputable and so far irreparable karma from Las Vegas's rough old days of gangsters and cowboys. I have a little ritual whenever I'm downtown: I pay my respects to Benny Binion's guns, then I walk across the street and visit with Steve Wynn's gold nuggets.

The nuggets are fine ones. One is the largest on display in the world, an Australian beauty unearthed with a metal detector from a vacant lot next to a trailer park in Victoria, Australia, weighed in *pounds*. Another is the second largest. There are also a couple dozen fist-size nuggets from Alaska and Australia and South Africa. The eagle beak–shaped rock is the one I want.

Guns and gold—both are symbolic of the Wild West, of which Las Vegas, with its casinos and saloons and cribs and neon and boardwalks, was the last living remnant as late as the 1930s. Both are extremely dear to the hearts of libertarians in Las Vegas and Nevada (and, for that matter, everywhere) who cling, for one, to the Second Amendment with a fierce possessiveness and can appreciate Benny's little display not only for its utility in the preservation of freedom, but also for the beauty of the technology and craftsmanship. And who pine, for two, for the days of the gold standard, when bankers, bureaucrats, brokers, and creditors couldn't simply materialize fiat currency out of thin air—one of history's great illusions.

But this isn't about credit bubbles or a well-armed militia or libertarianism. This is about dice.

Binion's Horseshoe is also the world's most popular dice house. It has the largest number of crap tables of any casino anywhere. And they're all hoppin' and boppin', 24/7. Like guns and gold, dice are a throwback—history's oldest living randomizer. They've recently been displaced by slot machines, the greatest gambling device ever invented, and we'll get to that. Meanwhile, however, let's talk a little bit about the evolution of gambling.

*The world's largest gold nugget, on display at the Golden Nugget. (photo by Kerrick James)*

The ankle bone, or astragal, of a sheep, an anatomical structure with six roughly equal sides, was the first real die. Evidence of this has been found in ancient Hindu literature dating all the way back to 2000 B.C.E. As soon as the astragal was adopted as an implement of wagering, it was gaffed: even the earliest dice were weighted to favor a particular side, and sleight-of-hand artists learned to manipulate them to their advantage. One of the Hindu Vedic hymns includes the first recorded mention of a crooked crap marathon, in which the loser, after losing everything else, wagered his wife and lost her, too.

The Greek gods shot dice for the universe. Poseidon won the oceans, Hades the afterlife, and Zeus the heavens (they were Zeus's dice).

Ivory cubes unearthed at Thebes, in Egypt, have been dated as existing since 1500 B.C.E.

Dice swept west from India through the Middle East, around Europe and North Africa, across the Atlantic to the Caribbean, and finally into North America via the port at New Orleans in the early 19th century. By then they were employed primarily in a game called "private (or alley) craps," wherein the players bet against each other (private craps is still played in charity casino events around the country). It only took another hundred years for "bank craps," wherein the players bet against a central bank, to evolve. Bank craps is the game that raises all that ruckus at Binion's Horseshoe's 14 crap tables.

On the surface, craps is the most complex game in the casino. There are upwards of 50 bets on a crap table. But the odds of every single bet can be calculated quite easily, and every payoff is designed to favor the house. Nick the Greek Dandolos summed it up succinctly: "The best long-term attack I know of at craps is to play the don't-pass line and lay the odds. Using that system I've lost millions of dollars."

The predictability and immutability of craps illustrate the mathematical Law of Independent Trials. Dice have no memory. In that way, they're just like roulette wheels, big six wheels, baccarat, keno, bingo, and even the new poker-based casino table games, such as Caribbean Stud and Let It Ride, where the cards are shuffled up (another great randomizer) every round. No matter what accouterments surround these games—dice and cards, balls and wheels, handles and reels—they're all just slot machines. Pull (or roll or spin or deal) and pray.

Because this isn't really even about dice. It's about slot machines. Dice, cards, and wheels are now relegated to increasingly more compact compartments in the

*Craps is the only dice game played on the casino floor. (photo by Michael Yamashita)*

## FREMONT STREET AT DAWN

*T*here are no innocent bystanders in Las Vegas. Nobody comes to Vegas to be innocent. Even the kids, who may or may not be born innocent, become savvy bystanders before long-and commit more suicides here than anywhere in the world. Desert dawns are delicate, light seems not to fall from the sky but to rise from the sands in soft and slowly swelling pastels. A dawn is coming that nobody wants, not in a gaudy city designed for night but so bleak in the bright day. Then comes the moment just before the neons flicker off: their buzzing piercing brightness dulls as the sun rises and you see how light's supposed to look-and you wish for some innocence to meet it with, but all that's left of what you brought here is the wishing.

Fremont Street just after dawn. Here and there somebody homeless walks uncertainly, drunk with fatigue if nothing else, after a chilly night spent begging between attempts at sleep in a city where sleep comes hard—a city intent on keeping you awake whether you can afford a room or not. In the casinos you know it's dawn only by how few people are around and by the dullness in their eyes. At that hour it doesn't matter whether they'resitting at the bar or pouring the drinks, dealing or playing; everyone's eyes share the same stare, the same sense that something that's happened once too often is about to happen again.

—Michael Ventura, *The Death of Frank Sinatra,* 1996

casino, in favor of reels. In fiscal 1998, statewide, coin-operated gambling devices accounted for 63.5 percent of casino revenues, roughly $5 billion. In fiscal 1999, they made up 64.7 percent, for $5.5 billion. On the Strip in 1999, they were 66.4 percent, for $250 million.

In other words, slots are hot. And they're not your father's one-armed bandits anymore, either. They're now digital, complete with oversized screens, animation, video, games within games, sophisticated bonusing, and electronic player tracking. They come with all kinds of theming: game shows *(Wheel of Fortune, Jeopardy),* board games (Monopoly), TV series *(I Dream of Jeannie, The Addams Family),* cultural icons (the Three Stooges, Elvis), and plain old greed (Filthy Rich, Win and Grin). Slots are also becoming more interactive, skill-based machines where you make choices about which symbols to hold or discard, predicated on a certain internal and intuitive logic (Hot Reels). In fact, the most advanced slot machines are starting to look like video poker machines. And here we get a little glimpse into the future of gambling.

Video poker is perhaps the most perfect gambling device ever invented. It's

# LAS VEGAS THRILL RIDES

Since its founding, Las Vegas has only been interested in the ups and downs of people's bankrolls. But in 1990, with the opening of Merlin's Magic Motion Machine at the Excalibur, that changed, and suddenly Las Vegas was also interested in the ups and downs of people's bodies. Today, probably no other city on Earth has a larger selection of physical thrills. The following latest and greatest rides are all on the Strip *(See map pages 44-45.)*

**Circus Circus:** *Adventuredome.* This five-acre indoor playground boasts the world's largest indoor roller coaster, along with a log flume, bumper boats, and kiddie rides.*800-634-3450.*

MGM **Grand:** *Grand Adventures.* The amusement park here offers a roller coaster, rapids and flume rides, Sky Screamer, bumper cars, and combination bungee jump/swing set. *800-929-1111.*

**Luxor:** *In Search of the Obelisk.* This show consists of two motion simulators. The first provides an unusual sensation even for these illusion machines: you feel like you're standing in an out-of-control elevator, free-falling down a shaft. On the second, you're made to feel like you're sitting in an out-of-control hovercraft, darting around a subterranean temple. *800-288-1000.*

**Stratosphere:** *High Roller and Big Shot.* These, if you haven't heard, are at the top of the Stratosphere—two of the highest, and arguably most hair-raising, thrill rides in the world. Though tame by ground standards, the High Roller is a hundred stories high! But the roller coaster is just a warm-up for the Big Shot, the "sky-thruster" attached to the tower's needle. You're launched 160 feet up the needle, squeezed by gravitational forces equal to four times your weight, with a moment of zero gravity at the top. *800-998-6937.*

**New York–New York:** *Manhattan Express.* You strap into your car and chug 20 stories above terra firma. The first dive is 75 feet—a great sensation, but tame compared to the main fall—150 feet at 70 m.p.h. Then you go right into a 360-degree over-the-head somersault and a 540-degree spiral. Finally comes the one-of-a-kind "heartline twist and dive." *800-693-6763.*

**Sahara:** *Speedworld.* This "ride" is two 3-D motion theaters (off-road and Indy races) and 24 three-quarter-scale Indy-race-car simulators. The cars are mounted on hydraulic platforms, surrounded by screens (displaying the race course) and speakers. The car accurately responds to the slightest pressure on the pedals and turn of the wheel.It's the fastest you'll ever drive without moving. *800-634-6666.*

**Forum Shops at Caesars Palace:** *Race for Atlantis.* This is a motion simulator with 3-D computer graphics projected onto an oversized dome-shaped IMAX screen. You strap in, don a headset complete with personal sound system and goggles, and go for a three-minute virtual rip and tear. *800-634-6661.*

**Las Vegas Hilton:** *Star Trek—The Experience.* This is the most expensive and extensive simulation deal in town. You're ushered into the theater, which consists of five separate environments, including two motion simulators. A cast of 10 live actors interacts with characters from "Star Trek—The Next Generation" on a life-sized high-rez video screen to advance the plot: you're kidnapped by Klingons and beamed onto the 24th century bridge of the *Enterprise.* The crew must get you back to the Hilton on a shuttle which, naturally, turns out to be a wild ride. *800-732-7117.*

derived from poker, the most popular card game in the world. It's unintimidating, just you and a machine. There's the possibility of a big jackpot. The investment to play is as low as a nickel—like slots. It's fast—like craps. And it plays on a screen—hypnotic, self-perpetuating, addictive. Best of all, it can be beaten—like blackjack.

Combine the great features of slot and video poker machines and you'll have a gambling device that could take over the planet. It'll be called a superslot. Everything—houses, cars, hotel rooms, stores, restaurants, etc.—will be hooked up to the global superslot network. Businesses will use spins as loss-leader come-ons, awarding a free play for every, say, load of laundry you do.

When you roll a strike at a bowling alley, the reels will spin. For every gallon of gas you buy, the reels'll spin. At the rifle range, the closer targets will spin the lower-denomination slots; the farther away you get the higher the stakes will be. I can see it now: only at the ATM will there be a fee to spin, on top of the fee for the cash transaction, on top of the interest charged from the nanosecond that you hit the spin button. But people all over town will stand at ATM machines spinning reels, which will actually have the reputation of being loose!

Booked and paid off by digital credits, the superslot would suck up money like a tax collector and redistribute it like a welfare state. The seat of superslot government, of course, would be Las Vegas. And when that happens, Las Vegas will rule the world.

## ■ RED ROCK CANYON

West of Las Vegas, stretching across the sun-setting horizon and hemming in the valley, are the mighty and rugged Spring Mountains. On the edge of this range is Red Rock Canyon, a multicolored sandstone palisade only 15 miles from downtown Las Vegas. Here you'll find 197,000 acres of outdoor splendor—as dramatic a contrast to the electrified cityscape as might be imaginable. The transition from city to suburb, exurb, and then wilderness is unforgettable. A mere 12 miles from downtown Las Vegas on West Charleston Boulevard (Highway 159), you're on open road through the outback Mojave; the view—thick stands of Joshua trees, backdropped by the precipitous Spring Mountain walls, with the sandstone Calico Hills standing sentinel— has been known to leave even *National Geographic* photographers speechless.

Start with the enormity of the semicircular scenery, swallowing crowds and dwarfing climbers. Then superimpose the gorgeous colors of the sandstone—yellow, orange, pink, red, purple—all overlaid by the stalwart and tempered gray of older limestone. Then add the narrow and steep-walled canyons, moist, cool, lush gashes between the cliffs for wonderland hiking, and the contoured, inviting boulders that have turned Red Rock Canyon into an international climbing destination. Finally, tack on the cooperative year-round climate, the proximity to the city, and the excellent visitor center, and it's safe to say that the nearly 30 million yearly tourists who don't make it to Red Rock Canyon simply don't see Las Vegas.

Orient yourself at the BLM Visitor Center's excellent 3-D exhibits of geology, flora and fauna, and then walk along the short nature trail out back. A 13-mile loop road is open 7 A.M. to dusk and features half a dozen overlooks, picnic sites, and trails leading to springs, canyons, quarries, and *tinajas* (tanks). There is a small per-vehicle entry fee to the loop road. Gas and food are *not* available either at the Visitor Center *or* on the road, so be prepared. With luck, you will see hikers and climbers dotted along the rock, demonstrating the amazing scale of the fiery walls.

*To reach Red Rock Canyon from Las Vegas, take I-15/US 93 south to Hwy. 160 (Blue Diamond ); take Hwy. 160 west to Hwy. 159; call 702-363-1921.*

*A Joshua tree frames sandstone bluffs and full moon at sunrise.*

# INTERSTATE 15 & US 93:
## SOUTH & EAST NEVADA

### ■ HIGHLIGHTS

### ■ TRAVEL OVERVIEW

An hour's run up Interstate 15 (northeast) from Las Vegas puts you in Mesquite, the fastest growing border town in Nevada, with its casinos, country clubs, and gorgeous basin and range scenery. A half-hour's run down the interstate (southwest) delivers you to Primm, a casino-resort destination, complete with thrill rides, golf course, and factory outlet mall, right on the California state line.

Not counting Boulder City (near where US 93 enters Nevada from Arizona) and Las Vegas, only eight towns break up the 520 miles of US 93 in Nevada—and only two of them have more than a few hundred residents. This route, which roughly parallels the ruler-straight Utah state line in eastern Nevada, is short on communities and culture, but long on wide-open country.

The contrast between the fast freeways of southern Nevada and the vast uninhabited reaches of eastern Nevada is akin to going from lunch at a dim sum counter in downtown Hong Kong straight to the meditation room of a Buddhist monastery. Outside of Las Vegas's octopus tentacles, you're in a zone where two cars traveling in the same direction constitutes a traffic jam, entering a tiny village is a major event, and the same few mountain ranges hem you in for hundreds of miles like some sort of Gaian police escort. It all adds up to the realization that you really are alone in this world.

Beyond the frenzied urban southernmost portion of US 93, the highway follows, for 175 miles, the surface evidence of an artesian aquifer so vast that no one has found the edge of it. The surprising lakes and warm springs of Pahranagat Valley, the hot springs of the early 20th-century railroad town of Caliente, the swimming hole of the Mormon farm town of Panaca, and the reservoirs just east of the 19th-century mining boomtown of Pioche are all part of the same plumbing.

From Pioche, it's 100 uninhabited miles to the bustling little burg of Ely *(covered in the US 50 chapter)*. From Ely, it's another 130 uninhabited miles to the crossroads town of Wells, where US 93 and Interstate 80 intersect *(covered in the I-80 chapter)*. And then it's 70 uninhabited miles to Jackpot, Nevada's own private Idaho.

What little traffic you encounter on the long stretches of existential highway is local—pickup trucks heading from the ranches to the towns and highway workers checking out the asphalt. You, and the occasional RV waddling along, will be the only long-distance runners on the road.

### Getting Around

At times, an enterprising Elyite tries to make a go running a public van between Ely and Las Vegas, but these operations come and go with the wind. You'll see railroad tracks on the Vegas-to-Caliente stretch, but they're only for freight trains; passenger service between Los Angeles and Salt Lake City was discontinued in 1996. Otherwise, there are no buses and hardly any trucks on the road, nor any planes overhead. To travel at all on US 93 in eastern Nevada, it's either your own wheels or Hertz's. Roadside help, in the event that you should need some, is far away and in no hurry.

### Food and Lodging

For food and drink, carry a cooler. In the big town of Ely, pride of east-central Nevada, you'll find a couple coffee shops, a couple sandwich shops, a couple velocity vittles, and a Mexican restaurant. Wells has even less. Jackpot has a buffet, a couple steakhouses, even a gourmet room, but Jackpot is also 11 hours from Vegas—if you make excellent time. It's infrequent road food the rest of the way.

On the other hand, Ely has a grand old hotel, a newish Holiday Inn, a big Motel 6, a Ramada Inn with an indoor swimming pool, and nearly 300 other motel rooms to choose from—plenty of lodging variety right in the middle of the state. Jackpot, as well, has a 300-room high-rise hotel, and several motels.

If you have some gourmet take-out along or are prepared for burgers and chicken-fried steak, you'll eat and sleep well on US 93.

# ■ INTERSTATE 15, EAST TO WEST

Interstate 15 enters Nevada after traveling through western Montana, eastern Idaho, the length of Utah, and 25 miles of Arizona, with its spectacular Virgin River Canyon. The superhighway slices through the southern tip of Nevada for 122 miles, the shortest main road in the state except for US 395 (which is just under 100). It continues southeast in California through Baker, Barstow, and San Bernardino, then turns south and ends in San Diego.

Upon crossing into Nevada, I-15 more or less parallels the Virgin River for 30 miles, then the long arm of Lake Mead that it feeds for another 30, and finally the route of the Colorado River south of Hoover Dam for the rest of the way, though 30 to 40 miles inland. It passes through the border town of Mesquite, the village of Glendale and the adjacent Moapa River Indian Reservation, Nellis Air Force Base, the Las Vegas metropolitan area from northeast to southwest, the small settlement of Jean, and the resort destination of Primm at the California state line.

The speed limit is 75 m.p.h. along the four-lane sections of interstate; it slows down to 65 in Las Vegas, where it widens to ten lanes briefly. Heading northeast from Las Vegas, it's 90 miles from the Spaghetti Bowl in downtown to Mesquite, a quick hour or so once you get rolling (more if you're the law-abiding type); traffic is rarely heavy. In the other direction, it's 40 miles to Primm and traffic is rarely *not* heavy. On Fridays, starting around 2 P.M. and continuing into the night, the northbound lanes of I-15 south of Las Vegas become

# INTERSTATE 15

congested with traffic arriving from southern California for the weekend. Like-wise, on Sundays starting at around 10 A.M. and continuing into the evening, the process is reversed, with L.A.–bound traffic snarled from Vegas to San Bernardino.

We'll start at the Silver State's border with the Grand Canyon State and work our way down to the Sunshine State.

## ■ MESQUITE  *map page 88*

On the east side of town, along Pioneer Boulevard behind the Virgin River Hotel-Casino, is one of the most spectacular contrasts you'll see in Nevada: the green green grass of Mesquite golf courses set against the red red rock of Southwestern hillsides. Interspersed are brand new redbrick and pale adobe mansions dotting the landscape. Subdivisions surrounding the golf course sport optimistic names like Enchantment, Highland Fairways, Red Hills Village, and Summer Ridge, filled with snowbirds and retirees and casino execs and Vegas nabobs and golf folk who've been living here for going on—geez! Has it been seven months already?

Mesquite is the fastest-growing small town in Nevada. Its population has exploded from less than 2,000 in 1990 to more than 10,000 today. A small-town

*The Casa Blanca Resort Casino in Mesquite.*

atmosphere, ground-floor home prices, three golf courses (one designed by Arnold Palmer), three major and three minor casinos, stunning scenery, and gorgeous weather year-round make for an irresistible combination when it comes to relocating from Worcester or Wilkes-Barre or Wilmington or Wheeling or Wichita. The bright lights of Las Vegas an hour down the road don't hurt the equation, either.

New commercial centers line Mesquite Boulevard on the east and west sides, while central Mesquite is obviously the original part of town. At the east exit ramp, very little is more than a few years old. **The Mesquite Star** is a small hotel-casino with a Western façade, coffee shop and buffet, and small sports book. **The Eureka Hotel-Casino** is a big barn of a joint with four pool tables in the sports book bar. Only the **Virgin River Hotel-Casino** has been holding down the east exit for more than a matter of months. A newer wing boasts 300 rooms (for a total of 1,000) a 24-lane bowling alley, snack bar, huge arcade, and bingo hall; in the older wing are the low-roller casino, poker room, coffee shop, buffet, cinema, and a 100-foot-long bar with 36 video poker machines. A utilitarian 47-space RV park is in the parking lot.

From the east exit ramp, you take a left and drive into town, making the big right turn at the venerable **Corner Bar**, passing the equally venerable **Chalet Cafe** on the left. The Polar Freeze, Harley's Garage, La Mesa Motel, and Mesquite Tire are holdovers from the old days. But then you come to new bank, condo, and shopping-center developments filling up most of the space along Mesquite Boulevard. But not all of it: there's still some ranchland left on the main drag, with cattle grazing behind barbed-wire fencing and a big ranch house or two in the fields.

At the west exit is the **Casa Blanca Resort-Casino.** The waterfall out front, with its faux rocks, flowing water, and palm trees on top, might remind you of the Mirage—all it needs is a volcano. Inside are 500 rooms, an upscale casino, coffee shop, buffet, steakhouse, and showroom. The pool area is also almost as large and luxurious as the Mirage's, while the spa outshines even most of those in Las Vegas, with warm and hot pools, mud baths, steam room, sauna, and plenty of therapies.

Across the street is the resort that put Mesquite on the map, originally the Peppermill (which, if you've seen the ones in Wendover and Reno, you'll recognize as soon as you walk in), but now known as the **Oasis Hotel-Casino.** The Oasis has all the usual casino games, restaurants, and deals, but it also has a big arcade, pedestrian skywalk across Mesquite Boulevard between the hotel tower/parking lot and casino, miniature golf, and a little racetrack in the parking lot.

## ■ VIRGIN VALLEY   *map page 88*

For a scenic drive out of Mesquite, turn onto Riverside Road, NV 170, just east of the Casa Blanca and Oasis, heading south. You cross the Virgin River, into the Virgin River Valley, toward the Virgin Mountains, with Virgin Peak rising to 8,075 feet. Contrary to popular belief, the namesake of the river, valley, range, and peak isn't a local virgin who drove all the cartographers crazy; it was this other Virgin, from Nazareth, whom the early Spanish explorers honored by naming the river after her. Today, the Virgin River is still "virgin" in that it's the only main river flowing through Nevada that isn't dammed.

Riverside Road follows the river as it travels through lush bottom-land dairy farms and cattle ranches, passing the small farm-to-market village of **Bunkerville** and crossing the river again at the little settlement of **Riverside**. From there it's a couple of miles north to I-15, where you reconnect at Exit 112.

Heading west on I-15, you climb up and out of Virgin Valley, onto a mesa at the south end of the Mormon Range. It's rugged country up here, big mountains in the distance, red rock all around, Joshua trees in the middle. It's 30 miles to Glendale, a small service center for the road and the Nevada Power generating plant here; it has a motel, cafe, grocery store, and bar. **Moapa** is the Paiute reservation village next door.

## ■ MOAPA VALLEY   *map page 88*

Backtracking three miles east of the twin towns, Exit 93 is the turnoff for NV 169, the road through Moapa Valley, which encompasses the towns of Logandale and Overton, then continues on through Valley of Fire State Park *(see page 93)*; it also connects with NV 167, the highway along the north shore of Lake Mead. The road, Logandale, and Overton are oriented to the Muddy River, which flows out of the Sheep Range to the west and collects the watershed from the Meadow Valley Wash, then empties into Lake Mead.

**Logandale** is a tiny settlement (cafe, post office, grocery store) in the midst of tidy farms and ranches spread along the loamy banks of the Muddy.

**Overton** is also a farming community, though larger and less languid than Logandale. It actually has a bar-casino gathering place called **Sugar's**; check out the local sports memorabilia and the wall map of Moapa Valley. There's also an ice cream parlor, community park, and big RV campground.

But the main attraction in Overton is the **Lost City Museum.** As early as 1,500 years ago, Native Americans, primarily the Anasazi, recognized and utilized the Moapa Valley's agricultural potential; thus the area is rich with ancient artifacts. The first serious archaeological excavations were begun in the 1920s, followed up by the Civilian Conservation Corps in the 1930s. The adobe museum has a log and brush exterior, reminiscent of the Anasazi's pueblo dwellings; you can also climb a log ladder into a replica pit house. Exhibits illustrate the lifestyle of the earliest Indians: their arts and crafts, tools and weapons, agriculture, and rituals; fossils and minerals uncovered during the various digs are also on display.

From Overton, it's nine miles south on NV 169 to the entrance to Valley of Fire State Park.

■ VALLEY OF FIRE STATE PARK   *map page 88*

Valley of Fire, Nevada's oldest state park, was established in 1935. It encompasses 46,000 acres, centered on stunning red-rock formations six miles long and three miles wide. Erosion has chiseled fantastic formations out of the characteristically colorful Southwestern sandstone—rock arches, sheer walls, jagged pinnacles, and

*(above) Petroglyphs on Atlatl Rock at Valley of Fire.*
*(opposite) Eroded sandstone creates a surreal landscape in and around Valley of Fire State Park.*

## PETROGLYPHS

Petroglyphs are prehistoric rock carvings representative of the culture and religion of ancient Indians. Though some of the shapes and figures of the artwork are recognizable today, their significance has mostly been lost with the ages. Scientists speculate that rock incision was one of the rituals performed by shamans before a hunt, special event, or life passage, or that the renderings served as graffiti, or a sort of community bulletin board.

The petroglyphs in Valley of Fire are particularly numerous and noticeable. The sandstone is coated with a layer of oxidized iron and magnesium which, when carved, becomes white, so the artistic possibilities were propitious. It's not hard to imagine how a smooth, flat, and high-hanging face such as Atlatl Rock would have been irresistible to the graffiti artists of the day, though one does wonder how the ancients *reached* it. The petrogylph of a ladder might shed some light on the question, and would point to a more recent Anasazi carver. But the incised *atlatl* above it returns the aura of mystery; this "spear-launcher" long predates the bow and arrow, which arrived here around A.D. 500.

Experts recognize certain "totems," or clan signs, in the petroglyphs; in fact, some Hopi clan symbols appear in Valley of Fire, supporting the theory that the Anasazi who migrated into Arizona and New Mexico intermingled their culture with that of their eastern cousins.

Some of the artwork's symbolism seems obvious: suns, snakes, animals, people. But you'll also see hieroglyphs that could represent mushrooms and cacti (with renderings reminiscent of the psychedelic peyote cultures farther south), butterflies, octopi and starfish, Greek letters, menorahs, tic-tac-toe games, spermatozoa, treble clefs, even the Great Prophet foretelling the arrival of 747s, roller coasters, and basketball. Road maps? Advertising? Headlines? Interpretations are limited only by the imagination.

smooth domes, as well as more intricate shapes—beehives, hoodoos, animal heads, even a grand piano. Red sand, petrified wood, and petroglyphs are also abundant. Elephant Rock, Seven Sisters, Mouse's Tank, Rainbow Vista, and the sandstone-brick Cabins are a few of the named attractions. Nevada's tallest outdoor staircase lets you climb up to **Atlatl Rock,** a flat sandstone billboard for prehistoric graffiti.

The visitors center, tucked into the base of a fiery escarpment, orients you to the geology, ecology, archaeology, and sightology of the park; two campgrounds back up against the red cliffs.

You can follow NV 169 through the park, out the west end, and back onto I-15 for a scenic detour. (You can also continue on NV 169 a mile past the park entrance and hook up with NV 167, Lake Mead's Northshore Road *(see page 100)*, with various turnoffs into Las Vegas at its terminus.)

Or you can backtrack from Overton the 12 miles north to I-15. A little farther south, the superhighway splits Nellis Air Force Base in half. Just beyond, you come over a rise and around a turn and suddenly, Las Vegas Valley is splayed out from one end of the horizon to the other. Stratosphere Tower presides over it all, like a giant welcome beacon or a giant middle finger, depending on your mood.

### ■ JEAN AND PRIMM   *map page 88*

Ten miles later, you and Interstate 15 are beyond the city. Phew!

It's drab desert for 25 miles, till you come to the little roadside stop of **Jean**. Two casinos grab southern California traffic on either side of the highway: **Nevada Landing** (southbound) and the **Gold Strike** (northbound). Both are owned by Mandalay Resort Group and known for bargain rooms (less than $20 most of the time) and cheap breakfasts and buffets.

Finally, at Exit 1, is **Primm**. This spot was claimed in the early 1950s by Ernest Primm; like Jim Smith of Wendover a couple decades earlier, Primm started with a service station and slots. Since then, the Primm family has developed the home-

*Buffalo Bill's resort and casino in Primm.*

stead into a respectable resort destination. With three sprawling casinos, more than one first-timer from So. Cal. has mistaken Primm for Las Vegas. **Whiskey Pete's** is the original joint, opened way back when; check out the bizarre exhibit of Bonnie and Clyde's "Death Car." **Primm Valley Resort** was next, unveiled in 1990; **Buffalo Bill's,** opened in 1994, made a big splash with the monster Desperado roller coaster. Also here are an 18-hole golf course, a factory outlet store, a 6,500-seat arena, amusement park rides, a monorail over the freeway, bowling center, motion-simulation theater, and a convenience store in California that sells more California lottery tickets than any other outlet in that state.

## ■ ON TO US 93  *maps pages 100 & 105*

US Highway 93 runs for 520 miles up the east side of Nevada, starting at the two-lane bottleneck where the highway crosses Hoover Dam at the Arizona border and ending at the two-lane bulge in the road at Jackpot on the Idaho border. It's a long, flat, and (mostly) straight shot that travels "with the grain" of the state—parallel to the mountain ranges—lengthwise from one narrow valley to the next, then the next, then the next.

Still, for all its elongation—roughly the distance from New York City to Raleigh, North Carolina—the length of US 93 in Nevada is relative: the span of 520 miles

*An aerial view of Hoover Dam and Lake Mead.*

is just a small portion, a mere blink and it's over, of one of the longest road systems in the world, stretching from Fairbanks, Alaska, to Panama City, Panama.

## ■ HOOVER DAM

*map page 100*

With its seven million tons of concrete (enough to pave a four-foot-wide sidewalk entirely around the globe at the equator), 300 miles of steel (enough to build a bridge from Key West to Havana), and nine trillion gallons of water (enough to flood all of Pennsylvania 12 inches deep), no-nonsense, hard-working Hoover Dam stands in stark contrast to the

*Construction of Hoover Dam, circa 1932. (Underwood Photo Archives, San Francisco)*

frivolous, show-biz casino architecture of Las Vegas.

In 1930, when Congress finally appropriated the first funds for the Boulder Canyon Project, the Great Depression was in full swing, and the country was embarking on its most massive reclamation effort to date.

The immensity of the undertaking boggles the brain. The closest civilization was at the sleepy railroad town of Las Vegas, 40 miles west. Two hundred miles of poles and wire had to be run from the nearest large power plant, in San Bernardino, California. Tracks had to be laid, a town built, men hired, equipment shipped in—just to prepare for construction. And then! The mighty Colorado had to be diverted. Four tunnels, each 56 feet across, were hacked out of the canyon walls. Thousands of tons of rock were loosened, carried off, and dumped, every day for 16 months. Finally, in November 1932, the river water was routed around the dam site. Then came the concrete.

For two years, eight-cubic-yard buckets full of cement were lowered into the canyon, five *million* of them, till the dam—660 feet thick at the base, 45 feet thick at the crest, 1,244 feet across, and 726 feet high—had swallowed 40 million cubic yards, or seven million tons, of the hard stuff. The top of the dam was built wide enough to accommodate a two-lane highway. Inside this Pantagruelian wedge were placed 17 gargantuan electrical turbines. The cost of the dam exceeded $175 million. At the peak of construction, more than 5,000 workers toiled day and night to complete the project, braving the most extreme conditions of heat, dust, and danger from heavy equipment, explosions, falling rock, and heights. An average of 50 injuries per day and a total of 94 deaths were recorded over the 46 months of construction.

The largest construction equipment yet known to the world had to be invented, designed, fabricated, and installed on the spot. Yet miraculously, the dam was completed nearly two years ahead of schedule. In February 1935, the diversion tunnels were closed, and Lake Mead began to fill. The dam was dedicated eight months later by President Franklin D. Roosevelt. A month after that, the first turbine was turned, and electricity started flowing as the Colorado River water finally came under control. Today, Hoover Dam cranks out enough kilowatt-hours of electricity annually for half a million houses, but only four percent of the total goes to Las Vegas.

*Shafts of hydroelectric generator turbines on the Nevada side of Hoover Dam.*

*The visitors center at Hoover Dam (brown tower in background).*

## ◆ HOOVER DAM VISITORS CENTER   *map page 100*

Roughly 115,000 Hoover Dam visitors take the dam tour every month, almost a million a year. The 35-millionth tour-goer, since the tour began back when Eleanor Roosevelt was First Lady, was recorded on September 11, 1999—making Hoover the most heavily visited dam in the world.

You can see the year-to-year visitor body counts in two charts, the first on a wall in the *old* visitors center, the second on a display board in the *new* one. (The old is across the road from the new.)

The main floor of the new visitors center hosts several exhibits on earth sciences, such as a flash-flood diorama, as well as dam history, engineering and construction, power generation and transmission. There are also some maps and signboards, but the exhibits are mostly focused on videos; visitors huddle, watching small screens.

On the third level is a small photographic exhibit and an outdoor deck overlooking the the lake, the dam, and the river. On the bottom floor are the tour elevators and the theater. The theater is round and the seats revolve on a platform, moving you through three different presentation areas. The show lasts 36 minutes (during which, as a federal employee firmly instructs, you cannot leave).

If you go on the 30-minute guided walking tour, you take a 75-second elevator ride into the bowels of the buttress, viewing the giant electrical turbines, the diversion tunnels, and the view up the face of the dam from the bottom. Special 60-minute "hardhat" tours delve more deeply.

## ■ LAKE MEAD

Two miles north into Nevada on US 93 is a turnoff (right) onto NV 146, also known as Lakeshore Drive, which hugs the western shore of Lake Mead. The largest manmade lake in the Western Hemisphere, Lake Mead is 110 miles long and 500 feet deep, with 822 miles of shoreline. The National Park Service's recreation area, at 1.5 million acres, is the largest in the Lower 48. The reservoir extends north along the long, thin Overton Arm, with its two fingers where the Muddy and Virgin rivers flow in. The Arm comes within a few miles of Valley of Fire; the red rock in the foreground and the blue lake in the background make for a surreal juxtaposition in the desert.

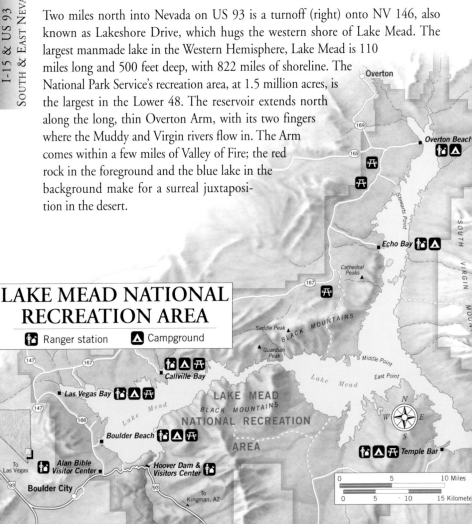

LAKE MEAD NATIONAL
RECREATION AREA

Ranger station    Campground

*Lake Mead is the largest resevoir in the Western hemisphere and one of America's most popular recreation areas. (photo by Kerrick James)*

Weekends from March through October, a veritable Vegas flotilla takes to the lake, everything from sailboards to speedboats, jet skis to houseboats. Anglers fish for bass, crappie, catfish, and trout; divers explore ruins, caves, even the Tennis Shoe Graveyard. Hiking routes (few actual trails in the desert) abound. And it's all located in Las Vegas's backyard.

Right at the intersection of US 93 and Lakeshore Drive is the **Alan Bible Visitors Center,** park headquarters for the recreation area, where you can pick up maps and books and catch a 15-minute movie about the lake. A mile north on Lakeshore Drive is Boulder Beach, the closest (and most popular) beach on the lake to the city (30 minutes from the Strip, depending on traffic). However, bring your zoris: it's all little boulders, no sand. There's a big trailer village and campground nearby.

Eight miles north of Boulder Beach is **Las Vegas Bay,** which has a campground on a bluff over the lake and no real beach. At the marina is where you catch the *Desert Princess,* the 250-passenger Mississippi-style sternwheeler that cruises the lake, steaming all the way to the dam.

A mile north of Las Vegas Bay is an intersection with NV 167, also known as Northshore Road; take a hard right to continue northeast along the shore of the lake (stay on NV 146 to loop back to US 93 in Henderson). In another two miles, you come to another intersection: take a hard left onto NV 147 (also known as Lake Mead Boulevard) to return to the city and hook up with US 93/I-15, or bear right to stay on Northshore Road.

Seven miles northeast of the intersection is the turnoff for Callville Bay, with an RV park, shady campground, visitors center, marina, houseboat rentals, and convenience store, but no beach. Unless you're boating, or want to stop into the visitors center (restrooms), it's better to invest the extra 20-30 minutes to get to Echo Bay, 20 miles along Northshore Road.

Echo Bay is the best development on the Nevada side of Lake Mead. Two campgrounds accommodate the few in-the-know RVers and tent campers who make it this far from Las Vegas (a whole hour!) to commune with the heat and sweat of summer; a motel, restaurant, bar, and houseboat rentals take care of the refugees who are reluctant to rough it. The beach is worth the extra effort to reach: sandy, shallow, secluded, and a bit of shade.

Roughly ten miles up the road is the intersection of NV 167 and NV 169. Three miles east of the intersection is Overton Beach, the northernmost resort area on the reservoir, farthest from the dam. It has an RV park, marina, convenience store, and some of the lake's best fishing off the shore, where the denizens of the deep congregate to swim in the fresh water, and feed off the fish food, delivered by the two rivers. The beach itself is only passable, kinda rocky and exposed.

■ FROM HOOVER TO BOULDER  *map page 105*

Back on US 93, heading toward Boulder City from Hoover Dam, the two-lane road twists and turns amid erector-set superstructures, electrical apparatus, high-tension cable, and rugged red rock—a surreal landscape. But you quickly emerge from the canyon, with views of the aqua lake below and gorgeous multi-million-dollar houses on both sides of the road overlooking it. You come to the one traffic light in town, at the corner of US 93 and Buchanan Boulevard; a left turn (east) on Nevada Highway takes you into the Boulder City historic district.

*Fan palms in Lake Mead National Recreation Area.*

## ■ BOULDER CITY *map page 105, C-6*

At the time construction of the Hoover Dam began, urbanologists across the country were exploring large-scale community planning. Boulder City was born of these unique factors. Today, generations later, it remains the most unusual town in Nevada.

Construction of Boulder City began in March 1931, only a month before work commenced at the dam site. Boulder City became one of the first "model towns" in the country, a prettified all-American oasis of security and order in the midst of a great desert and a Great Depression. The U.S. Bureau of Reclamation controlled the town down to the smallest detail. A city manager, who answered directly to the Commissioner of Reclamation, oversaw operations, and his authority was nearly total.

After the dam was completed in 1935, many thought Boulder City would become a ghost town, but visitors to the dam and Lake Mead began to turn it into a service center for the new tourist attraction and recreation area. For 30 years, the government owned the real estate, even the cemetery, but in early 1960, an act of Congress established Boulder City as an independent municipality. A city charter was drawn up, the Feds began to sell property to the long-term residents, and

*Boulder City soon after its founding. (Underwood Photo Archives, San Francisco)*

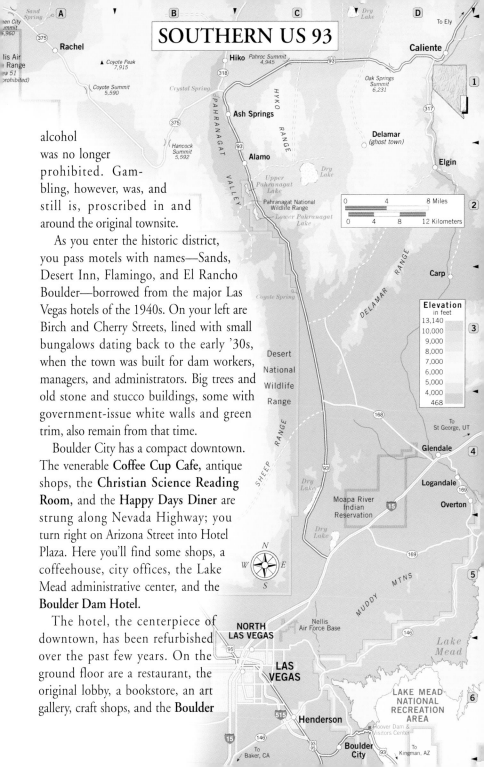

# SOUTHERN US 93

alcohol was no longer prohibited. Gambling, however, was, and still is, proscribed in and around the original townsite.

As you enter the historic district, you pass motels with names—Sands, Desert Inn, Flamingo, and El Rancho Boulder—borrowed from the major Las Vegas hotels of the 1940s. On your left are Birch and Cherry Streets, lined with small bungalows dating back to the early '30s, when the town was built for dam workers, managers, and administrators. Big trees and old stone and stucco buildings, some with government-issue white walls and green trim, also remain from that time.

Boulder City has a compact downtown. The venerable **Coffee Cup Cafe**, antique shops, the **Christian Science Reading Room**, and the **Happy Days Diner** are strung along Nevada Highway; you turn right on Arizona Street into Hotel Plaza. Here you'll find some shops, a coffeehouse, city offices, the Lake Mead administrative center, and the **Boulder Dam Hotel**.

The hotel, the centerpiece of downtown, has been refurbished over the past few years. On the ground floor are a restaurant, the original lobby, a bookstore, an art gallery, craft shops, and the **Boulder**

City/Hoover Dam Museum, at the end of a long the hall. Poster-size historic photographs fill the walls; tools, hats, cameras, and other artifacts of the day are exhibited in display cases. The video of the building of Hoover Dam is shown on request. On the upper floors of the hotel are the chamber of commerce and various offices.

West of downtown on Nevada Highway, Boulder City has expanded substantially in the past 10 years. Around the intersection of Buchanan Boulevard, and on the other side of it, are strip shopping centers, fast-food outlets, gas stations, supermarkets, and the like.

Just beyond Boulder City's exurbia, you pass the exit off US 93 for US 95 and Laughlin; heading toward Las Vegas, these two US highways merge and travel as one for a while. You climb Railroad Pass (2,367 feet), a saddle at the north end of the McCullough Range. Just beyond the pass is the Hacienda Hotel-Casino. Formerly the Railroad Pass Hotel-Casino, that joint burned down in July 1998, was rebuilt, and reopened in November 1999. Inside are a few hundred rooms, classy casino and steakhouse, coffee shop, buffet, snack bar, and Dairy Queen.

■ HENDERSON   *map page 105, C-6*

From the Hacienda, you descend a few hundred feet down the hill into Las Vegas Valley and the city of Henderson. Henderson is not quite, but almost, contiguous now with Boulder City. Railroad Pass will forever remain between them (unless it's imploded), but Henderson is creeping all the way up to the west side of the pass, and Boulder City has expanded almost all the way up to the east.

Driving along the freeway (here known as US 93/US 95/I-15), you look out over a sea of red-tile roofs with air-conditioning units sticking up from them, off-white stucco walls, windows that don't open, what my grandmother called "stickim-uh" trees, streetlights, and the occasional commercial strip. This is the fastest-growing subdivision of the fastest-growing metropolitan area in the country: in 1999, Henderson eclipsed Reno as the second largest city in Nevada, having absorbed 75,000 new residents in five years, for a total of 176,000.

You also pass a huge industrial complex built during World War II to process magnesium from mines in Gabbs, Nevada, for its use in aircraft components and bombs. Just as Boulder City was built in the '30s for dam workers, Henderson was built in the '40s for magnesium workers; the dam, in fact, supplied the prodigious amounts of electrical power necessary to process the 16 million pounds of Henderson magnesium that eventually found its way into the war effort. Today, the vast factory houses large chemical companies and small manufacturing firms.

Taking the Henderson exit off the freeway, you can cut over to the commercial artery, Boulder Highway. Stop off at the **Clark County Heritage Museum.** The largest historical museum in southern Nevada, the Heritage has extensive displays on the people, production, and progress of the area, from Native Americans to dam builders, from the military to magnesium, with a special emphasis on railroading. Several vintage buildings, one dating back to the 1890s, have been moved in their entirety to Heritage Street, which you can tour and appreciate. Also wander the grounds behind the museum, where you can view all manner of ghost town accouterments and mining and railroading machinery.

From the Heritage, continue toward Las Vegas and turn left onto Water Street to see downtown Henderson. The big action downtown is the Eldorado Casino; the small action is the Rainbow Club. The convention center, library, and a park are nearby, along with rows of shops in the original '40s storefronts.

### ■ AVOIDING LAS VEGAS

From Henderson, you hurdle headlong into Zoom Town. At the central "Spaghetti Bowl" interchange downtown, under continuous construction since just after the wheel was invented, US 93/I-15 heads off to the northeast and US 95 cuts northwest. If you'd like to pretend the whole thing is a hallucination, a mere mirage in the Mojave, you can barrel right through Las Vegas on the freeway (stay in one of the two left lanes). But don't turn your head: it's an illusion only if you see it with one eye.

Leaving the city, you drive along I-15 for 20-odd miles up to exit 64, where I-15 and US 93 part company, the former continuing northeast toward Mesquite *(see pages 89–91)* and Salt Lake City, the latter veering north toward Lincoln County.

For the next 45 miles, US 93 is one of the straightest roads you'll ever have the pleasure to patronize. If your front wheels are properly aligned, you won't even have to steer. Dude! I'm tellin' ya'! You can read a book and go 90 at the same time. At the sign for Lincoln County, however, the road turns immediately rough. Till then, you hadn't realized how smooth your sailing had been. Ain't that the way it always is?

## ■ PAHRANAGAT VALLEY *map page 105*

In another 10 minutes or so, you notice that the land is turning gradually greener. You're entering Pahranagat Valley, home of **Pahranagat National Wildlife Refuge.** This is the southern end of Meadow Valley Wash, which you'll come to know and love on your travels in Lincoln County. The wash is where an underground aquifer (whose extent is still largely unknown) interfaces with the surface of the Earth.

For example, the water from the aquifer appears at the north end of verdant little Paharanagat Valley at Nesbit Lake; from there, a series of springs percolate southward to **Upper** (large) and **Lower** (small) **Pahranagat Lakes.** Keep an eye out for a host of migratory and permanent waterfowl and predatory birds. Signs point you toward the National Wildlife Refuge adminstration office where you can pick up brochures, and down to the shoreline of Upper Lake, where you can picnic, camp, and launch a (non-motorized) flotation device.

Four miles north of Upper Pahranagat Lake is the small ranching community of **Alamo,** the backstreets of which you might want to explore for a few minutes; on the highway are gas stations, the Meadow Lane Motel, and a couple of mini-marts. You can also turn off on Richardville Road to take the scenic route, which parallels US 93 north through the cultivated bottomlands, past ranches, ranch

*The underground Meadow Valley Wash makes Pahranagat Valley greener than surrounding areas.*

houses, alfalfa fields, and tall cottonwoods, almost all the way to the next little settlement of **Ash Springs.**

There's no real village here, just a reduced-speed zone and a couple of service stops, including R Place at the Texaco station, a hoppin' mini-mart with a whole back wall's worth of cold beverages and lots of microwave road food.

Directly across US 93 from R Place, three log posts mark the start of a small dirt road (to the right as you're heading north). Drive in 50 yards to an idyllic little hot springs, one of the most accessible such attractions in the state. The springs have been developed over the years. Along with some vibrant young and some gnarly old cottonwoods, there are a bricked-in pool, picnic tables, garbage cans, and restrooms, everything but overnight camping (and a proper sign pointing the way from the road—look for the logs).

North of Ash Springs is a junction called **Crystal Springs,** marked by road signs and some tall cottonwoods. Here, US 93 does a 90-degree to the east, toward the population centers of Lincoln County; NV 318 continues north 150 miles to Ely, passing the ranching villages of Hiko, Preston, and Lund; and NV 375 heads generally west 100 miles to Warm Springs, passing the small UFO town of Rachel, to which we'll take a worthwhile 100-mile roundtrip detour.

<sub>SOUTH & EAST NEVADA   I-15 & US 93</sub>

*Red volcanic cinders were used to pave US 93 in Lincoln County.*

# ■ RACHEL  *map page 105, A-1*

Nevada is made up of all kinds of towns: casino towns, border towns, farming towns, ranching towns, mining towns, railroad towns, fishing towns, reservation towns, even an ammunition-depot town and a gun town. But Nevada boasts a type of town that's unique not only to the state, but also to the country, and possibly the world.

A UFO town.

Welcome to Rachel, closest civilian settlement to the top-secret, yet notorious, Area 51, where the Air Force reportedly has test-flown experimental aircraft, and stowed and studied unidentified flying objects and extraterrestrial beings themselves. Naturally, the vast mythology emanating from the sketchy details that have leaked out about Area 51 (also known as Groom Lake and Dreamland) since the late 1980s has affected the fortunes of Rachel. This tiny town of 80 souls has become the latest promised land for UFO pilgrims from all over the globe—many of whom claim to have seen some strange fast-moving and quick-turning lights, or heard unearthly noises in the big sky in the direction of the Air Force base.

Talk about illusion country! Everyone sees something different around here—generally, what they want to see. According to Glen Campbell, author of the *Area 51 Viewer's Guide,* the people of Rachel have been "living under bizarre aerial displays for years. Nearly everyone in town has seen unusual lights." But, he maintains, "Recognizing a flying saucer or exotic aircraft here can be immensely difficult amid the vast circus of routine military activity, the optical illusions of the desert, and the confusing swamp of speculation brought here by believers." Campbell continues,

"Most visitors have already made emotional investments and bear private grudges that they expect UFOs to support, and it takes very little evidence to confirm their views. UFO proponents expect to see flying saucers, and they do. Hardened skeptics expect to debunk the saucer stories, and they do. Spiritualists see spirits. Doomsdayers see the end of the world."

*The Extraterrestrial Highway has been given official status by the Nevada Highway Department.*

*The Area 51 Research visitors center in Rachel. Terrestrial vistors also welcome.*

The federal government, of course, denies every single bit of it. The secrecy, however, only encourages the UFO cult. Somehow or other, Rachel, a cameo character that makes one fleeting appearance in the cursory Nevada chapter, has come to strongly symbolize both substance and shadow in the great American novel.

Rachel was a tiny mining settlement set up in the early '70s (named, the story goes, for the first baby born there), which might have dried up and blown away in the late '80s were it not for the UFO craze that has yet to let up. In 1996, the state Department of Transportation designated NV 375 the "Extraterrestrial Highway" and erected several road signs to that effect, though when I passed through four years later, only one remained, right in Rachel.

Today, as you enter town from the east, you come to the Kwik Pik mini-mart, the first of three commercial establishments in town; here you can buy gasoline from an aboveground tank, Area 51 guides, T-shirts, maps, an alien-autopsy board game, flying-saucer postcards, and limited food and drink.

Cruising the backstreets, you'll see single- and double-wides, a few quonset huts, a senior center, and a day park with swings and kids' apparatus.

Directly across from the Kwik Pik is the Area 51 Research Center, housed in a distinctive yellow trailer. The proprietors of the Center have taken the high road, the academic approach—*data*—to the whole local controversy. They sell maps, and books on UFOs, abductions, psychic phenomena, the military, and local travel, including the intelligent and heavily researched *Area 51 Viewer's Guide;* also check out the photo albums full of the fetching and far-out phenomena. The Area 51 Research Center is open every day.

On the other side of Rachel, about a quarter-mile away, is the renowned **Little A'Le'Inn,** formerly the Rachel Bar and Grill, the Oasis, and the Watering Hole. Check out the cute little sign advertising self-parking sign for UFOs, the time capsule planted by the state out front, and the purple extraterrestrial staring out the front window. Inside are the bar and restaurant counter, a pool table, three video poker machines, and a whole wall of photos and clippings from magazines on UFOs and flying saucers, including some interesting ones over California and Hawaii. You'll want to pay close attention to the panoramic view of the Groom Lake facility from the nearby Freedom Ridge overlook, which was accessible to the public until the government fenced it off in 1995. If we can say the research center has taken the "high road," the Little A'Le'Inn has taken the "low road," the consumer approach—*souvenirs*—to the phenomenon: They sell burgers and booze, motel rooms, along with Little A'Le'Inn ashtrays, bumperstickers, ashtrays, refrigerator magnets, mugs, shot glasses, even menus, and an entire collection of Area 51, Extraterrestrial Highway, and Little A'Le'Inn T-shirts.

Continuing northwest on NV 375, it's 50 miles to the junction with US 6 at Warm Springs (no services), and another 50 miles west to Tonopah and US 95.

*Even aliens must eat.*

LITTLE A'LE'INN

**DINNER**

| | |
|---|---|
| York Steak (12 ounces) | $8.99 |
| Pork Chops | $6.95 |
| ast Beef | $5.95 |
| ast Turkey | $5.95 |
| ried Chicken (3 pieces) | $5.95 |
| 3.B.Q. Half Chicken | $5.50 |
| Baked Half Chicken | $5.50 |
| Chicken Fried Steak | $5.50 |
| Fried Fish | $5.95 |
| Liver & Onions | |
| Hamburger Steak | |
| Chicken Fingers | |

(above served with soup or salad, choice of potato, and vegetable)

**Beverages**

| | |
|---|---|
| Coffee (regular or decaf) | .47 |
| Tea (hot or iced) | .47 |
| Milk (small) | .94 |
| Milk (large) | $1.95 |
| Fruit Juice (orange, tomato, grapefruit, cranberry) | .61 |
| Soda Pop | .94 |
| Hot Chocolate | |

**Soup of the Day**

| | |
|---|---|
| Cup | $1.25 |
| Bowl | $2.25 |

**Chili**

| | |
|---|---|
| Cup | $1.75 |
| Bowl | $2.95 |

**Desserts**

| | |
|---|---|
| Cake | $1.50 |
| Pie | $1.75 |
| | $1.00 |

EARTHLINGS WELCOME
Rachel, Nevada
*Your Hosts Joe & Pat*

## ■ CALIENTE

*map opposite, A-6*

Back on US 93 at Crystal Springs, you turn due east, cross Six-Mile Flat, crest Pahroc Summit (4,925 feet), then climb into the Delamar Mountains and over Oak Springs Summit (6,327 feet). From there, you drop through Newman Canyon, with its high and sheer sandstone walls, into Caliente. This is the first of three settlements that time has forgotten, in a small conservative county with no gambling to speak of, no prostitution, and little crime, in an undiscovered corner of Nevada that's nonetheless packed with attractions.

Unlike northern Nevada, with its series of railroad towns strung along the Southern Pacific mainline, Caliente is the only true railroad town remaining in southern Nevada, founded in 1903 when the San Pedro, Los Angeles & Salt Lake track was being laid through Nevada. Little has changed here since. A classic Spanish-California passenger depot was built in 1923; today it houses City Hall, the chamber of commerce, the library, and a museum of sorts in the oak-trimmed lobby.

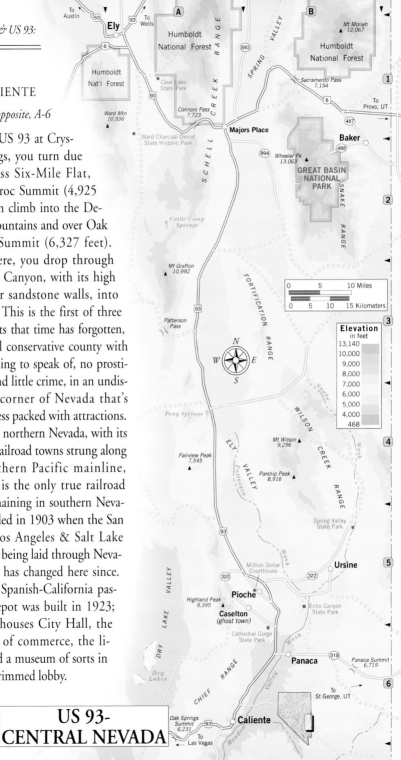

Elevation
in feet
13,140
10,000
9,000
8,000
7,000
6,000
5,000
4,000
468

## US 93-
## CENTRAL NEVADA

Around town, the post office is original, as are the elementary school, a church, and even an apartment building (the Underhill Apartments, off Clover Street); lining US 93 beyond the bend are railroad bungalows, built circa 1900. Downtown Caliente has four motels and an RV park, three eateries, a couple of bars and gas stations, a supermarket, a hardware store, and the Lincoln County hospital. Every time I've been to Caliente, a county sheriff's cruiser has been either sitting on the side of the road or tooling up and down the main streets, making sure everyone does 25 m.p.h. through town.

At the south end of town, across from the Latter-day Saints church, is a turnoff (NV 317) that follows Meadow Valley Wash (more evidence of the vast aquifer that also feeds Pahranagat and Ash Springs) past Kershaw-Ryan State Park and through **Rainbow Canyon.**

The sheer polychrome cliff walls of Rainbow Canyon consist of mineralized volcanic tuff: iron (red), copper (green), manganese (black), and ash (white). Two miles from the intersection is the turnoff (left) into **Kershaw-Ryan State Park,** nestled in the steep-walled and seep-filled Little Kershaw box canyon. You first come to the restrooms and picnic area; a nearby wading pool, built by the Civilian Conservation Corps in the mid-1930s, is surrounded by 100-year-old fruit trees. Hiking trails lead you around the old ranch, homesteaded in the 1870s and donated to the state in the early 1930s to become one of Nevada's earliest state parks. Check out the hanging gardens of wild grapevines.

Continuing down Rainbow Canyon on NV 317, you pass idyllic ranches, old railroad trestles, some historic sites, and access to the rugged backcountry, all bordered by the massive cliff walls and babbling brook of the wash. In another 20 or so miles, the canyon flattens, the creek dries, and the pavement gravels. Good place to turn around. All in all, it's worth an hour's detour; this drive will drop your chin—and you won't close your mouth the whole way.

■ PANACA  *map page 113, B-6*

Back on US 93 beyond Caliente heading north, you continue your travels through Meadow Valley Wash—well-watered, fertile farm and ranch lands on the east side of the highway, a couple of modern housing subdivisions hidden in the Chief Range foothills on the west side.

Five miles north of Caliente is the turnoff (right) to Beaver Dam, the most remote state park in Nevada. It's a 27-mile haul on a graded gravel road that twists and turns through the piñon-juniper country of the Clover Mountains, across the

*Spring wildflowers bloom in Pahranagat Valley.*

railroad tracks at the Acoma Siding, and down a steep slope into the park. There are no concessions or centers or amenities, barely a ranger on duty. You can camp at the campground or in any likely place, fish and swim in Beaver Dam Reservoir (stocked with rainbow trout), amble up to old Hamblin Ranch, shoot wild turkey (with a camera only), or get lost in the rugged canyon country on either side of the Nevada state line. You won't bump into many other people.

Nine miles north of the Beaver Dam cutoff on US 93 is the road to Panaca, possibly the most timeless town in the state. Panaca is the only Nevada town I can think of that hasn't changed, at all, in recent memory. It was established in 1864, which makes it one of the oldest settlements in the state; it was then, and is still, a tiny village in the midst of family farms and ranches.

Meandering around town, you'll see the Panaca Mercantile (established in 1868), the post office, a gas station, and several interesting old houses. But it's the solid and ageless brick school buildings and expansive playing fields that dominate Panaca, befitting the very solid and far more ageless **Court Rock**, an incongruous chalk outcrop that sits in the middle of it all. About a mile north on Fifth Street is Panaca Spring, the local swimming hole, shaded by grand old cottonwoods.

■ CATHEDRAL GORGE   *map page 113, A/B-5/6*

A mile north of Panaca on US 93 is Cathedral Gorge State Park, as accessible and accessorized as Beaver Dam is remote and remedial. Right on the highway at the entrance into the park is the visitors center, built in 1996. Outside are signboards on regional history, communities, and state parks, along with a variety of vegetation (labeled) common to the area: dogwood, wood rose, shrubby cinquefoil, buffaloberry, golden currant, bright clematis, western red birch, snowberry, and smooth sumac, to name a few. An enclosed cinderblock amphitheater is attached, the concrete benches focused on a big-screen TV behind glass; push the button for videos on the state parks and natural history of eastern Nevada. Inside is a small room full of photographs of the local state parks, a cross-section of a bristlecone pine trunk, a taxidermied owl, coyote, gray fox, bobcat, and rattlesnake, and books, posters, and postcards for sale.

Cathedral Gorge itself consists of sediments deposited at the bottom of an unimaginably large lake over tens of thousands of years in the dim mists of history. The silt, ash, and rock sediments rose 1,500 feet, while the lake dried up and disappeared. Millennia of erosion carved the soft bentonite into today's variety of elaborate rococo forms—many, as the name implies, in visible ecclesiastical shapes. Trails traverse the face of the gorge, enter cavelike openings, disappear into narrow corridors, and connect with the campground out on the desert flats. The campground has shade trees, water pumps, flush toilets, showers, and pay phones.

It's good fun to stand back and pick out facsimiles of recognizable structures in the gorge's formations. If you try hard enough, and you're in the right imaginative frame of mind, you can almost see the spirits of the shapes in the rock.

■ PIOCHE   *map page 113, A-5*

Pioche completes the Lincoln County triumvirate of railroad town, farming town, and mining town, all within 25 miles of each other. Pioche has seen little mining for roughly 70 years, but the original boom was so fulsome that its echoes have resonated for several generations. Mining boomlets have visited Pioche over the years, though not for several decades. Indeed, a headframe, aerial tramway, and mill erected in the 1920s only operated for a dozen years or so, but all the machinery remains in place, exactly as it was the moment everything stopped running; empty ore buckets have hung suspended from the tramway cable, a couple above US 93, ever since.

*Eroded clay formations in Cathedral Gorge State Park.*

Over the years, Pioche has attracted retirees, recluses, and families getting away from it all. It's certainly the most thriving old-time boomtown in southern Nevada, and perhaps boasts more amenities, packed into the smallest space, of any town in the state. The old part of Pioche, which claims most of the commercial establishments, is on a hillside below the original mines; the newer part of town is on the flats just off the highway, closer to the mill.

To start with, Pioche is the seat of Lincoln County, claiming not one, but two, county courthouses. The 125-year-old **Million Dollar Courthouse** has a history as fascinating as it is corrupt. The county had to go into debt, to the tune of $10,000, to complete the courthouse in 1876; by the time it was paid off nearly 70 years later, the total cost had reached the eponymous million smackeroos, the building had been abandoned, and the new courthouse had been built down the hill. Open April through October, a docent will take you through the structure and show you the county offices, courtroom, judge's chambers, and jailhouse. Many of the furnishings are original.

Along sloping Main Street, you'll find nearly every other attraction and amenity in Pioche. The two rooms of the **Lincoln County Museum** are as packed full of

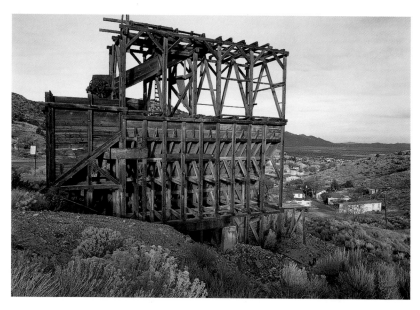

*An ore hopper and aerial tramway are perched above the town of Pioche.*

interest as Pioche itself; exhibits include pioneer artifacts, mining and mineral displays, antique guns, historic photos, and more. Next door is the library.

Up the street is the Pioche Chamber of Commerce Cottage, with its requisite handful of handouts; an informational sign out front on the street tells the story of the building. Down the street is the **Gem movie theater,** without a doubt Nevada's oldest motion-picture hall. It's only open three nights a week for one showing a night, but if you get the chance, check out the original box office, 300-seat auditorium with balcony, original 1930s' projector and screen, and "crying room" (glassed-in sanctum for fussy youngsters). Next door to the Gem is the old Thompson Opera House, recent focus of restoration fundraising.

Also downtown are more historical buildings and signs, the Overland Hotel, several bars and cafes, a dinner house, grocery store, hardware store, gas station, and motel. Around the suburbs are the **Book Mine** used book store, free RV parking, old Pioche Elementary School and Boot Hill cemetery down Austin Street in the vicinity of the (working) courthouse.

Within 20 miles of Pioche, east on NV 322, are two small state recreation areas, **Echo Canyon** and **Spring Valley,** at the upper end of Meadow Valley Wash. Echo Canyon (12 miles from Pioche) has a 34-site campground and a reservoir stocked with trout; it's impounded by primitive 50-foot-high earthen Echo Canyon Dam. Spring Valley is a state park (20 miles) with a larger campground, larger dam and reservoir, and larger fish.

■ THROUGH LAKE VALLEY  *map page 113*

Make sure you have at least a half-tank of gas before heading north on US 93 toward Ely; the next services are few and far between. It's a long straight shot up Lake Valley into central Nevada. The speed limit is 70, but everyone does 80 or more, though you might not see another car for an hour. If you happen to get stopped by a cop, don't bother trying to worm out of a ticket by saying, "But officer, I thought 70 was the road number and 93 was the speed limit!" They've heard it many times before (once from me).

Seventy miles north of Pioche, on the east side of the valley, is the south end of the mighty Snake Range, home of Great Basin National Park; on a clear day Wheeler Peak, at 13,083 feet the second highest mountaintop in the state, towers over the low-lying landscape. Right around here is also where you depart Lincoln County and enter White Pine County.

*(following pages) The fantastic forms of Cathedral Gorge are eroded bentonite, a soft sandstone.*

## DESERT SURVIVAL TIPS

Southern Nevada's Mojave Desert is not to be taken lightly. From Las Vegas, even nearby day-trips and short hikes in the desert can, unless proper precautions are taken, turn into perilous situations. Before heading into the Mojave, a few simple preparations might spell the difference between a routine and a life-threatening experience.

First, make certain that your trusty steed has had the best care. Fuel and fluids should be full. Carry at least a gallon of water for the car (some coolant is also good to have), along with spare belts and hoses, spare tire and jack, tool kit, flashlight and flares, and shovel. Baling wire and super-glue often come in handy. Don't forget a rag or two. And a well-stocked first-aid kit is essential.

If the car gets hot or overheats, stop until it cools off. Never open the radiator if the engine is steaming. After a while, squeeze the top radiator hose to check the pressure; if it's loose, it's safe to remove the radiator cap. Never pour water into a hot radiator. You could crack your engine block. If you start to smell rubber, your tires are overheating, which makes them highly susceptible to blow-outs. Stop, in the shade if possible, to let them cool.

If you're exploring the backcountry, it's not a bad idea to inform a friend, park ranger, or even a highway patrol officer where you're going and when you'll be back. (Don't forget to check in upon returning.) Carry double the amount of water you ordinarily would on such an outing, plus an extra five-gallon containerful. If your vehicle gets stuck in the sand, don't panic! Just take it easy and seriously. Let some air out of the tires for traction. If you can't get moving again, stay with the vehicle until after the sun has gone down, then try to dig out.

Wear dark glasses. Cover up to avoid burning. Drink regularly, but not to excess. Minimize conversation. If outside help is required, send the strongest member of the party to the main road, but only after the sun is down. Most desert deaths occur from dehydration by walking too long in the midday heat.

Your life expectancy—in extreme heat, resting, in the shade—will be: three days with no water, four days with one gallon of water, five days with two-and-a-half gallons, one week with five gallons. Try not to verify these statistics.

*Perhaps the most resilient of desert survivors is the desert tortoise* (Gopherus agassizi), *shown here about one quarter life size, and making its way through a bed of woolly daisies.*

*Snow blankets sagebrush and juniper in east-central Nevada. Freezing temperatures occur every month of the year in this region.*

Eighty miles north of Pioche is a rare junction of three US highways: 93, 50, and 6. Major's Station, a small roadhouse, services traffic at the intersection. From there, the three highways share the same two lanes, which turn west and climb into the piñon-juniper heights of the Schell Creek Range, cresting at Connors Pass (7,723 feet). It's all downhill from there, another 20 miles or so, into the bustling crossroads town of Ely. *(Ely is covered in the US 50 chapter on pages 299–301.)*

■ MCGILL   *map page 123, B-6*

The Ely area was originally settled in 1900 when gold was found, but it was copper that supported the region for the next 75 years. The thing about copper is that it's extremely abundant, therefore it's extremely inexpensive, therefore it takes a lot of it to make any money. In the early 20th century, to process ten dollars worth of usable copper, you had to dig up 15 tons of ore, sift out three tons of paydirt, and smelt it down to 60 pounds of refined metal. The refining part required big blast furnaces in a huge smelter, and McGill, 12 miles north of Ely on US 93, was selected as the site of the factory and accompanying company town. Here's how prodigious was the output: steam from the furnaces heated every house in McGill via underground ducts, and the two smokestacks that cleared the rest of the heat were 750 feet tall.

The copper gave out in the late '70s, after more than 70 years, and a billion dollars, worth of production; the mine at Ruth closed in 1979. The smelter shut down soon thereafter, leaving McGill a typical company town without a company. First one tower, then the other, was knocked down (the latter in a public implosion in 1993). Today, McGill is a funky little town with US 93 passing right through. There's a market, cafe, Frostee Stand, bank, and a big old derelict rec center. **The McGill Bar** is worth a peek to see its 100-year-old back bar and display of servicemen and women from McGill who participated in World War II.

During the summer, the main action in town is at the McGill pool, a big spring-water swimming hole dredged out for local aquatics decades ago. It has a high slide, a high diving board (into 15 feet of water), and a shaded shelter. For $1.50, it's a cheap and refreshing break on a hot afternoon of traveling around—perfect for spending yet another day in the Ely area.

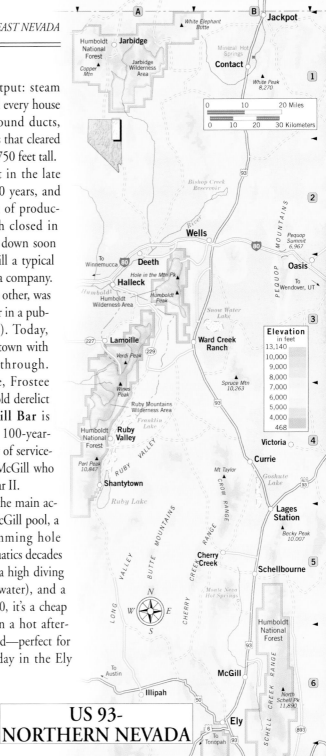

US 93-
NORTHERN NEVADA

*A cabin sits abandoned in Steptoe Valley. Many settlers passed through this area in the middle of the 19th century on the Overland Trail.*

## ■ STEPTOE VALLEY TO JACKPOT *map page 123*

McGill is the last settlement of any size for nearly 125 miles. Forty-five miles north on US 93, straight up Steptoe Valley, is Lages, the junction where Alternate 93 veers off northeast to Wendover (60 miles). The Stage Stop Bar, Cafe, and Texaco are at Lages. From there it's roughly 60 miles, straight up Goshute Valley, into Clover Valley, at the bottom of the mighty East Humboldt Mountains. For a bucolic scenic drive and an unusual peak experience, go left on NV 232, which loops through the bottomlands of the valley, with its luxuriant ranches and farms, till it rejoins US 93.

First though, four miles north on NV 232 is **Hole in the Mountain Peak** (11,306 feet), named for a natural window through the top of it; the 750-square-foot hole is as clear as, well, the daylight that you can see right through it.

Continue up NV 232 or rejoin US 93 (roughly six miles from Hole in the Mountain) into Wells. (Wells is covered in the I-80 chapter.)

From Wells, it's another 68 miles north on US 93 through the mainly unpopulated northeast corner of Nevada. Fifteen miles south of Jackpot you come into Salmon Falls Creek country. This watershed runs north into Idaho, eventually draining into the mighty Snake River. That's just one of the many elements of this corner of the state that belong more to Idaho than Nevada; Idaho time (set your watches ahead an hour), Idaho utilities, and Idaho taxes are others. The only detail that keeps this area in Nevada is that it's south of the state line. That, and the brightly lit casinos of Jackpot.

### ■ JACKPOT   *map page 123, B-1*

All Nevada border towns are a little startling, especially at night, driving into the neon and hubbub through the dark desert on every side. Jackpot is even more so—a shiny nail stuck to the wide baseboard of Idaho.

Especially surprising is its main casino, **Cactus Petes,** which would be right at home at the other end of US 93. The 10-story tower holds 400 rooms, respectable for a locals joint and huge for here. Petes' pits sport dozens of table games, and the slot floor is modern, well-equipped, and comes with decent slot club benefits; there's even positive-expectation video poker (if you look hard enough). The four restaurants include a coffee shop, buffet, snack bar, and gourmet room—all of them recommendable—plus cocktail and dinner shows in the 400-seat show-room. Keno, poker, sports book, lounge, convention center, 18-hole golf course, and RV park—Petes is nothing short of Little Las Vegas near Idaho.

Directly across the highway from Cactus Petes is its sister hotel-casino, the **Horseshu.** It's smaller, funkier, and, as you might infer from the name, has a Western theme. There's some blackjack, craps, and decent video poker, along with a dance hall–saloon that rocks on weekends and a coffee shop that usually features prime rib and breakfast meal deals. Right next door is the only market in Jackpot.

North of the Horseshu is **Barton's Club 93,** with a dozen or so table games, 500 slot and video poker machines, 60 hotel rooms, two restaurants, and an RV park. The Pony Express (located on a bluff above Barton's, closest to Idaho) and the Four Jacks (last gambling stop before the 70-mile drive to Wells) are small slot-only joints with bars and coffee shops.

Cruise around town (during the day) and you'll see a handful of real houses, plus four-plexes and rows of single- and double-wides, all on streets named with gambling terms. Schools (K-12), a couple of municipal buildings and a post office, an RV park, and a water tank round out the infrastructure.

Needless to say, Cactus Petes and the other casinos attract Idahoans, especially from the large town of Twin Falls 50 miles north on US 93, to Jackpot like lambs to the... oat bucket. And they come not only to play, but also to service the players: Just check out the license plates in the parking lots and the nametags on the employees. And that, after all, is the sole purpose of border towns, to empty other states' wallets and purses into the casino coffers. Jackpot, however, to keep them coming back, offers a lot in return.

On the other side of Jackpot is another author's state.

# US 95: WESTERN NEVADA

## ■ HIGHLIGHTS

## ■ TRAVEL BASICS

US 95 is the longest (700 miles) and most meandering road in Nevada. Starting close to the southern tip of the state near Needles, California, a 20-mile side road leads down to Laughlin, the 20-year-old casino town on the banks of the Colorado River. Road parallels river (Lake Mojave, more accurately) right into Boulder City, and from there cuts northwest through Las Vegas, passes the Spring Mountains and Mount Charleston Wilderness Area, and threads a needle between the state line to the west and the massive Nellis Test Range to the east, almost all the way to Tonopah.

From Tonopah, US 95 stair-steps—west, north, west, north—into western Nevada, where the main route strikes due north through Fallon (covered in the US 50 chapter) and up to join Interstate 80 at Exit 83. Those two highways run together to Winnemucca, where US 95 cuts off and continues north, past the big Santa Rosa Range and into remote southeast Oregon at the tiny border town of McDermitt. Meanwhile, Alternate 95 cuts west off the main route at Walker Lake, then heads north through the sweet little town of Yerington and terminates at booming Fernley and Interstate 80, which heads west again for 35 miles to Reno.

### Getting Around

Tour buses ply the 90-odd miles between Las Vegas and Laughlin daily; the coupons and rebates that await at the Laughlin casinos make the ride as good as free. K-T Bus Line has one bus in each direction between Las Vegas and Reno, via Carson City, daily. Greyhound rolls along on Interstate 80 between Reno and Winnemucca, while Amtrak chugs along next to it.

Most traffic on US 95 is local, and most of the non-local traffic is traveling the 440 miles between Las Vegas and Reno. But a handful of travelers do use the highway as a north-south through route, given the lack of superhighways that link together the western states.

### Food and Lodging
Both are few and far between. North of Las Vegas, only a half-dozen towns of any size break up the drive to Reno, and motel rooms and road food are the order of the day. Other than a Mexican restaurant in Tonopah, steakhouses in Hawthorne and Yerington, and a few taco shacks along the way, you're a captive of casino coffee shops and snack bars. Even fast food is limited—McDonald's in Tonopah and Hawthorne, and a Dairy Queen and some pizza in Yerington. Lovelock, on I-80, has a McDonald's; Winnemucca has some variety, though minimal. North of Winnemucca, Mc-Dermitt has the only travelers' facilities for at least 100 miles in every direction.

Laughlin, Las Vegas, and Reno are full of hotel rooms. But on the long rural stretches of the highway, only Tonopah has a bona fide hotel, the 95-year-old Mizpah (with wonderfully restored rooms). Otherwise, check into any motel room anywhere along US 95 and you might as well be in any other motel room anywhere else along US 95.

*Mohave pineapple cactus flowers.*

# ■ LAUGHLIN *map page 123*

Off the main pit in the old wing of the Riverside Hotel-Casino in Laughlin is the show lounge that dares to point out that the emperor isn't wearing anything. It's called the **Losers Lounge**. The setting is typical: stage, dance floor, balcony, bars, barstools, and tables. But the decor is atypical, especially for a casino town: an homage to bust-outs. The ornamentation is of many of recent history's most famous fall guys and gals, who wound up on the wrong side of some track or other and went down in high-visibility flames.

John Belushi, for example. His image is framed and hangs on a wall. On his face is one of the most desperate expressions ever photographed.

A presidential-campaign mirror decorates the main bar, touting "Nixon and Agnew—a team of honesty and integrity." The Hindenburg, Ma Barker and her boys, General Custer, Moamar Khaddafi, Buffalo Bill, Mike Tyson—lots of shooting stars are captured in this room.

Famous flops are represented by big movie posters of, for example, the unforgettable Attack movies: *Attack of the 50-Foot Woman* (take a good look at that body, boys) and *Attack of the Puppet People,* to name a couple.

On the stairs are displays of Timothy McVeigh, Tonya Harding, OJ Simpson and Marcia Clark (side by side), and Ted Kazcynski. The balcony walls are (dis) graced by Imelda Marcos, Ethel and Julius Rosenberg, Eddie Fisher and Debbie Reynolds (in an old poster for a movie they co-starred in), Edsel Ford, Bonnie and Clyde, and Gary Hart.

Whenever I have occasion to blow into Laughlin, I try to stop first at the Losers Lounge at the Riverside. I'm always a little surprised that my picture isn't up on those walls.

Why? Simple. I'm a loser. I lose. Most of us who live in gambling towns, or visit them frequently, are net losers year in and year out. To win, you have to be so skilled, dedicated, and willing to spend your life in casinos that only a tiny minority of the total gambling population even try. And it's only a tiny fraction of those people who succeed. From what I can tell, after a decade of running with professional gamblers in Las Vegas, worldwide there are only a few hundred who actually make their entire livings at gambling.

To win year in and year out, you have to be part mathematician, part probability theorist, part banker, part actor, part computer geek, and part martial artist. The winners play high-level blackjack (sometimes in teams) and rarely get caught.

They pounce on progressive video poker machines (sometimes in teams) the minute the meter makes them playable. They enter all the big-money gambling tournaments (often in teams) and win regularly. They factor comps and cashback into the positive expectation.

They have iron self-discipline, managing gigantic bankroll swings without going on tilt (easy to succumb to) and blowing the whole wad. They take the big losses in stride and the big wins for granted. And they're able to get away with it. The casinos, managed by some of the most suspicious people in the private sector, breathe down their necks every minute of their working day. Their families and friends—many times wives and children—wonder what kind of life they've chosen for themselves.

They eat, sleep, and dream gambling theory. They spend all their time in casinos, carry a lot of cash (and flash it when necessary), and chase small edges with big bucks. The best ones stay healthy in unholy environments, alert under the most distracting conditions, and cool as an early-spring breeze under the heat of scrutiny.

The rest of us? Tinhorns. Pikers. Grinds. We keep going to the casinos, which keep grinding us into chopped meat. And I'm not even talking about slot pullers or crapshooters or keno players, who are, after all, mathematically destined to lose. I'm talking about those of us who play blackjack and video poker. For the pros, these are proven beatable games. For the rest of us, the idea of beatable is entirely theoretical.

## LOOKING LIKE A LOSER

*W*hen I first sit at a table and the dealer or a player asks me how it's going, I'll moan about having played in four casinos that day and having lost in all of them. So even if I win, it's considered an aberration. The last thing I want to do is announce that I've been killing them all over town with my super card-counting method. Out of necessity, lying in casinos soon becomes a way of life. People fib about everything from their real names to their winnings, or lack thereof. When you look at pit bosses who pretend to want you to win, counters using aliases and cover plays, dealers who wear a painted smile while imagining ways to dismember the players, and hookers moaning with one eye on their watch, partial truth is about the best you can expect in Nevada.

—Barry Meadow, *Blackjack Autumn, A True Tale of Life, Death, and Splitting Tens in Winnemucca,* 1999

At blackjack, even playing perfect basic strategy is no easy feat, and you still give up a little edge to the house. And card counting? Fuhgeddaboudit. It takes months of study even to attempt to count cards under casino conditions, and years to perfect the comportment required to get away with the joint's money—and still be welcome back to play another day. It also takes a high-roller bankroll.

Video poker, what most of us play, is the automated version, assembly-line gambling. You become a part of the machine, the part that feeds it with coins, for which the machine has a voracious appetite. Sometimes it gets full and returns some, but more often, the machine is ravenous. So our play is a series of 10-cent wins and 20-dollar losses. What's more, to get even you have to hit the royal flush, an event that happens on average every 60 hours or so. Worse, even factoring in the royal flush, the edge is tiny, fractions of percentage points. Strategy-card perfect play at the "loosest" video poker machines gives you an edge of a tenth or two of one percent.

So we lose. But still we keep on playing. Why? For a lot of reasons. We're supposed to be in it for the fun, the recreation value, the social interaction. For us it's about spending the same money on gambling that we'd use to buy tickets to a ballgame, a concert, or an amusement park. It's about risking our gambling bankrolls for the excitement of the casino, the adrenaline of the action, and, to some extent, the dream of the once-in-a-lifetime monster run. It's about seeing how our luck is holding up lately. It's about fading the chronic pain of losing for the acute fun of winning.

So I always tip my cap at the Losers Lounge when I first arrive in Laughlin.

Because I'm a desert heat kind of guy, I generally gravitate to the southern tip, and the lowest point (400 feet), of the state in July or August, when it's 115 or 118 or 120 or even 125 degrees Fahrenheit (which it reached on June 29, 1994, setting a state record; Laughlin claims the second highest number of record-high temperatures in the United States, behind Laredo, Texas).

Laughlinites like to say that they have only two temperatures in the summer: hot (anything from 100 to 120 degrees) and damn hot (anything above 120). Life is a bit strange when it's damn hot. For example, you can literally fry an egg on the sidewalk. Also, the asphalt gets soft. It feels like you're walking on moss. And it would be an interesting sensation, except that the pavement is burning the soles of your feet through the bottom of your shoes.

Most people do their shopping, golfing, and running around in the early morning, before the ground begins to give off the heat it's been absorbing during the day. Shorts are considered proper business attire, and you won't see a suit jacket or nylon hose within 50 miles, not even on casino bosses. Any clothing chafes every inch of your skin and you desperately want to throw off anything you're wearing. Occasionally you do, but then you just as desperately want to throw off your skin. You have thoughts like, "Wouldn't it be great just to lie around in your bones?"

■ THE STRIP   *map page 133*

You can cool off a little down by the river—where it might be only 118 degrees or so. One place to access the river is at the edge of the parking lot on the north end of the Riverside. While you're here, look up at the Riverside hotel towers, which have sliding patio doors and outside balconies—rare for Nevada high-rise hotels.

Inside, on the first floor, is the sprawling casino, built in several phases over the past 30 years or so by Don Laughlin, the owner of the casino and the founder and namesake of the town. Laugh-

lin founded Laughlin in the mid-1960s, after he'd bought a bait shack and an eight-room motel for $250,000 ($35,000 down). He's since grown the Riverside to megaresort status, while Laughlin has grown into Nevada's third largest casino destination.

On the second floor of the old section are a movie theater, Don's Hideaway Lounge, the Riverside box office, bingo, restaurants, and shops. On the second floor of the new tower is the Western Ballroom, with its 1,400-square-foot dance

*Hotel-casinos line the Colorado River in Laughlin.*

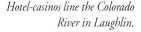

floor, free live entertainment from up-and-coming country acts, great drink specials, and bargain dinners. You can take country dancing lessons or play pool at the tables outside the front door. Also on the second floor are the race and sports book and bar, a bowling alley, and a good cheap snack bar.

**Don Laughlin's Classic Auto Exhibition Showroom** is a fair-sized collection of vintage vehicles, and it's free (the only one of its kind in Nevada that doesn't charge admission). Of interest are the 1880 stagecoach, one-of-a-kind 1983 four-wheel-drive Cadillac Coupe de Ville, and a '66 International Travelall custom-built for John Wayne and his Arizona ranch. Lots of motorcycles are also on display, including 1914 and 1924 Harley Davidsons and a '45 Indian military model.

The Riverside runs the RV park across the street; with 806 sites, it's the largest RV park in the state. The Laughlin Visitors Center is across the street from the RV park, on the corner of Casino Drive and Laughlin Civic Drive. Across Laughlin Civic Drive is the Horizon Factory Outlet center.

Across Casino Drive from the factory outlet is the **Flamingo Hilton.** It has the signature pink-plumage neon, 2,000 rooms (the most in Laughlin), a big casino, the Beef Baron steakhouse and Alta Villa ristorante, plus a '50s-style coffee shop (usually serving a $1.99 lunch special), and a Dairy Queen.

Next door is the **Edgewater**, a Mandalay Resort Group joint. Like the Riverside, its tower rooms have sliders and patios. The Edgewater has a sprawling casino, a steakhouse, buffet, and coffee shop. The snack bar advertises the biggest shrimp cocktail on the river. Not true: The Pioneer snack bar's is bigger. But the Edgewater does have the biggest *cocktail shrimp* on the river. Next door is the Mandalay Resort Group's **Colorado Belle,** sister joint to the Edgewater and the only riverboat-themed casino in Nevada that's actually situated on a river.

**Ramada Express** is the only hotel-casino on the east, non-river, side of Casino Drive. The Express has the most theming of any joint in town. Old Number 7 chugs between the front "depot" and the back parking lot on a mile-long track, a fun little diversion—check out the fog machine (for the smoke) and the steam-engine sound effects. Also look around the train store at the end of restaurant row. Model trains run in the display window and overhead; for sale are train track, train sets, train books, train magazines, model-train controls, train magnets, train pins, train calendars, train videos, train tapestries, train prints, train greeting cards, train wrapping paper, train whistles, train—I could go on, but I won't. If you can, try to get a look at the pool from above; it's in the shape of a cartoon train engine. The Ramada Express also offers the standard Italian restaurant, steakhouse, coffee shop, and buffet.

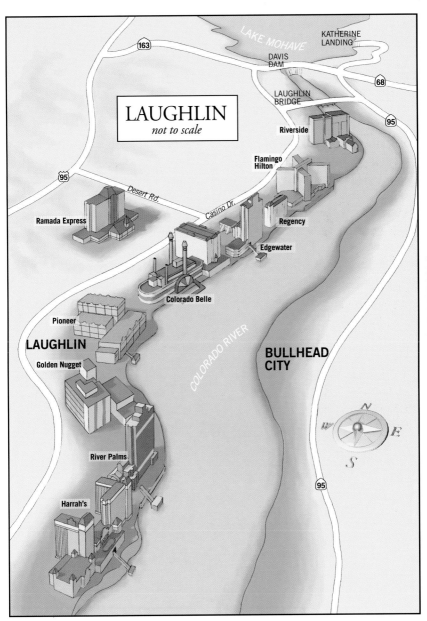

LAKE MOHAVE

163

KATHERINE
LANDING

DAVIS
DAM

68

LAUGHLIN
BRIDGE

95

LAUGHLIN
*not to scale*

Riverside

Flamingo
Hilton

95

Desert Rd.

Casino Dr.

Ramada Express

Regency

Edgewater

Colorado Belle

Pioneer

COLORADO RIVER

LAUGHLIN

BULLHEAD
CITY

Golden Nugget

River Palms

Harrah's

95

N
W    E
S

**The Pioneer** is Laughlin's grind joint. It's always packed—full of video poker players and people waiting to eat at the popular coffee shop/buffet. Granny's gourmet room is also renowned for its atmosphere and quality. And 50-foot-tall neon River Ric waves along the water, Laughlin's counterpart to Vegas Vic.

**The Golden Nugget** is a tiny Mirage Resorts' afterthought. You walk in through a tropical atrium reminiscent of the Mirage, but then it's just a casino with a few hundred rooms, a coffee shop, buffet, and deli (good pizza, shrimp cocktail, chili, hot dogs, and sandwiches). In the lobby is a big cage in which animatronic birds do French showtunes a là Maurice Chevalier.

Not only players can be losers. Plenty of loser casinos have come and gone through history. **The River Palms** is one of them, having gone bankrupt and changed hands several times over the past ten years. But this joint finally seems to have hit a winning streak, now that Allen Paulson and his Full House casino company (whose passive partners are rumored to be Jack Nicholson, Kenny Rogers, and Lee Iaccoca) have taken it over. It's always been an interesting building, with three stories, including a mezzanine and balcony overlook of the pit; the main floor, with Madeleine's Lodge restaurant, the fanciest room in town; and the river level, with the coffee shop, Italian restaurant, and doors to the dock.

*At one time, paddle steamers cruised the Colorado River, carrying supplies into and bullion out of mining camps. (Nevada Historical Society)*

But Paulson has really spruced up the place. He's launched a pirate theme; a big old pirate ship sits atop the central bar. He's upgraded the buffet and remodeled the main lounge—now called the Bermuda Club, which sports great lighting, a good sound system, an adequate dance floor, ass-kicking rock 'n' roll, and dollar happy-hour drink specials with all the appetizers you can eat. Last time I was there, a live reggae band with a steel drum sound was playing on the mezzanine and a jazz pianist was tickling the ivories in the bar at Madeleine's. The full-pay deuces wild and 10/7 double bonus video poker throughout don't interfere with your inclination to stay and play at the River Palms.

Last but not least along Casino Drive is **Harrah's**, with its festive south-of-the-border flavor. There's a decent Mexican restaurant, a great steakhouse, and the Fresh Market Square Buffet, the only superbuffet in Laughlin, with Mexican, Chinese, American, and Italian serving stations. The sports book has a unique feature: Four of the screens are the lowest you'll ever see; sitting right on the floor, the heads of the people in front of you are in the way. Harrah's also offers the only public beach on the river, a fine place to cool off between, believe it or not, February and November.

*The only "sternwheeler" on the Colorado today is the Colorado Belle casino—firmly anchored to the ground on which it was built.*

*A windmill framed by Joshua trees lies still in the afternoon heat of the Highland Range Habitat Area just north of Searchlight.*

## ■ LAUGHLIN AT LARGE *map page 137*

The actual town of Laughlin is inland, up the hill from the river on the back road to and from US 95. The sprawling condos and townhouses, shopping center, schools, and public buildings have all arrived within the past six or seven years, and it shows. The Mojave Generating Station is the big power plant with the tall telltale smokestack on Edison Way.

Three-quarters of the local population lives in Bullhead City, across the river in Arizona. Like Laughlin, Bullhead City has undergone an extensive expansion up the slope on the east side of the Colorado over the past decade. Arizona Highway 95 is the commercial strip, a long stretch of motels, used-car lots, Mexican restaurants, marine parts stores, burger shacks, pawn shops, bars, RV parks, and Ski- and Sea Doo rentals—you get the picture. Bullhead Community Park, near the north end of AZ 95, hosts a playground, little league baseball field, and a chamber of commerce. This park is especially pretty at sunset, when the sky is pink and the neon lights of the casinos are reflected in the river.

Several of the casinos, most notably the Riverside, own riverboats that cruise up to Davis Dam, which controls the water about a mile north of the strip, and down toward the Nevada, Arizona, and California tip of the state. You can take a self-guided tour of Davis Dam, 200 feet high and 1,600 feet wide, built in 1953 to impound industrial, irrigation, and recreational water in

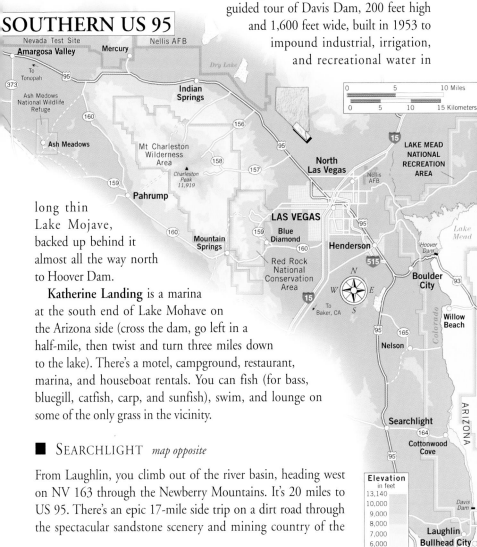

## SOUTHERN US 95

long thin Lake Mojave, backed up behind it almost all the way north to Hoover Dam.

**Katherine Landing** is a marina at the south end of Lake Mohave on the Arizona side (cross the dam, go left in a half-mile, then twist and turn three miles down to the lake). There's a motel, campground, restaurant, marina, and houseboat rentals. You can fish (for bass, bluegill, catfish, carp, and sunfish), swim, and lounge on some of the only grass in the vicinity.

■ SEARCHLIGHT *map opposite*

From Laughlin, you climb out of the river basin, heading west on NV 163 through the Newberry Mountains. It's 20 miles to US 95. There's an epic 17-mile side trip on a dirt road through the spectacular sandstone scenery and mining country of the

Newberries and the Mojave Desert. The turnoff is a little more than three miles west of Laughlin on NV 163 on the right. The rough road passes Grapevine Canyon, which you can hike into to see a series of petroglyphs, continues up to Christmas Tree Pass, then heads down to US 95 about a mile south of Cal-Nev-Ari. A high-clearance four-wheel-drive is preferred, but you can negotiate the trip in just about any vehicle that rolls on rubber.

**Cal-Nev-Ari** is a tiny desert town that grew up around an old World War II airfield. A string of single-wides and shade trees hug the highway; in "town" are the main cafe/bar/post office across the highway is the motel/RV park/mini-mart/laundromat.

Ten miles north of Cal-Nev-Ari on US 95 is Searchlight, founded at the turn of the century to service the surrounding gold-mining district. The mining continued into the 1940s and the highway has helped keep the town alive ever since. Here you'll find a couple of motels, a diner, a parade of billboards for Laughlin,

and the two main attractions: the Nugget casino-coffeeshop and the town's museum.

**The Searchlight Nugget** is full of little gems to occupy your interest as you stretch your legs, wandering. By the cage is an old **Mills Black Beauty** nickel slot machine; this is the original "one-armed bandit," in the shape of a cowboy with one amputated arm and the other arm—the slot handle—holding a revolver. It was restored in

*A trio of original one-armed bandits. (Underwood Photo Archives, San Francisco)*

1985. Also check out the big banner for the 1964 Nevada Centennial hanging in the poker room, an aerial view of Searchlight, turquoise cow skulls over the hearth, and a half-dozen Calgary Stampede posters. The coffee shop serves typical road food at typical prices, except for one anomaly: the Nugget is known statewide as the home of the 10-cent cup of coffee. There's a nice houseboat mural on the coffeeshop wall.

Drive a long block east on NV 164 to the **Searchlight Historic Museum and Mining Park,** a big-time muse-

*Cottonwood Cove and Lake Mohave.*

um for such a small town. Searchlight has had a long and interesting history, even claiming several celebrities as original residents, and it's all here in the displays, photographs, and "ghost narrations."

Continuing east along NV 164 (Cove Road), it's another 14 miles down to **Cottonwood Cove** on Lake Mohave. On the way, notice the teddy-bear cholla forest. The Cove is a large facility in the Lake Mead National Recreation Area. It has a Park Service interpretive center and a discovery trail, cafe, campground, picnic area, RV park, mini-mart, gas station, and marina, not to mention a nice beach on a big lake. This is a great secret getaway, a little more than an hour from downtown Las Vegas.

## ■ MOUNT CHARLESTON  *map page 137*

From Searchlight, it's 36 miles north on US 95 through Eldorado Valley to the junction with US 93 on the east side of Railroad Pass, where you take a left and head west into Henderson and Las Vegas. If you want to stop and spend some time exploring the metropolitan area, you probably won't regret it; I've heard there are a few things to do and see in the city. *(See pages 36–85.)*

Otherwise, you can blow through on US 95; pay attention to the signs approaching the Spaghetti Bowl downtown so as not to find yourself, a few hours later, in Los Angeles or Salt Lake City. Our road parallels the mighty Spring Mountains, which stand to the west. Continue roughly 30 miles north to the turnoff (left) on NV 157 to Kyle Canyon, which climbs forthwith up into the 43,000-acre Mount Charleston Wilderness Area, controlled by the National Forest Service.

### ◆ KYLE CANYON  *map page 137*

About 20 minutes up NV 157 is the elegant **Mount Charleston Hotel,** sitting in a bowl at a little under 7,000 feet elevation, the closest mountain lodge to Las Vegas. The hotel has 63 rooms, restaurant, bar, slots and video games, and a nine-hole golf course. It's always 25 or so degrees cooler up here than in the valley, making it a great place to beat the summer heat in fresh alpine air, or warm up on a winter afternoon in front of a sizzling hardwood fire in the stone hearth in the lobby.

Farther up NV 157 you'll come to: the junction with NV 158; **Kyle Canyon Campground,** with 25 campsites, piped drinking water, and plenty of vegetation, including tall conifers; **Mount Charleston village,** a pretty alpine hamlet with year-round homes inhabited by Vegas commuters, summer houses inhabited by Vegas diluters, and a Forest Service ranger station; **Fletcher View Campground,** about half the size of Kyle Canyon (though a little more crowded); and funky **Mount Charleston Lodge,** with restaurant, bar, and cabins. The road ends at the Lodge parking lot, from which trails spider-web into the mountains, one heading off nine miles to the top of Mount Charleston, at 11,918 feet the eighth tallest peak in Nevada.

Backtracking on NV 157, turn on NV 158, which takes you north for six miles on a ridgeline, connecting the Kyle Canyon Road (NV 157) with the Lee Canyon Road (NV 156). Halfway between the two is **Hilltop Campground.** At 8,400 feet on the ridge, it's more exposed than the campgrounds in Kyle Canyon, but has fine views of the valley floor and mountain ranges on the other side of it, as well as a paved access road, 35 sites, and running water.

◆ LEE CANYON  *map page 137*

At the junction with NV 156, go left and climb three miles to the top of Lee Canyon. You pass two nearly identical campgrounds, **McWilliams** (40 sites, piped drinking water, tall but sparse pine and cedar, and a flush toilet) and **Dolomite** (31 sites). Just up from Dolomite is **Las Vegas Ski and Snowboard Resort,** only a short hour from, and 7,000 feet higher than, one of the hottest cities in the world. Ski Lee, as it's affectionately known, is a full-service downhill resort, with a day lodge (coffee shop, lounge, and rental shop), ski school and beginner chairlift, and three double chairlifts. Base elevation is 8,500 feet; the top of the main run is 9,500 feet. You'll find mostly locals on the slopes up here, crowded on the weekends, especially after a productive winter storm; weekdays you'll have the place practically to yourself.

*Highway 158 heads toward Mummy Mountain in the Spring Mountains.*
*Charleston Peak would be just off to the left.*

You can retrace your route, via Hilltop and Kyle Canyon, back down to US 95, or drive 17 miles down NV 156 through Lee Canyon. You'll be 14 miles north of where you turned off US 95 onto NV 157.

It's also 14 miles, but north, to **Indian Springs**, a small settlement and military outpost right on the highway. Here you'll find a runway for Nellis Air Force Range (with attending control tower, green equipment, and barbed wire), two gas stations and convenience stores, and Indian Springs Casino.

### ■ MERCURY  *map page 137*

From Indian Springs, it's another 19 miles to the turnoff to Mercury, the operations center for the Nevada Test Site, the huge chunk of forbidden territory (roughly the size of Rhode Island) where the U.S. military exploded approximately 1,250 nuclear warheads (that we know of) between 1951 and 1992, 126 of them above ground. At the height of the testing era, Mercury was one of the largest "cities" in Nevada, housing upwards of 10,000 workers, with its own power and water plants, administration offices, labs and shops, dormitories, cafeteria, a hospital, gymnasium, swimming pool, even a

*During the 1950s, at least 126 above-ground tests were made at Yucca Flat on the Nevada Test Site range outside of Mercury. The 2.2 kiloton device exploded here was suspended from a balloon and then detonated 1,500 feet above the valley floor. (photo from the collection of Stanley W. Paher, Reno)*

US 95:
WESTERN NEVADA

bowling alley and a movie theater.

Today, since the United States no longer tests nuclear weapons, the staffing has been reduced to 1,500 or so, most of whom are working on Yucca Mountain, the federal government's only candidate to become the permanent repository, or disposal site, for the nearly 20,000 metric tons of high-level radioactive waste that has accumulated over the years from nuclear-power plants nationwide. A "study" of the Yucca Mountain area has been on-going for years—its costs in the billions of dollars, as opposing factions battle it out in Congress, the courts, scientific journals, and the mainstream media.

You can take a tour of Mercury, as well as Frenchman Flat, site of the first nuclear tests in 1951, the crest of Yucca Ridge, and the repository's field-office buildings; you're even led into one of the tunnels to see the huge boring machines that drill the holes deep into the mountain that will eventually store up to 70,000 metric tons of radioactive waste. Conducted by the U.S. Department of Energy (DOE), the tour is free, takes place six times a year (once a month in September, October, November, March, April, May), and is extremely popular. The seven busloads of seats are booked weeks in advance.

You have to show ID and receive something of a temporary security clearance; your bags are searched for weapons, cameras, telescopes, and the like. But it's worth the little bit of cloak-and-dagger to go to the least accessible "state," and its "capital city," in the country, a place the increasingly secretive federal government doesn't really want us to see, but obviously feels it's necessary to let a few of us in, in order to garner public support for the waste dump.

Just north of Mercury, the four-lane freeway narrows down to two lanes, which it remains for the next 350 miles until you hit Interstate 80. Five miles north of Mercury is a junction with the northern terminus of the road to Pahrump, NV 160.

■ FRONT SIGHT   *map page 137*

The southern terminus of NV 160 is at exit 33 off Interstate 15, ten miles southwest of Las Vegas. From there, the road heads due west toward the southern edge of the Spring Mountains, then climbs into them on a good three-lane road. You crest the pass at Mountain Springs Summit (5,493 feet), affectionately known as "the hump to Pahrump." Up here is the venerable Mountain Springs Saloon, the focal point of the small hamlet of Mountain Springs. From there, you drop down to Pahrump Valley, bordered on the east side by the Spring Mountains, and follow the route of the area's earliest explorers, Franciscan missionaries blazing a trail from Santa Fe, New Mexico, to Los Angeles, California, in the 1770s. The road is arrow straight, the speed limit is 70 miles an hour, and Nye County sheriff's deputies patrol heavily.

In about eight miles is a turnoff onto the Tecopa (California) road. Four miles south of the junction on the Tecopa road is another turnoff to Front Sight, the newest and most unusual "town" in a state full of unusual towns.

Allow me to introduce Front Sight by saying that Nevada, with its 70-year-old tradition of wide-open gambling and 130-year-old traditions of legal prostitution,

open-pit mining, no state income tax, and general distrust of the federal government, is perhaps the most live-and-let-live libertarian state in the country.

And that's not even including the gun laws. Nevada is an "open-carry" state, meaning that you can legally walk around most places with a holstered sidearm strapped to your belt, and a "shall-issue" state, meaning that you can get a concealed-carry permit, which allows you to walk around with a loaded gun in your pocket, just by asking for it (and taking a cursory course and passing a shooting test). Also, Nevada residents can own Class III fully automatic submachine pistols and machine guns.

Which is one reason why Front Sight wound up in Nevada. The other reason is

that there's still enough inexpensive open land to build what Front Sight is eventually slated to become: the world's largest non-military gun range.

When it's built out (by 2002), Front Sight will be a $25 million, 550-acre master-planned firearms training institute, community, and resort. Think of it as a typical golf facility, except that bullets replace the balls, targets replace the holes, firearms replace the clubs, and "un" replaces "olf." It will consist of 171 homes on one-acre lots, several hundred townhouses, a community center and pool, a school, and an airstrip, along with retail, meeting, and administrative areas, and a guarded front gate.

This is in addition to the extensive firearms facilities: 12 shooting ranges from 25 to 150 meters, a 400-meter rifle range, video and live-fire training simulators, a defensive driving track, classrooms, gunsmith and armory, and pro shop.

That's the vision, anyway. As of this writing, there are a half-dozen training ranges (with protective earthen berms completely surrounding the perimeters), large canvas tents for shade on the ranges, and a classroom building.

Two- and four-day classes in handgun, shotgun, rifle, or submachine gun are currently offered; they run $500–1,200. But one-day and even half-day classes are in the works for people who just want to see what it's all about. You bring your own weapon and ammunition to train with.

Front Sight is aimed at anyone who wants to become more proficient in the responsible, safe, and effective use of firearms; everyone from SWAT cops to soccer moms have trained here. I've trained here, and I highly recommend it.

■ PAHRUMP   *map page 137*

In the middle of downtown Pahrump is **Terrible's Town Casino.** The front-door handles are in the shape of Colt revolvers (with eight-inch *Dirty Harry* barrels). The interior decor represents an entire town, with façades such as Dolly's Doll House, Laura's Bordello, Lisa's Western Wear, Roy's Hotel, and Poncho's Bar. Also packed in are neon cactus, a whole stagecoach, wagon wheels, hats and guns, taxidermied buffalo, elk, and deer, along with clanking slot machines, raucous table games, a rowdy race and sports book, a smoky bingo hall—and an eight-foot-tall round aquarium full of tropical fish, with a fake shark sitting on the bottom and a guide to Hawaiian oceanlife posted nearby.

*(previous pages) A desert sunset lights the evening sky over Nevada.*

The scene at Terrible's about sums up Pahrump: part *Wild Wild West,* part modern casino, and part stuff for which there's no apparent explanation.

(There is, in case you're curious, an explanation for the "Terrible" in the name of the joint. Terrible's Town is owned and operated by the Herbst family of Las Vegas, lately of the Herbst Oil Company, whose gas stations were called Terrible Herbsts. Old Man Herbst was nicknamed "Terrible" due to his fiercely competitive nature in the rough-and-tumble wildcat oil business in the 1930s and '40s. On a side note, my wife incorporated the term into her lexicon years ago and now uses it for whatever ails her, as in, "All this drinking is gonna give me a Terrible Herbst in the morning!")

Pahrump is a bizarre little boomtown 60 miles west of Las Vegas, just over the Clark County Line in Nye County. As such, it has one foot in Las Vegas's sphere of influence, serving as a bedroom community, both literally (people commute an hour to work in the city) and figuratively (prostitution is legal in Pahrump, where there are two famous brothels). It also has one foot in the far southern corner of Nye, the third largest county in the country. It's a long 160 miles from the county seat in Tonopah, 250 miles from Nye's far northwestern town of Gabbs, and almost 300 miles by road to Duckwater, Nye's far north*eastern* town. To its strange location, add an unincorporated status (with no zoning to speak of), and you can get a glimpse of some method to the madness.

★  OFFICIAL PROGRAM  ★

"*Pahrump Wedded to Civilization*"

**HIGHWAY OPENING**

Water flowing at the rate of more than 1800 gallons per minute from the Hafen well in Pahrump. Wells like this keep Pahrump's cotton and hay fields growing.
(Photo by Clark County Extension Service)

**Sunday, September 26, 1954**

PAHRUMP, NYE COUNTY, NEVADA

Sponsored By

PAHRUMP - ASH MEADOWS IMPROVEMENT ASSOC.

LAS VEGAS CHAMBER OF COMMERCE

★  Price 25c  ★

*This broadside celebrates Pahrump being "wedded to civilization" thanks to the completion of a new highway.*

Across the street from Terrible's Town is a Day's Inn. No more than six or seven years ago, this was the western edge of the commercial strip in Pahrump. Today, the Days Inn is smack dab in the middle of it. This well-watered valley, especially its central core, has exploded with development over the past few years. West of Terrible's is a shopping center called Pahrump Valley Junction. All lined up are about a dozen franchises—EZ Money Check-Cashing, Cigarettes Cheaper, Hollywood Video, Canyon Rent-to-Own, fast fooderies, jewelers, etc.—the quintessential New Nevada strip mall. Perfect for Pahrump.

Across the street is a different kind of commercial experience, little box-like buildings containing an old-time crafts store, used-book store, bike store, bail-bondsman, chiropractor, and law office. Between those and Terrible's Town are more fast-food joints.

A bit east of Terrible's on Hwy. 160 is the old **Saddle West**, Pahrump's original action-central, though it's been expanded and remodeled a couple times over the years. Check out the cool three-way neon sign of a bucking bronco. There are also a couple of old nickel slot machines, including a rare console model, by the restrooms.

Pahrump is also famous for billboards, brothels, and Art Bell. Almost all the billboards are for development-oriented businesses: realtors, equipment rentals, pipe wholesalers, subdivision road builders, house-pad installers, aggregate asphalt suppliers, and on and on.

The brothels huddle on one of Pahrump's many edges (heading west, turn right on Homestead Road and drive eight miles). Sherri's Ranch and the Chicken Ranch are side by side in a kind of Hatfield-McCoy apposition. **The Chicken Ranch** is probably the most famous house of delight in southern Nevada. The original Chicken Ranch opened in Texas in the 1840s (it took chickens in payment for services rendered); the Broadway play *The Best Little Whorehouse in Texas* was based on it. In 1976 it was relocated to Pahrump, and it's been Visa and Venus ever since.

**Sherri's Ranch** is famous for a different reason: It's the subject of the book *Madam—Chronicles of a Nevada Cathouse*. The author, Lora Shaner, was a full-time madam (a combination greeter–hostess–shift manager–den mother) at Sherri's for five years, and she tells all in the most revealing and poignant look at Nevada's legal sex industry ever written from the inside.

And then there's Art Bell, who until very recently broadcasted from a modest

*Prostitution has long been legal in Nevada. This photograph was taken in Goldfield in 1907 and shows the working ladies' "cribs" in the town's red-light district.*
*(Nevada Historical Society, Reno)*

home studio, also on Homestead Road somewhere, via nearly 400 AM radio stations around the country, reaching an audience estimated at up to 20 million, for five hours most nights. Bell's call-in show focused on the lunar and the lunatic, his content ranging from aliens and mysticism to political, economic, and climatological disasters. Just your average Nevadan attitude, coming to you live, direct from Pahrump.

## ■ ASH MEADOWS  *map page 137*

At the western edge of Pahrump is a turnoff (heading west, take a left) on Belle Vista Road (aka County Road 210), which travels 24 miles till reaching a dirt road into Ash Meadows National Wildlife Refuge. This little park, in the wilds of the Nevada desert just this side of the California state line, is an internationally renowned desert wetlands. Here, a powerful artesian aquifer gushes to the surface, feeding dozens of springs and seeps and supporting an amazing array of flora and fauna, some found nowhere else on the planet.

*A National Park Service diver passes the alabaster walls of calcite crystals and descends into the darkness of Devil's Hole Cave. (photo by John D. Brooks, National Park Service)*

Meander along backroads till you get to the visitors center; from there, walk along the Crystal Springs boardwalk to immerse yourself in this virgin habitat (rare major natural springs that haven't been tapped for industrial or residential water). Depending on the season, scores of different waterfowl make these springs and reservoirs a stop on their migratory routes or home for the winter; a species of local water beetle occupies a habitat that's about 100 square yards; also look for endemic three-foot-tall poppy plants. There's nothing quite like clear blue water in the desert, of which Ash Meadows National Wildlife Refuge is the epitome.

Nearby is **Death Valley National Monument,** a non-contiguous annex of the national park in the state next door. The monument is the home of **Devil's Hole,** a deep limestone shaft containing warm spring water. The top 60 feet of the Hole host the entire earthly population of Devil's Hole pupfish, direct descendants of a prehistoric fish that has survived, for tens of thousands of years, in one of the most restrictive and isolated habitats of any living creature on Earth. Both the national wildlife refuge and the national monument are well worth the two-hour detour between Pahrump and Beatty.

*Early morning shadows play across the dunes in Amargosa Valley.*

Map labels:
To Reno
6 95
Tonopah
Tonopah Summit 6,033
6
To Ely
Silver Rush 1902
Mud Lake
0 Miles 10
0 Kilometers 15
Montezuma Peak 8,376
Gold Rush 1903
Goldfield
Goldfield Summit 6,087
95
Mt Jackson 6,394
Stonewall 8,390
Nellis Air Force Range (travel restricted)
266
To Big Pine
774
Gold Point (ghost town)
Scotty's Junction
267
SARCOBATUS FLAT
95
Rhyolite (ghost town)
Death Valley National Park
374
Beatty
BARE MTNS
N W E S
Nevada Test Site (travel restricted)
CALIFORNIA
AMARGOSA DESERT
95
Amargosa Valley
To Las Vegas
373

An eight-mile gravel road runs due west from the national monument and dead-ends into NV 373, which heads due north for 16 miles back to US 95. At the intersection and the small settlement of Amargosa Valley, go left (west) and continue 30 miles into Beatty.

## ■ BEATTY

In downtown Beatty, at the corner where US 95 makes a dogleg (right), is the **Exchange Club.** This casino, with bar and coffee shop, dates back to just after the turn of the 19th century, when Beatty was developing as a supply stop on the railroad line from Las Vegas for the gold-mining district of Rhyolite, four miles west. Rhyolite died when the gold ran out, but Beatty survived off the railroad, then the highway, and a resurgence or two of gold fever.

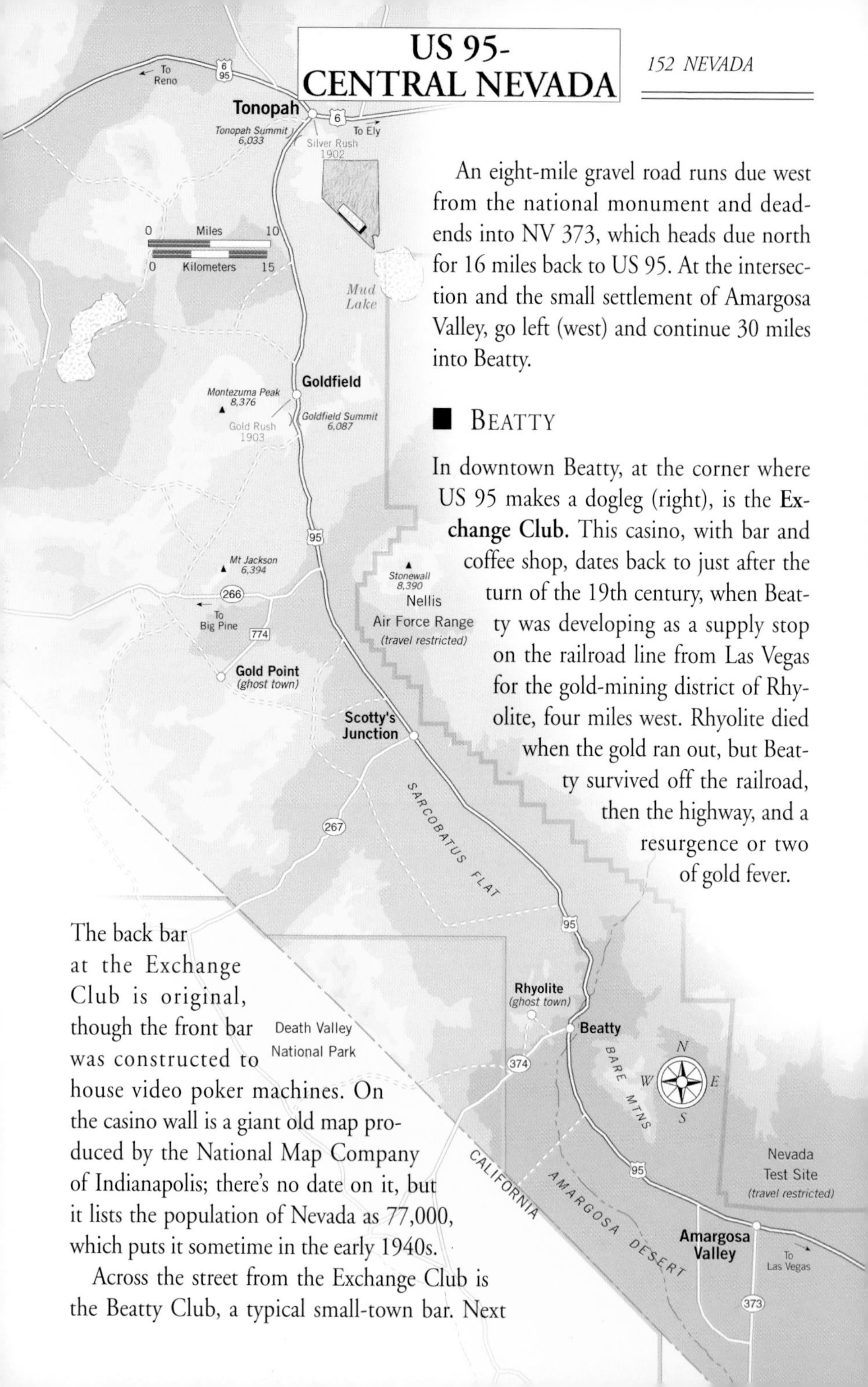

The back bar at the Exchange Club is original, though the front bar was constructed to house video poker machines. On the casino wall is a giant old map produced by the National Map Company of Indianapolis; there's no date on it, but it lists the population of Nevada as 77,000, which puts it sometime in the early 1940s.

Across the street from the Exchange Club is the Beatty Club, a typical small-town bar. Next

*Rhyolite (above), during the peak of the gold boom in 1908; and (below) as it looks today.*
*(Nevada State Historical Society)*

door is the Sourdough Saloon, a pizza place and bar. Next door to the Sourdough is a cute little old-fashioned ice-cream shop, complete with pink trim and an awning. Across the other side of the street is the Lost River Trading Company, selling turquoise, rocks, and whatnot. Next to that is Beatty General Store, the main market in town. That about sums up downtown Beatty.

Surrounding downtown are a couple of RV parks, right next to each other, a burger shack known as the Classic Diner, and two other casinos, the **Burro Inn,** a crowded little joint with one blackjack table and a coffee shop, and the **Stagecoach Inn,** a surprisingly airy and uncluttered joint with four blackjack tables, the only crap table between Tonopah and Las Vegas, and a coffee shop that serves excellent soup for a buck. Beatty's a good lunch stop if you're driving north from Las Vegas; otherwise you'll have to wait another 90 minutes or more to get to Tonopah.

Rhyolite (take a left at NV 374 at the junction in downtown Beatty) today is a ghost town, with just a few ruins left standing. On the way, you pass a huge gold-mining operation, so big that it's literally terraced one entire slope of the Bullfrog Hills. Since 1986, more than two million ounces of gold (roughly $600 million at today's spot price) have been unearthed by Bond Gold, an Australian mining

*Just south of Beatty a primitive desert road follows what used to be the Carrara Hills cable railway to Bear Mountain, a former marble quarry.*

*The northern wall of Tom Kelly's Bottle House in Rhyolite.*

company, and Barrick Gold, a Canadian mining company that bought out Bond.

Skirt the tailings and leach fields, then go right and climb up the hill to the ghost town. Here are a **Bottle House** (constructed in 1906 from 50,000 Busch beer bottles), the remains of the jail, school, bank, and mercantile, and a well-preserved train depot (behind a cyclone fence). The proud stone-and-brick buildings were erected by prosperity for posterity, but it was all an illusion: Rhyolite lasted only five years or so (1904–09) before it was deserted, left to the mercy of the elements.

About ten miles north of Beatty is **Bailey's Hot Springs**, an RV park with his and her bathhouses sheltering hot springs (about 105 degrees); pony up a couple of bucks for a soak.

■ SCOTTY'S JUNCTION AND NELLIS AIR FORCE RANGE

*map page 152, A/B–3/4*

From the Hot Springs, it's another 25 miles to Scotty's Junction and the turnoff (left) onto NV 267, which heads southwest for 21 miles through Grapevine Canyon into Death Valley National Park and its northern attractions, Scotty's Castle and Ubehebe Crater.

Also at Scotty's Junction, US 95 comes closest to, and almost touches at one point, the Nellis Air Force Range. Actually, cars skirt the western edge of this three-million-acre military reservation (nearly five percent of the total land area of Nevada) from about 30 miles north of Las Vegas, and continue to do so almost all the way to Tonopah.

This huge chunk of real estate is a legacy of World War II. It was parceled off by the Feds in 1940 to use as a practice range for fighter pilots, bombardiers, and air-to-air and air-to-ground gunners; at the height of the war build-up, classes of 4,000 bombers and gunners were graduating every six weeks. Though the government, which had invoked the wartime emergency to appropriate the range, was supposed to return the land to the public trust after the war, that never happened. Sixty years later, not only do the feds "own" it lock, stock, and barrel, but it's off-limits to civilians. We're talking about an area the size of Connecticut here, a stretch of US 95 equivalent to driving from Manhattan almost all the way to, well, Washington D.C.

From Scotty's Junction, it's 32 miles to Goldfield.

*The Esmeralda County Courthouse.*

■ GOLDFIELD  *map page 152, A–2*

Smack in the middle of Goldfield, the largest and most authentic semi-ghost town in the west, is the **Esmeralda County Courthouse.** This solid stone building, which looks like a castle thanks to the ramparts on its roof, dates back to 1907 when Goldfield was roaring with the noise of machinery mining and refining the precious yellow metal, lining the pockets of two generations of Nevada power-brokers-to-be, and enshrining itself as the largest population center in the state. But like Rhyolite and hundreds of boomtowns-turned-ghost-towns before it, Goldfield's heyday was relatively short-lived: by 1910, the gold thinned, a flash flood in 1913 washed away one side of town, and the Great Fire of 1923 put the finishing touches on much of the other half.

Still, thanks to its status as county seat, a handful of die-hard miners, and the US highway, Goldfield remains more than a

*(above) Goldfield in 1903. By 1905, the town had a population of 25,000. A Fourth of July drilling contest (below) draws a crowd in the Goldfield of 1907. (Nevada Historical Society)*

wide spot on the road, complete with many stone and brick monuments of its golden, so to speak, era. The courthouse, in fact, is one of the best preserved century-old buildings in the state (even though it serves a

county of barely a thousand souls, smallest county population in Nevada): all the fixtures, including the Tiffany lamps, are original.

Tooling around town, you'll see the four-story 150-room Goldfield Hotel, which has fallen just short, several times recently, of being renovated and reopened; the three-story boarded-up Goldfield High School and the Goldfield elementary school in use behind it; and the beautiful brick Southern Nevada Consolidated Telephone Company building.

Both bars in town are chock full of character and local color. **The Columbia Bar** is one block off US 95 (turn at the shuttered Mozart Club). **The Santa Fe,** four long blocks down Fifth Street (turn at the courthouse), dates to 1905 or so, with the original wood floor, lots of historical photos and articles on the wall, and an old mining headframe outside (as well as a four-room motel and laundromat).

Otherwise, Goldfield consists of regular single-wide mobile homes, old aluminum-frame double-wides, fancy brick and wood houses, junk and satellite dishes in most of the yards, a couple of big old falling-down barns, and a handful of headframes scattered around the scarred hillsides to the east of town.

From Goldfield, it's 25 miles north to Tonopah.

## ■ TONOPAH

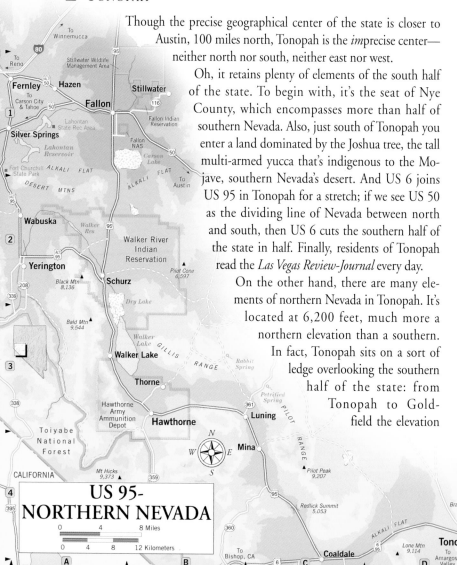

Though the precise geographical center of the state is closer to Austin, 100 miles north, Tonopah is the *im*precise center—neither north nor south, neither east nor west.

Oh, it retains plenty of elements of the south half of the state. To begin with, it's the seat of Nye County, which encompasses more than half of southern Nevada. Also, just south of Tonopah you enter a land dominated by the Joshua tree, the tall multi-armed yucca that's indigenous to the Mojave, southern Nevada's desert. And US 6 joins US 95 in Tonopah for a stretch; if we see US 50 as the dividing line of Nevada between north and south, then US 6 cuts the southern half of the state in half. Finally, residents of Tonopah read the *Las Vegas Review-Journal* every day.

On the other hand, there are many elements of northern Nevada in Tonopah. It's located at 6,200 feet, much more a northern elevation than a southern. In fact, Tonopah sits on a sort of ledge overlooking the southern half of the state: from Tonopah to Goldfield the elevation

US 95-
NORTHERN NEVADA

*The Mizpah Mine headframe and hoistworks, Tonopah Historic Mining Park.*

drops nearly 1,000 feet; from Goldfield to Beatty, it drops another 1,500 feet; from Beatty to Las Vegas is another 1,000 feet. Its winters—frigid and snowy—are definitely northern Nevadan. And Sierra Pacific, the northern Nevada utilities company, services Tonopah (though Sierra Pacific and Nevada Power, Las Vegas's utility company, recently merged).

In short, Tonopah occupies a place all its own in the geography of Nevada.

As you might expect for such a central cross-roads location, Tonopah is a respectably sized town, even though two strong elements have conspired against it being so: its origin as a mining boomtown (silver was discovered here in 1900, triggering a resurgence of Nevada mining and ending the 20-year hiatus that began when Virginia City went bust) and its climate (elevation, tough winters, and windswept exposure on the slope of Mount Brougher). Downtown are two six-story brick buildings from the turn of the century; one is the **Mizpah Hotel**, tallest building in the state when it was erected. And the major **Central Nevada Museum** boasts an extensive collection of artifacts from around the region and an outdoor exhibit of mining machinery and a replica townsite; meet here to take the one-hour tour of Tonopah's 70-acre **Historic Mining Park**. Tonopah also boasts one of the state's largest rural hospitals, the Nye County Courthouse, and a good library.

*A stock certificate from a Tonopah mining company issued at the Tonopah Stock Exchange in 1905. (collection of Stanley W. Paher, Reno)*

**The Station House** on the south edge of town is Tonopah's full-scale casino. The four blackjack and one mini crap tables open at night, but there's positive video poker while you wait. A couple dozen antique slot machines are on display downstairs by the restrooms; they're mostly from the 1940s, but a few date back to the 1930s and '20s. The Station House also has a coffee shop and snack bar. The Banc Club is a slot house and coffee shop in a converted bank building.

Tonopah has 600 or so motel rooms, which line both sides of the highway through town. It's a little light in the dining department—mostly hotel and motel coffee shops, a Mexican restaurant, burger joints, and fast food.

## ■ NORTHWEST TO HAWTHORNE  *map page 158*

In the middle of Tonopah, US 95 meets up with US 6, then makes a wide left turn. The two US highways head west for 40 miles to Coaldale Junction, where they split. US 6 continues west toward California, climbing into the White Mountains, cresting **Montgomery Pass** (7,132 feet), and passing in the shadow of **Boundary Peak**, at 13,143 feet, the highest point in the state.

Our faithful US 95, meanwhile, turns northwest. In 30 miles is **Billie's Day and Night**, a small roadside hole-in-the-wall open 24 hours, advertising massage and sauna; more is probably available, though I couldn't say so from personal experience (really, honey!).

A couple miles north of Billie's is **Mina**, an early 20th-century railroad town at the southern terminus of a Southern Pacific spur line that no longer runs, but was

*The Tonopah Stock Exchange, circa 1905. (Central Nevada Historical Society, Tonopah).*

*A view of Boundary Peak and Montgomery Peak as seen from the west.*

once the closest any train car came to Tonopah. Mina might not be pretty, but it boasts well-kept homes on three streets running parallel to the highway and a handful of surviving, if not thriving, businesses. Surrounding the Mineral County municipal building and sheriff's substation and the Nevada Department of Transportation yard are the Mina Club (bar, slots, pool), two convenience stores and gas stations, the Silver King Cafe, and the shady Sunrise Valley RV Park.

Nine miles north of Mina is **Luning**, an old mining and train town, with a bunch of old railroad buildings on one side of the road, a junkyard and a few houses hugging the highway on the other, and a rest area in middle of town. Two streets run parallel to US 95, and there are no commercial services.

Just north of Luning, US 95 turns due west again and continues 24 miles to Hawthorne.

■ HAWTHORNE *map page 158, A/B–3/4*

On the north side of Hawthorne are the town cemetery and park. At the front of the cemetery is a row of bombs, while at the entrance to the park is an anti-aircraft gun. Hawthorne is a typical rural Nevada town, with one little difference: stored here, in thousands of bunkers, warehouses, and *entrepots,* is a sizable percentage of the United States Army's entire supply of conventional armaments. **The Hawthorne Army Ammunition Depot,** which covers nearly 150,000 acres in the vicinity, is the largest ammunition storage facility in the world.

Is Nevada a wild state or what?

At the north edge of town is the old army base (to enter, tell the guard you want to take a look at the golf course). Near the entrance are the fire station, power plant, and administration offices. Beyond those is the typically orderly housing of a military facility (though the army itself is 20 years gone and the base is run by a private contractor): narrow paved roads lined with tall old elm trees; single-story brick quarters with front decks and two-story houses with glassed-in second-floor porches; playgrounds, old theater building, and the nine-hole golf course—everything spic-and-span and looking more like New England than the Great Basin.

Heading out of the base, if you cross US 95 onto Thorne Road, you can

*Tree-lined Maine Avenue in the Hawthorne U.S. Army Ammunition Depot in autumn.*

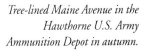

WESTERN NEVADA

US 95:

drive into the middle of one section of the sprawling ordnance-storage facility. You'll see strange sights, such as restricted gated areas, "Explosives Crossing" and "Safety First" signs, electronics-calibration shops, fire and emergency-services training area, air strip and control tower, water tower, property warehouses, and numbered depot buildings. Whenever you're ready, hang a U-ee and return toward the highway; you can take a left on Bonanza Road for the back route into town.

As for the rest of Hawthorne, it's fairly similar to Tonopah in a municipal sense, except that its history is about munitions instead of mining. The **Mineral County Museum** is here, packed with eclectic and interesting historical exhibits; so is the Mineral County Courthouse. **The El Capitan** (Hawthorne touts itself a gateway to Yosemite) is the full-service casino, going on 60 years old; it has blackjack, craps, slots, and video poker, free self-serve coffee in the casino, and a coffee shop.

Across from the El Capitan is **Joe's Tavern**, the old local-color licensed premises, which hasn't changed for decades. Check out the cute little mural on the outside wall, as well as the 25-foot-long shuffleboard table against the back wall inside. Ed's Bait and Tackle, the Walker Lake Guide Service, and the gun and tackle shop cater to the outdoor-recreation market; the golf course is called **Walker Lake Country Club.** A dozen motels, a steakhouse, a couple Chinese take-out counters, a taco shack, and an ice-cream/pizza place round out the amenities.

You'll see a vintage '60s sheriff's car parked permanently outside the Texaco station on the north side of town—a clever and gentle way of reminding people to slow down through town. Mount Grant of the Wassuk Range towers above, casting a late-afternoon shadow over it all.

■ WALKER LAKE *map page 158, A/B–3*

Once upon a time, about 15,000 years ago (give or take a few millennia), much of northwestern Nevada, roughly 8,400 square miles, was underwater. In fact, the entire route that US 95 follows, from Hawthorne all the way to Nevada's northern border with Oregon, was flooded by the last of the great Wisconsin Ice Age lakes, remembered today as Lahontan. Walker Lake just north of Hawthorne, Pyramid Lake a little north of Reno-Sparks, and Honey Lake just east of Susanville, California, are the last remnants of mighty Lake Lahontan.

Walker Lake has been shrinking for the past 15,000 years, and it's still shrinking. But it's been disappearing a lot faster during the last century, ever since the

*Sunset over Walker Lake at Tamarack Point.*

Walker River, which flows east in two main forks out of the central Sierra Nevada, was over-allocated to upstream local farmers and ranchers, and even faster yet since the river was dammed in three places, creating Bridgeport Lake in California, and Topaz Lake and Weber Reservoir in Nevada.

A coalition of activists has been working to "save" the lake, warning that it will "die" any year now if someone doesn't do something. But so far, Mother Nature has had her way—some years wet (with fresh water reviving the lake) and some years dry (when the lake level lowers)—and as of this writing, Walker Lake is still very much with us. It's stocked with a quarter-million trout a year. You can boat, fish, water-ski, swim, camp, and picnic, all on the west shore off the highway, and unless there's a derby or event, you'll probably have the whole schmear to yourself.

■ TOWN OF WALKER LAKE   *map page 158, A/B–3*

Ten miles north of Hawthorne is the lovely little settlement of Walker Lake, the only true fishing village in Nevada. Take a short detour off the highway to wander around the back streets and you'll see a beached houseboat or speedboat or two, rowboats, lots of jet skis, driftwood, fishing nets, lakeside homes from funky to fabulous, cabins, a motel, an RV park, and the **Cliff House** restaurant, famous for its rock lobster. Up on the road is the **Buffalo Stop** mini-mart, and above the road on the lower slope of the Wassuks are more homes with great views.

**Walker Lake State Recreation Area** is at the north end of town: 12 picnic tables under space-age shelters, outhouses, boat ramp, camping on the beach, free. A bit north of there is **Sportsman's Beach,** also right on the water: 17 picnic tables and shelters, outhouses, camping. A bit north of there is **Tamarack Point**, a BLM picnic area with tables and shelters. Finally, Twenty-Mile Beach has no facilities and no shade, but plenty of water and sand, good for tenting. Just past Twenty-Mile Beach is the north end of the lake, where the Walker River sloughs into it; there, you enter the Walker River Paiute Reservation.

**The Walker River Reservation** is the oldest, and the second largest, reservation in the state, established in 1859 and given official status in 1874. Schurz is the name of the village. Paiute have been fishing, farming, and ranching hereabouts for seven generations, though the farming and ranching are scant these days, and unemployment is through the roof. The Walker River, which is dammed at Weber Reservoir on the rez, supplies irrigation water to the few remaining alfalfa fields and cattle. The Walker River Paiute hold a three-day Pine Nut Festival in September, with a pow-wow, rodeo, queen contest, and parade. The elementary school in town is new, and the Four Seasons Market, right at the intersection of US 95 and Alternate 95, sells convenience-store sundries, some tribal crafts, and, of course, cheap cigarettes and fireworks.

At the junction of US 95 and Alternate 95, US 95 heads due north 40 miles to the reclamations and military town of Fallon. *(Fallon is covered in the US 50 chapter, pages 285–287.)* If you take this route to get Reno, it's another 60 miles to the city, 100 altogether.

From Fallon, US 95 runs for another 34 miles straight north to where it joins Interstate 80 at Exit 83. US 95 and I-80 share asphalt in a northeasterly direction for nearly 100 miles, all the way to Winnemucca. At Winnemucca, I-80 darts east, while US 95 veers off to the north and continues another 75 miles to the small border town of McDermitt, where it crosses into Idaho. *(The stretch of US 95 from Exit 83 to McDermitt is covered in the Interstate 80 chapter.)*

From the junction at Schurz, Alternate 95 cuts 25 miles west to Yerington. If you choose this route to Reno, it's another 80 miles from Yerington, 105 miles altogether.

■ YERINGTON  *map page 158, A–2*

The last time I drove around Yerington, a big gray coon cat, with the distinctive "M" marking in its forehead fur, was lying in the middle of one of the residential streets, and it wasn't even dead. Cars simply crept around the cat, which twitched its tail once or twice in response. I mean, a dog, sure, but a cat? That image says all there is to say about the pace of life in Yerington.

Yerington is one of the sweetest little settlements in Nevada, with as quaint a three-block downtown as exists in this state. Cars park diagonally on wide Main Street outside the old-time Rexall Drugs, Shear Shed barber shop, Olden Rule antique store, brick Oddfellows Hall and City Hall, Lyon County Courthouse and Museum; the town owns not a single parking meter (or traffic light).

The Crescent Garage opened in 1918 and is still going strong; the wooden Hillygus gas station was built in 1939 and is scheduled to shut down in 2002 (the federal deadline for a too-costly gasoline storage tank upgrade). Around the corner, the three-story brick Yerington Grammar School, built in 1912, has been refurbished into a performing arts center. And on the south side of town is the

town's pocket shopping, with a Scolari's supermarket, McDonald's, and Dairy Queen; Bootlegger deli and pizza place is across Bridge Street in Goldfield Plaza.

**Dini's Lucky Club** is downtown, a small slot house with bar, coffee shop, and Giuseppe's steakhouse; it's owned by Joe Dini, who's served in the Nevada Assembly for 17 or 18 terms (I've lost track). Then there's **Casino West,** the big-city casino that fills half of downtown with slots, craps, and blackjack, a coffee shop, 12-lane bowling center, big pizza parlor, convention center, and 79-room motel across the street. When you ask, of an afternoon, at the Casino West cage for a souvenir chip, you're told, apologetically, that you'll have to buy one at a blackjack table, which doesn't open till 4 P.M. However, after walking around town for 15 minutes and returning to your car outside the casino, the Casino West manager might come out onto the street to flag you down, saying someone just cashed in some chips, so they have one for you at the cage. Certainly, casinos love to sell chips for five bucks that cost only 35 cents apiece, but what casino manager anywhere else is going to come outside looking for you?

Yerington is that kind of town.

*(above) Cooling off in the Walker River in Yerington. (photo by Jean Dixon, Reno Gazette-Journal)*

*(opposite) The West Walker River flows through Wilson Canyon in Lyon County, 10 miles south of Yerington.*

The whole population area, both in town and surrounding agricultural Mason Valley, is as tidy and productive as Mennonite country in Pennsylvania. Even Weed Heights, the Anaconda Copper company town built in the 1950s on a bluff two miles west of Yerington, isn't unattractive. It now overlooks the huge open-pit copper mine (which closed in the '70s) and huge berms of green-tinged tailings.

### ■ ACROSS THE WALKER RIVER  *map page 158*

Bridge Street crosses the Walker River on the west side of town, lined by big cottonwoods (and teenage boys jumping from the bridge into the river on summer days). You turn right (north) and head into Mason Valley, with 100-year-old trees lining the two-lane thoroughfare, and all manner of ranch houses, lush green alfalfa fields, grazing horses, cattle, and sheep, rolling irrigation pipe, feed lots, silos, barns, and tractors keeping you company on your drive. The Pine Nuts are the big mountains hemming in the valley on the west; on their other side is Carson City.

The Yerington Indian Reservation is in the middle of it, with its requisite smoke shop; Wovoka, the Paiute prophet and religious leader who led the second messianic Ghost Dance movement, lived here. In 1889, Wovoka claimed that during a trance, God had told him that in two years, his people's ancestors would rise again and that the white men would disappear. To achieve this, he preached, the Indians must remain peaceful and participate in a "Ghost Dance" ritual. Growing increasingly fervent, the movement spread quickly, most notably to the more militant Lakota tribes, who used the prophecy as a rallying cry against whites. As fear among local settlers grew, so did hostility between Indian and white—leading ultimately to the massacre at Wounded Knee, in South Dakota.

About 25 miles north of Yerington is **Fort Churchill State Historical Monument,** an idyllic 700-acre park that preserves what's left of the first and largest army base built in Nevada (1860). There's a visitors center, walking trail through the ruins, picnic area, loop road, and a gorgeous campground near the banks of the Carson River in the heart of what was once Buckland's Ranch and Overland Stage station. The whole area is stunning in the fall, with bright orange leaves on a veritable forest of 100-year-old cottonwoods lining the Carson River.

Six miles north of the river is a turnoff for Lahontan State Recreation Area *(covered in the US 50 chapter, page 287);* two miles north there is the little crossroads settlement of **Silver Springs.** Here you cross US 50; there's a gas station, minimart, and Piper's, a locals bar and slot joint. From Silver Springs, it's 14 miles north to Fernley and Interstate 80.

■ FERNLEY  *map page 158, A–1*

On the east side of Fernley, along the interstate and the railroad main line, is Nevada Pacific Industrial Park, a 5,000-acre development that's barely four years old and already claims the western operations center for Quebecor, one of the world's largest printing companies; a big Trex manufacturing plant, which produces artificial wood out of plastic bags and sawdust; and a giant warehouse belonging to Amazon.com, which loses a ton of money on every book and product it sells over the Internet (but makes it up on market capitalization). **The Silverado Casino,** at the big Super 8 motel, has just doubled in size. The new Best Western Fernley Inn has an indoor pool and spa. The McDonald's drive-through window is backed up day and night.

On the south side of Fernley is Desert Lakes Golf Course, surrounded by a new 800-home subdivision.

And in town is the ultimate symbol of modern urbanization: the Get Fit Health Club.

Fernley's booming.

What for 50 years was a tiny agricultural settlement built around the first desert reclamations project in the country is now the greatest industrial boomtown in northern Nevada. Some things, however, are as they've always been. **The Wigwam** restaurant, for example, is a local landmark, run by the same Fernley couple for going on 40 years. The state's most extensive collection of arrowheads, baskets, and implements, all from nearby Indians, fills nearly every inch of wall space; Western art occupies the rest.

**The Truck Inn,** across the interstate on the north side of town, has also been around a long time. This quintessential truck stop covers 40 acres; its sign is a full-sized tractor-trailer sitting on a 60-foot-tall pole. Motel with jacuzzi, slots and video poker, two bars (with free popcorn), a big market, truck wash and scales, repair shops, Truckers Gallery, and a coffee shop are contained within. Annie B's (complete with phones at the counter) serves a five-egg breakfast special (no splitting, please).

A playground, baseball field, and tennis courts mark the end of Alternate 95, at the intersection with Alternate 50, an 18-mile stretch of road from west of Fallon. You can get on Interstate 80 at Exit 48 or 46; from Fernley, it's a quick 30-mile run west into Reno.

# US 395: RENO &
## SILVER COUNTRY

■ HIGHLIGHTS

■ TRAVEL BASICS

Smaller, slower, prettier, and friendlier than Las Vegas, Reno is one of the best-kept urban secrets in the West. It's nestled in a basin at the bottom of the north end of the Sierra Nevada, with 8,000- and 11,000-foot peaks in the background. Four distinct seasons also surround the town: In winter, 20 ski resorts within an hour's drive offer the most concentrated and varied downhill and cross-country opportunities anywhere; festivals and special events are held non-stop throughout the summer; spring and fall are beautiful, uncrowded, and inexpensive. The casinos don't completely dominate the area, but plenty of action, bargains, and entertainment satisfy the five million annual visitors.

Also within an hour's drive are Virginia City, one of the best preserved 19th-century mining boomtowns in the country; Carson City, the state capital; Genoa, the oldest town in the state; Tahoe, one of the world's great alpine lake resorts (covered in the US 50 chapter); and Pyramid, a stunning desert lake (covered in the I-80 chapter).

Most of all, the high quality of life in western Nevada is unmistakable, even to casual visitors. It's why I live here.

## Visitor Information

Greater Reno-Sparks Chamber of Commerce, 405 Marsh Ave., 89505, 775-686-3030; info@reno-sparkschamber.org; www.reno-sparkschamber.org. Reno/Sparks Convention and Visitor Authority, 4950 S. Virginia St., 89502, 775-827-RENO or 800-FOR RENO; www.playreno.com.

## Getting Around

The Reno area is served by Reno-Tahoe International Airport, conveniently located five minutes from downtown. It's also on Amtrak's northern transcontinental line; two passenger trains, one eastbound, the other westbound, roll through downtown daily. Bay Area and Sacramento-area visitors roar in on Interstate 80, over the Sierra Nevada's 7,200-foot Donner Pass, in a few hours; far-flung northeastern Californians drop in via US 395, which continues south through Washoe Valley, Carson City, and Carson Valley, then back into California at Topaz Lake—hugging the base of the eastern scarp of the Sierra the whole way.

Citifare is the local Reno bus service. K-T Bus Line sends coaches south on US 395 to Carson City (and all the way to Las Vegas on US 95). Gray Line conducts tours to area attractions.

## Food and Lodging

The Reno area isn't the culinary capital that Las Vegas has become, but it's making some strides in that direction. The latest expansions at several of the large hotels (especially the Peppermill) have added fancy fare and rooms at affordable prices. But Las Vegas has nothing on Reno in the bargain department; 99-cent bacon and egg breakfasts and good cheap buffets are readily available. Also look for early-bird specials in the casino gourmet and ethnic eateries.

Reno has upwards of 25,000 hotel and motel rooms, enough to handle the crowds most of the time. But beds can be hard to come by, and dear, over holiday weekends and during the festival-packed summer months. Also, the National Bowling Stadium hosts six-month-long tournaments, attracting steady hordes of bowlers who suck up as many rooms as they do lanes.

The rest of the area's lodging is in motels, plentiful in Carson City (except on Saturday nights), adequate in Minden and Gardnerville, and precious in Virginia City.

US 395: RENO &
SILVER COUNTRY

*Harold's Club was the nation's first famous casino. (Underwood Photo Archives, San Francisco)*

# ■ GREATER RENO

In a no-fanfare implosion during the witching hours of a cold December 1999 night, Controlled Demolition knocked down Harold's Club in downtown Reno. Harold's Club was the country's first famous casino, the one that popularized Nevada's legal gambling, making it palatable to the middle-class masses. Although razing the 65-year-old Club was a blow to local history buffs and some of the charm of downtown Reno, it wasn't that great a loss: Harold's Club had lived out its last years as a casino based on a memory of its heyday—a money-loser—and it spent a few humiliating post-casino years as a discount store. Its time was up.

Harrah's, which bought Harold's Club and the old Nevada Club next door, quickly got rid of them both, cleared out the rubble, and paved the property for a pedestrian plaza, while it finalized plans for a new attraction. At press time, rumor had it that Harrah's intended to build a mini-version of Las Vegas's Rio Suite Hotel-Casino, which it owns. A Reno Rio, over and above having a sweet ring to it, would do more to revitalize downtown Reno than would all the riverwalks, movie theaters, retail centers, thrill rides, artist lofts, even high-tech entertainment venues that have been proposed over the years to anchor, or catalyze, the "Renovation" of downtown.

And this is a downtown in dire need of a catalyst. Within a relatively short time span over the past few years, casino after downtown Reno casino closed for good. Joining, in shuttered limbo, the old Mapes (closed in 1982, standing vacant for 18 years, till it was mercifully imploded in early 2000) and Riverside (closed in 1986, standing vacant ever since) were Harold's Club, the Nevada Club, the Virginian, the Riverboat, and the Holiday. As a result, great gloomy gaps darkened the neon grin of Virginia Street.

This state of affairs was the culmination, it can be argued, of Reno's ambivalence, manifest over the past 50 years or so, toward its image as a devil's playground. Early in the 20th century, when Las Vegas was just a dusty whistlestop,

US 395: RENO & SILVER COUNTRY

**NEWS ITEM: "RENO HAS A MARRIAGE BOOM TOO!"**

"Dateline: August 6, 1943: You never get rich in the Army, but you can get hitched in Reno. Soldiers, sailors, and marines stand in line like this to get their marriage licenses. Reno has no physical examination or delay law."
*(Underwood Photo Archives, San Francisco)*

Reno was the country's most notorious town, a veritable Sin City full of gambling, prostitution, mobsters, and—most scandalous of all—liberal divorce laws. While Las Vegas was dreaming of lights, action, and buffets, Reno was already learning some hard lessons about fame and fortune. So when Las Vegas's star began to rise and shine in midcentury, Reno wished its upstart young sibling to the south all the best and was content, for most of the second half of the century, with its new status as a dusty whistlestop.

However, by the late 1990s, after eight years of the unstoppable boom—the tumescence, in effect—of southern Nevada and the spiraling bust in the fortunes—the emasculation, so to speak—of northwestern Nevada, Reno finally woke up one morning with an obvious case of Vegas envy. This triggered a mini-boom of casino expansions around the Truckee Meadows, the long valley between the massive granite batholith known as the Sierra Nevada on the west and the historic Virginia Range, home of the Comstock Lode and Virginia City, on the east.

And the implosions of the useless Harold's Club and Mapes, with the possibility of a Little Rio being built in the critical and ailing heart of downtown Reno, make official the positive developments occurring in the greater Reno-Sparks area.

## ■ THE SOUTH RENO DUO

On South Virginia Street, about two miles from downtown, stand the Peppermill and the Atlantis, practically across the street from each other, in a sort of Macintosh-IBM rivalry. Both started out as small motels in the early 1970s. Both have grown into formidable resort-casinos over the past 30 years. Both have exciting casinos with good-looking dealers and cocktail waitresses, positive video poker, similar slot clubs (no cashback), and a steady stream of promotions. Both are known for good food. And both have recently completed major expansions.

### ◆ THE PEPPERMILL

The Peppermill is glitzy for Reno; hell, it would be glitzy for Vegas. If neon made noise, the Peppermill would sound like Handel's *Messiah*—as sung by the Chipmunks. You really have to see it for yourself.

A few years ago, the Peppermill spent a cool $70 million on 465 new rooms, including several different varieties of suites, additional raucous casino space, the fine Steakhouse, and the White Orchid, a AAA Four-Diamond recipient and one of the fanciest gourmet rooms in town. The Peppermill also expanded and renovated the pool area, complete with a faux mountain and animatronic "wildlife."

*A view from the Virginia Range of the Reno skyline and Truckee Meadows at dusk. At center is the Peppermill.*

On Christmas Day 1999, the Peppermill completed another $55 million expansion project. The new neon noise sounds like Metallica—enhanced by jet engines. The new buffet is Nevada's fanciest and most expensive outside of Las Vegas; where the old buffet used to be is now the expanded keno lounge, sports book, poker room, and high-limit slots area. The new Italian restaurant, **Romanza,** is situated in a gorgeous circular room with 360-degree curtains closing off the visuals, though not the aurals, from the casino. And there's a new bar in the middle of it all with four of the largest video screens ever seen in Reno. Outside are a big new sign and a new little dancing-waters display.

The Peppermill has also announced another two phases of growth that, when completed, will render it the largest hotel-casino in Nevada outside of Las Vegas, with 2,200 rooms.

### ◆ ATLANTIS

Across and down South Virginia Street a bit, Atlantis spent $75 million on its last expansion. A colorful new 27-story tower added nearly 400 rooms, for a total of almost 1,000; now Atlantis's trademark glass elevators provide a mini-thrill ride to the top of both sides of the joint—on the north side of the old tower with the view of downtown and Peavine Peak, and on the south side of the new tower with the view of the south valley and Mount Rose. On the third floor is the health spa, centered on a big circular swimming pool and backed by a three-story faux-rock waterfall, all of which is contained under a stunning glass dome.

The expanded casino boasts all the new electronic slots and multi-play video poker machines, plus a decorative (and loud) wave pool by the quarter 10/7 double bonus machines. On the second floor is the 220-seat **MonteVigna** Italian restaurant, in a classy room with a grand piano at the entrance and big windows overlooking the mountains.

The most visible (and aromatic) manifestation of the Atlantis expansion is the **Skyway,** a greenhouse-style pedestrian bridge that connects the parking lot across Virginia Street to the casino. Two colossal towers, which look like giant chess pieces, support the overpass; gas-fed flames shoot out of the top of the rooks regularly after dark. Inside the solarium are an Italian seafood restaurant with an oyster bar (the garlic-oyster smell is stimulating to discerning tastes, nauseating to the rest), a video poker bar, a pastry counter, an espresso and cocktail lounge, and live plants cutting some of the glare off the slot and video poker machines.

■ SPARKS FLY IN SPARKS  *map page 192*

On the other side of the Meadows, in downtown Sparks, is John Ascuaga's Nugget, whose latest expansion, in 1997, kicked off the local mini-boom. The 45-year-old Nugget divides Sparks in half, both geographically and historically.

Though both Reno and Sparks originated as railroad towns, the former was founded more than 30 years earlier than the latter, when the Union Pacific was pushing its transcontinental train tracks east from California in 1868; railroad executives named Reno after General Jesse Reno, a Union general who'd been killed a few years earlier in the Civil War. Reno was never a railroad division point per se, merely western Nevada's main stop on the main line.

Sparks was founded in 1905 by the Union Pacific's successor, the Southern Pacific, to accommodate a switching yard and roundhouse. Unlike Reno, Sparks was a railroad company town for nearly 60 years, till the SP consolidated its maintenance facilities in California. Still, the railroad didn't completely close up shop; the Sparks yard switches upwards of 800 cars a day on the Oakland-Chicago line.

*A fountain and theater at Victorian Square in Sparks.*

Over the past quarter-century or so, Reno has expanded east, Sparks has expanded west, and the two have grown contiguous. But if the boundary between the sister cities is now indistinct, Sparks itself is basically two separate towns, divided along an I-80 Mason-Dixon line. North of the freeway is the residential area, now spreading northward beyond the Truckee Meadows into the valleys between the metropolitan area and Pyramid Lake Paiute Reservation. South of it is a sprawling railroad, warehouse, and light-industry district.

### ◆ JOHN ASCUAGA'S NUGGET

And John Ascuaga's Nugget actually straddles the division line: it's the only casino in the known universe that has a six-lane highway rumbling right over its roof.

The Nugget opened in 1955, at the same time that the railroad packed up and moved away, and it's now Sparks's largest employer by a long shot. The 1997 expansion included a new 980-room tower and a casino annex and dining complex, featuring **Orozko**, a stunning 300-seat Mediterranean restaurant, designed to resemble a village square in northern Spain's Basque country. A previous expansion included a big parking garage and skywalk, a sports book, and a deli.

Currently, the Nugget has 1,980 rooms, a big casino, a 750-seat showroom, a glass-walled indoor pool and spa on the recreation floor (fifth), and a 206-troy-ounce Golden Rooster on display in the hotel lobby. Ascuaga's is renowned throughout greater Reno for its restaurants: the Rotisserie Buffet, the Steakhouse (which has served nearly four million steaks since it opened in 1956, and which sells its steaks locally at the Nugget Meat Packers), the Oyster Bar (best in Nevada), Trader Dick's Polynesian restaurant (with a 6,000-gallon aquarium bubbling above the back bar), Orozko, two coffee shops, and the deli.

### ■ DOWNTOWN RENO *map page 182*

Between 1973 and 1979, Eldorado, Fitzgeralds, Circus Circus, the Comstock, the Sundowner, the Sahara (now Flamingo Hilton), and several smaller hotel-casinos opened. Nothing much happened for another 15 years, when Circus Circus and the Eldorado combined forces to open the Silver Legacy, in 1995. The Legacy is located in the center of Nevada's only "casino mall." Covering five city blocks, the complex contains three casinos (Eldorado, Silver Legacy, and Circus Circus) connected by two second-story pedestrian skywalks. Inside, thanks to the seamless design, it's hard to tell where one casino ends and another begins; outside, the three bridgeways give the streets a subterranean feel.

◆ DOWNTOWN CASINOS  *map page 182*

With 1,700 rooms, the **Silver Legacy** is the third largest hotel-casino in Reno-Sparks. Its main claim to fame is Reno's only Las Vegas–type spectacle: a 120-foot-tall mining-themed rig, a sort of combination train trestle, headframe, stamp mill, and Rube Goldberg machine. It's housed in one of the world's largest composite domes, and it mints dollar slot-machine tokens. The Legacy's more interesting, and relevant, display is a small portion of the 1,600-piece silver dining service, fabricated by Tiffany, for John Mackay, one of the Bonanza Kings of the Comstock and the namesake of several local institutions, including UNR's Mackay Stadium and the Mackay School of Mines (in front of which his statue stands). The Legacy has the requisite steakhouse, coffee shop, and buffet, along with a seafood restaurant and oyster bar, and a new comedy club, opened after a recent renovation.

Next door to the Silver Legacy on the north side is **Circus Circus,** a veritable clone (though cleaner and smaller) of its older sister in Las Vegas. With big-top acts performed continuously throughout the day and night, a midway of carnival games and stuffed animals, inexpensive rooms, and consistent crowds of low rollers, tourists, and kids, Circus Circus is the best place for cheap thrills, people watching, and free entertainment in Reno. An automated monorail shuttles patrons from the parking garage to the hotel towers and the casino—the only "ride" downtown.

A short while after the Silver Legacy opened, Circus Circus added the trendy **Art Gecko** Southwestern restaurant on the mezzanine skywalk and, in 1998, spent $80 million to spruce up the long-declining property, with a complete makeover of all its hotel rooms, the addition of a 3,000-space parking garage, a remodeled casino, and the replacement of the venerable Hickory Pit steakhouse with Amici's, a pasta and pizza eatery.

On the other side of the Silver Legacy is the **Eldorado,** owned and operated by the large Carano family, which has been in the area since the 1860s. The grandfather of Don Carano, the current patriarch of the family and Eldorado CEO, invested in a 50-foot parcel at the corner of Virginia Street and Fourth in 1929. The family added on to the property with land purchases over the years and opened the Eldorado in 1973 with 282 rooms. Today, the resort has 800 rooms, a sprawling casino, five restaurants, and an excellent food court. The Caranos also own Ferrari-Carano, an award-winning winery in Sonoma, California.

**Brew Brothers** at the Eldorado is one of Reno's busiest meet markets and the only microbrewery in a casino in Reno (also the only one downtown). The Eldorado recently turned its lounge into a 600-seat showroom and opened **Bistro Roxy,** a

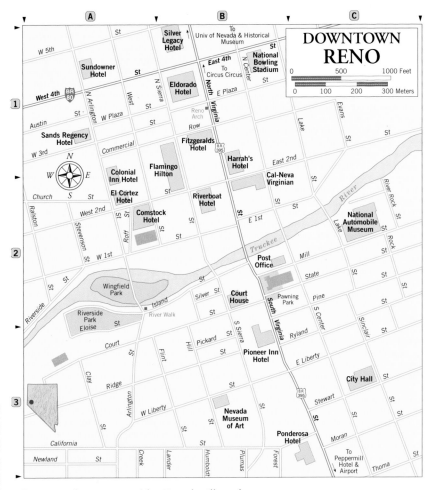

Continental restaurant with a French-village theme.

**The Cal-Neva Virginian** is the most clamorous, and the least glamorous, casino downtown, the quintessential old-time Reno sawdust joint. It opened in 1947 and has been owned by the same team since 1961. This joint is the place in Reno for low rolling, meal deals, and rammin'-jammin' action. The video poker is full pay, the crap and roulette minimums are less than a buck, and the race and sports books are the busiest in town. Cal-Neva is also home to Reno's longest-running 99-cent breakfast (serving more than a million of 'em a year), as well as other meal deals. For 37 years, Cal-Neva hadn't had a single hotel room; then, in the summer of 1999, it took over the Virginian, with its 300 rooms, and the Riverboat, with another 300. It also reopened the Virginian steakhouse, adding it to its own buffet, bargain gourmet room, bustling coffee shop, and rock-bottom snack bars.

And then there's **Harrah's**, the most extensive hotel-casino downtown, covering two-and-a-half city blocks (including the pedestrian plaza), as well as the oldest, now that Harold's Club is gone. It boasts a three-wing casino, more than 1,000 rooms (counting the attached Hampton Inn), the popular Steakhouse, a Fresh Market Square Buffet similar to the ones in Las Vegas and Laughlin, Sammy's Showroom, a coffee shop, a deli, and Planet Hollywood.

**Fitzgeralds** is a small version of its counterpart in downtown Las Vegas; the casino occupies two stories, with a buffet on the third floor.

Likewise, the **Flamingo Hilton** is a small version of its counterparts on the Las Vegas and Laughlin Strips. There's a small slot annex on Virginia Street, from which a skywalk connects with the second floor of the main casino on Sierra Street. The Flamingo might not be a Hilton hotel much longer (it's for sale for a bargain $20 million), but for now, it has a 600-seat showroom, a coffee shop –buffet, food court, Benihana, and Top of the Hilton, the highest (and one of the best) restaurants in Reno.

**The Comstock,** two blocks west of Virginia Street, has come up with one of the most creative uses of neon in the Neon State. On the exterior walls of the hotel

*"The Biggest Little City in the World": downtown Reno at night.*

tower is a display that comes as close as electric lights can to simulating fireworks. Inside are a mining theme, smoky casino, Mexican restaurant, coffee shop, and deli. Though Harold's Club and the Nevada Club are gone and the Virginian has reopened, downtown Reno is still a bit derelict at the core. High hopes are pinned on urban redevelopment, the plan for which has been partially implemented.

The first major phase was completed in 1995, when the **National Bowling Stadium** opened. This $35 million 80-lane bowling center is primarily dedicated to American Bowling Congress and Women's International Bowling Congress tournaments, which take place every year or two for months at a time. The Stadium offers public bowling on occasion, usually in conjunction with a major event downtown, though there's no set schedule and no advance notice. Kicks, a nightclub/diner owned by Paul Revere (of Paul Revere and the Raiders fame), a 100-seat geodesic Omnimax theater, and the Reno-Sparks Convention and Visitor Authority visitors center are also housed in the Stadium.

In November 1999, the second phase kicked in, when a 12-plex Regal Theater opened on Sierra Street, right on the south bank of the Truckee River. This was such a major event that on the day it opened, the daily *Reno Gazette-Journal* actually printed a map of the movie theater's interior on the front page, lest people get lost on the way from the popcorn counter to the screens.

## ■ THE BIG, THE SMALL, THE FUN

### ◆ THE RENO HILTON

The Reno Hilton is the largest hotel-casino in Nevada north of North Las Vegas, though its 2,001 rooms rank it as only the state's 20th largest hotel. Still, this behemoth, under almost continuous renovation since Hilton bought it from Bally's in 1992 for a bargain-of-the-century $83 million, lacks for no amenity that I can think of.

Start with the 100,000-square-foot casino, with 1,000-plus slot machines, nearly 100 table games, a 275-seat race and sports book, and a 150-seat keno lounge. Then add a 450-seat buffet, a "fresh-Mex" coffee shop, a steakhouse, an Italian restaurant, a noodle house, and a '50s diner, plus several fast-food outlets in the lower-level retail area. Throw in three bars, a 2,000-seat showroom, comedy club, outdoor summer concerts, movie theater, bowling alley, and giant video arcade. Now include the Garage, the Hilton's recently opened hip night spot with a 1950s service-station theme.

And that's not all. There's a wedding chapel, 450-space RV park, Olympic-sized swimming pool, eight tennis courts and a pro shop, his-and-her health clubs, even a golf driving range in a reflecting pool. Oh, and did I mention the Ultimate Rush? Reno's only major thrill ride is (where else?) at the Hilton.

## ◆ BALDINI'S

Baldini's is as diminutive as the Reno Hilton is substantial. Still, it packs a pretty solid punch as the Reno area's most popular locals joint. Tucked away in an obscure corner of west Sparks, Baldini's is a non-hotel full-service casino with plenty of table games and positive video poker, a 24-hour coffee shop/steakhouse, a poor-man's superbuffet complete with Mongolian grill (get 25 percent off in perpetuity just for signing up for the slot club), and the greatest bargain snack bar in town.

Baldini's is also the only "Pepsi Historic Landmark" in Nevada. For the past dozen years, Baldini's has awarded a six-pack of Pepsi each time a video poker player hits a natural 4-of-a-kind (no wild cards) with max coins played. The floor is literally littered with Pepsi (and Slice and Mug root beer and Mountain Dew) and floor people hustle around the joint with six-packs in hand or on hand trucks. What's more, Pepsi is actually a coin of the realm at Baldini's: you can trade in your six-pack at the redemption center for a "six-pack credit," worth a dollar in cash. Five credits get you a turkey between Thanksgiving and Christmas.

In fall 1999, Baldini's opened the $6 million Grand Pavilion a block from the casino. On the five-acre property are northern Nevada's largest convenience store, with four fast-food outlets served by a drive-up window, 32 fuel pumps, a self-service car wash, detail shop, and shuttle to and from the slots.

## ◆ BOOMTOWN

Finally, there's **Boomtown**, out on Interstate 80, 10 miles west of the city adjacent to the old logging town of Verdi. This could be Reno's top resort-casino when it comes to family fun. In the early '90s, a 40,000-square-foot amusement complex was built next to the casino, one of the best places in the area to take kids. There's a classic carousel, a mini Ferris wheel, Ghost Town miniature golf, the state's only motion simulator outside Las Vegas (hair-raisingly realistic), and enough arcade games to keep any 11-year-old happily occupied for a week.

Boomtown also has 300 rooms, a 203-space RV park, a good buffet (expanded in 1998), a popular steakhouse, and a 24-hour coffee shop. On the drawing board is a massive addition that will give Boomtown 2,100 rooms, a 150,000-square-foot casino, an outdoor amusement park and amphitheater, and a wildlife habitat a la the Las Vegas Mirage, all scheduled for completion sometime in 2002.

## ■ MUSEUMS AND PARKS *map page 182*

So much for casinos. Museums in Reno are a bit more, um, conventional and proper than the crop in Las Vegas. Rather than exhibits devoted to soda, chocolate, wax figures, world records, pharaohs, money, and magic, Reno's offerings include history, slot machines, art, and minerals—and, of course, the requisite classic-car collection.

### ◆ HISTORICAL MUSEUMS

In 1999, the state spent a million dollars to upgrade and refurbish the **Nevada Historical Society Museum and Research Archives,** next to the Planetarium near the top of the hill on the University of Nevada-Reno campus. The exhibits trace the history of Nevada from the ice ages through last Thursday.

Reno is especially fortunate to have Frank and Marshall Fey as residents and restaurateurs. The owner-operators of the **Liberty Belle Saloon** are two grandchildren of Charlie Fey, an engineer and inventor who came up with the first workable and mass-produceable slot machine in the early 1900s. The Fey brothers have a number of the earliest slot models, including their grandfather's first machine.

Marshall Fey is also the author of the definitive book on mechanical slots.

### ◆ NATURAL HISTORY MUSEUMS

**The W. M. Keck Minerals Museum** is on the UNR campus in the Mackay School of Mines building next door to the library; on display are hundreds of specimens of the precious metals and minerals wrested from the Nevada earth over the past 140 years, along with historical photographs, antique tools and machines, and geology exhibits.

*Charles August Fey (1862–1944) was a pioneer in the invention and manufacture of slot machines.*

**The Wilbur D. May Museum and Arboretum** houses the collection of Wilbur May, a wealthy traveler, hunter, collector, and philanthropist who owned the 2,000-acre Double Diamond Ranch in south Reno (now a Las Vegas–like subdivision); the arboretum next to the museum hosts a number of different gardens, including xeriscape (low water).

**The Nevada Museum of Art** at 160 West Liberty is Nevada's only state-operated fine art museum. Its permanent collection contains some interesting categories of art, among them works by Sierra Nevada and Great Basin artists; photographers and environmental artists focusing on altered landscapes; and artists whose work portrays the American work ethic.

*Installed at the main entrance to the Nevada Museum of Art is Celeste Roberge's sculpture* Cairn. *The piece is composed of a welded steel frame filled with rocks from the Truckee River. (courtesy of the Nevada Museum of Art)*

◆ NATIONAL AUTOMOBILE MUSEUM

The external design of the National Automobile Museum reflects the sleek curves, flawless finish, and tinted glass of, say, a 1913 Pierce Arrow, a 1921 Rolls, or a 1938 Corsair. Inside you can see those self-same vehicles, along with nearly 200 other fantastic makes and models. The cars are the stars of Bill Harrah's collection, and are arranged in four galleries according to the date they were manufactured.

The pièce de résistance of the museum is the 1907 Thomas Flyer, which has a gallery all its own. This is the car that won a grueling around-the-world race in 1908, starting in February in Paris, and rolling through Berlin, St. Petersburg, Irkutsk, Vladivostok, Yokohama, San Francisco (with a side trip to Valdez, Alaska), Chicago, Buffalo, and crossing the finish line in New York City in early August. The whole story is told in signs on the wall of the gallery; also on display are the Paris–New York Cup, at 1,600 pounds the largest sporting trophy ever produced, and the poster from the 1965 movie *The Great Race*.

Cars of interest in Gallery One include an 1899 Locomobile; a 1913 Pierce Arrow at 15 feet long and with a price tag of $6,000, the largest and most expensive car for sale in its day; and the 1912 Rambler used in the 1997 movie *Titanic*.

Gallery Two starts off with a Chevy Corvair exhibit and continues with a 1914 Fiat; a 1921 Ford camper, the original RV; and a 1921 Rolls, assembled using sheets of solid copper, nickel, German silver, and ebony trim. Galleries Three and Four contain a number of Caddies; a 1934 Dymaxion designed by Buckminster Fuller; plus John Wayne's '53 Chevy, Elvis's 1973 Eldorado, Sinatra's 1961 Ghia, a 1960 Flying Caduceus, and on and on.

### ◆ GREENBELTS AND PARKS

Also unlike Las Vegas, which is somewhat public-park challenged, Reno has a full complement of urban outdoor-recreation areas, both large and undeveloped and small and cultivated. Within walking distance of casino row downtown are the **Riverfront Plaza, Riverwalk,** and **Riverside Park,** a three-block greenbelt along the Truckee River west of the Virginia Street bridge, at the old Riverside Hotel. This stretch of riverbank is a fine place to stretch your legs and lungs anytime of year, but especially during the summer, when an almost continuous series of events, programs, and concerts is held here. An amphitheater in Wingfield Park, on an island connected to Riverside Park by footbridges, hosts many of the events; during the winter, a seasonal ice-skating rink is set up in the park.

About a mile farther along the Truckee is **Idlewild Park,** christened in 1927 for an exposition celebrating the completion of the transcontinental Highway 40, or Victory Highway, which passed through Reno (the first Reno Arch was also erected on Virginia Street to memorialize that event). Almost anything you can think of to do in the great out-of-doors is available here: a playground, picnic pavilions, skateboard ramps, baseball fields, volleyball courts, duck pond, rose garden, municipal swimming pool, even a kiddie amusement park with a merry-go-round, Tilt-A-Whirl, mini-roller coaster, giant slide, and narrow-gauge choo-choo that circles the pond. Half of Reno hangs out here of a summer Saturday or Sunday afternoon.

Then there's **Rancho San Rafael Park**, a sprawling plot of public land just north of downtown (around the intersection of North Virginia Street and McCarran Boulevard). The section south of McCarran has a few facilities, such as playing fields, a fitness circuit, and picnic areas, while the north section has a one-mile hiking trail, a Basque monument, and access to Peavine Mountain, the 8,260-foot peak that presides over, and provides a lumpy backdrop to, downtown.

Finally, in eastern Sparks right off the interstate is **Wild Waters**, the local water park. There's a "Lazy River" ride, big wave pool, two monster thrill-ride slides and two gentler water slides, kiddie pools and slides, snack bars, and arcade, open late May through mid-September. In the same complex are a 36-hole miniature golf course, big arcade, and racing-car track, open year-round.

## ■ FESTIVALS IN THE CITY

Reno is especially magnetic June through September. While Las Vegas bakes under oppressive 100-plus-degree heat, Reno basks in balmy daytime temperatures and cool blanket-warmed nights. It's perfect weather for the non-stop outdoor activities that attract travelers from all over the country: a big rodeo, hundreds of hot-air balloons, thousands of classic cars, 30 tons of barbecued ribs, and vintage-plane races—and those are only the major affairs. They're interspersed with an almost continuous string of community events.

The excitement gets rolling, appropriately enough, on the first day of summer with the venerable **Reno Rodeo**, one of the oldest, wildest, and richest rodeos in the West. This rodeo first came to Reno in 1919, when the prize purse was $5,000. The 80th annual show in 1999 attracted more than 75,000 fans, watching hundreds of world-class cowboys compete for more than $350,000 in prizes, the country's second largest purse after the National Finals Rodeo in Las Vegas. Buckaroo breakfasts, barrel races, horse sales, bronc riders, steer wrestlers, calf ropers, even a 300-head cattle drive right down Virginia Street fill the nine days of festivities. There's also a parade, a carnival, and country music concerts. It all takes place at the Reno Livestock Events Center.

In August, Reno gears up for **Hot August Nights**, when more than 4,000 vin-

US 395: RENO &
SILVER COUNTRY

*The Reno Rodeo has gained international acclaim.*
*(photo by Jean Dixon,* Reno Gazzette-Journal)

tage automobiles and 100,000 vintage-automobile enthusiasts cruise in for a four-day blow-out of auto mania and the lifestyle of the 1950s and '60s. The whole hullabaloo kicks off with a formal prom, where poodle skirts, bouffants, and tuxedos are de rigeur. Then it's a perpetual party: parades, concerts, sock hops, a massive automobile swap meet, the largest classic-car auction around, and "show 'n' shine" car displays held in parking lots all over town. Hula hoops, winged sunglasses, doo-wop, days of wine and Elvis—you can do anything at Hot August Nights, but lay off my blue suede shoes.

Renoites like to hold onto summer till the last possible day, which is why September is the biggest big-event month of all. **Sparks's Victorian Square** is the setting for a literal pig-out over Labor Day weekend when the **Rib Cookoff** comes to town. Veteran barbecue pork and beef rib cookers from 20 states grill 60,000 pounds of meat-on-the-bone as they compete for the title "Best in the West." At the same time, they cater to hordes of carnivores, who often wait in line for 20 minutes to get their fill of ribs, beans, corn on the cob, sourdough rolls, and beer or lemonade. There's also an arts fair with clowns, face painters, and bargain crafts, and a big concert on Sunday night.

The weekend following the Rib Cookoff, the nation's top hot-air balloonists vie for cash and prizes in the three-day **Great Reno Balloon Race.** The main event is the Dawn Patrol, which offers a stunning light show as 150 polychrome balloons—many in such bizarre shapes as grizzly bears, beer cans, and cartoon characters—are all fired up and take to the sky at the same time. The colorful spectacle is free to the public and can be seen from all over the valley.

Finally, the autumn-equinox sky heats up with the **National Championship Air Races,** the world's largest and longest-running air-race event; the 2000 event was the 37th annual. The Air Races are the fastest motor sport on Earth, and the only event of its kind to feature all four race classes. The biplane class consists of mostly restored antiques from the Lindbergh era. Formula Ones are small home-built planes that reach speeds of up to 250 m.p.h. on a three-mile race course. The AT-6s are World War II warplanes that can fly up to 225 m.p.h. on a five-mile course. All have their following, but most people come out to see the big Unlimiteds—restored World War II–era P-51 Mustangs, F4U Corsairs, and Hawker Sea Furies that fly a nine-mile course as fast as 500 m.p.h. and as low as 50 feet off the ground. In addition to the race events, the 100,000 spectators are treated to skywriters, skydivers, spectacular fly-bys, and astounding aerobatics performed by steely-nerved flight jockeys. The races are held at Reno-Stead Airport, 12 miles north of downtown.

These are just the main events in Reno's summer party season; minor celebrations fill in the gaps all summer long. **Celebrate the River** in early June is a weekend-long festival along the Truckee that spills into downtown. **The Nevada State Fair** is held in mid-June, with livestock and agricultural exhibits, rides, midway games, and carnival confections. **Street Vibrations** in mid-September is a motorcycle event that draws thousands of Harley-Davidsons and custom tour bikes with music, crafts, a parade, and a 300-decibel "burn-off." And the fun continues through October, with a **Chili Cookoff** where 200 chili cooks vie for a $35,000 purse; a **Great Italian Festival,** featuring grape stomps, pasta-eating contests, and food booths; and the **Grand Prix,** Reno's biggest racing event of the year, which takes place in the Reno Hilton parking lot (!).

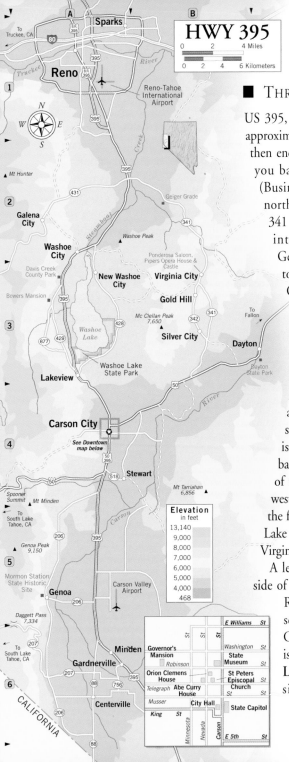

## ■ THROUGH WASHOE VALLEY

US 395, as a six-lane freeway, runs for approximately 10 miles south of the city, then ends. The second-to-last exit puts you back on South Virginia Street (Business 395) heading south, just north of the intersection with NV 341 (left), which takes you eastward into the Virginia Range, over Geiger Grade, and into the historic mining village of Virginia City. The freeway's last exit feeds right into NV 431, the road to Incline Village and the north shore of Lake Tahoe.

South of the intersection of Business 395 and NV 341, US 395, as a four-lane surface artery, picks up and continues south into **Washoe Valley.** This is a classically gorgeous Nevada basin, with the sheer eastern scarp of the Sierra Nevada rising to the west, ranches and mansions dotting the foothills, the 3,000-acre Washoe Lake filling the flats, and the rolling Virginia Range to the east.

A left turn heads around the east side of the lake on NV 428 (Eastlake Road), which passes by a little settlement called New Washoe City. A few miles down the road is a turnoff (right) into **Washoe Lake State Park,** with 49 campsites right on the lake, little shade, and a lot of wind. Washoe Lake itself is actually a playa, meaning it contains more or less water depending on the recent precipitation situation; it completely dried up in the 1930s and again in 1995, after an eight-year drought. There are also picnic facilities and a boat ramp. A few miles farther south, Eastlake Road rejoins US 395, at the south end of Washoe Valley.

Back up at the north end, a right-hand turn on NV 429 (Davis Creek Road) takes you down to **Davis Creek County Park**, with a large 63-site campground (closest camping to Reno), a day-use area, and duck pond (which freezes for ice skating in the winter); a number of trails, from a half-mile nature stroll to an eight-mile trek into the Sierra, criss-cross the park.

Immediately south is **Bowers Mansion,** a 16-room house built in 1864 by Sandy Bowers, a nouveau-riche Comstock miner, the only one of the earliest Comstockers ever to make serious money from the ensuing silver boom. Take the 20-minute tour to hear the gory details of Bowers's marriage to Eilley Orrum, an unstable pioneer woman, their trip to Europe to furnish the house, his death in 1867, the death of Eilley's adopted daughter, and her slow descent into destitution and mild madness. The house went through numerous changes and owners

*The historic Bowers Mansion in Washoe Valley, south of Reno.*

between 1874 and 1968, but today it's restored and filled with antiques, some of them actually original to the house. Next door to Bowers Mansion is another county park, with extensive grassy areas, a big kids' playground, and a public swimming pool.

Continue south on NV 429, then take another right on **Franktown Road** for a stunning drive past modern mansions and ritzy ranches in the Sierra foothills. Franktown Road rejoins NV 429, which rejoins US 395. From there it's another five miles into Carson City.

But first, we need to backtrack a bit to the intersection of Business 395 and NV 341 just south of Reno, the road to Virginia City. You travel through an extensive residential area known as the Virginia Foothills, then start climbing up into the Virginia Range. The road twists and turns for seven miles to Geiger Overlook, with a lofty view of the Truckee Meadows and Mount Rose across the valley. Shortly you arrive at Geiger Summit (6,800 feet), and from there it's seven more miles to Virginia City.

■ VIRGINIA CITY   *map page 192, B-3*

Portraits of several celebrities of the Comstock decorate a side wall of the Ponderosa Saloon in the heart of Virginia City, one of the old-time barrooms on C Street, the six-block boardwalked main drag that's usually crowded with history buffs, day-trippers, and locals. One is of Henry Comstock himself, a loud-talking, paper-waving horsetrader who, when gold was discovered high up on a desert hillside in October 1859, proclaimed the entire side of the mountain his "ranch." Comstock not only demanded a cut of the action, but also proceeded to name the day-old mining district after himself. Comstock sold his percentage some months later for a few thousand dollars. Had he held onto his share for another year or two, his fortune would have been as large as his fame was wide.

Next to the namesake of the Lode is a portrait of the namer of the city. James Finney was a drunken prospector whose three loves were gold, whiskey, and his home state of Virginia. One night Finney dropped and smashed a bottle of hooch on a rock, accidentally christening the early settlement; soon, all the miners were calling the tent camp Virginia Town. As soon as news of the strike, which turned out to consist of the purest sulphuret of silver to be discovered since the fabled Ophir Mines of King Solomon, reached California a few weeks later, a few thousand boomtowners rushed to Virginia Town, transforming it into Virginia *City* almost overnight.

### ◆ MARK TWAIN IN VIRGINIA CITY

A more familiar face than Comstock's or Finney's also adorns the Ponderosa Saloon wall. Samuel Clemens arrived in Virginia City in 1862 to take a job as city editor at one of the city's several newspapers, the *Territorial Enterprise.* Though he later told a different story or two about the origin of his famed pseudonym, hereabouts it's believed that he was nicknamed by barstool buddies for his habit of ordering two drinks at a time and telling the bartender to "mark twain" on his tab.

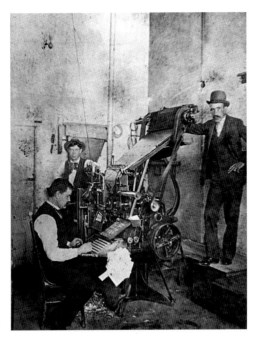

*The composing room at the* Territorial Enterprise *made famous by Mark Twain's tenure at the paper. (Nevada Historical Society)*

Today, Clemens's newspaper pressroom, with its antiquated printing equipment, is on display in **Mark Twain's Museum,** one of several among the bars and souvenir stores of C Street. There's also a **Mark Twain Saloon** and a **Mark Twain Books.** The latter is one of the highlights of Virginia City, with its large display of titles about ghost towns, gunfighters, prostitutes, the military in the west, railroads, Native Americans, gambling, mining, local travel—and, of course, Mark Twain. There's a wall of rare books and first editions, along with a Mark Twain mannequin sitting in a chair and a couple of antique orchestrions that actually play tunes for a quarter.

By the time Clemens left in 1864 (legend has it he snuck out of town one night to avoid a duel with someone he'd insulted in print), Virginia City was already one of the most illustrious cities in the country—glamorous, prosperous, magnetic. Perched precariously on a steep slope, the town was laid out along literal lines of wealth, status, and race.

*Pictures of Virginia City business offices frame this 1861 panorama of the two-year-old town. (Library of Congress)*

◆ THE STREETS OF VIRGINIA CITY

Stewart, Howard, and A Streets, highest up on the hill, flaunted the brick mansions of bankers and mine owners; several of them remain.

Below on B Street were the homes and offices of the mine superintendents, lawyers, engineers, stockbrokers, and the like. Today, **the Castle** on B Street epitomizes the luxurious milieu of the nabobs. This 16-room mansion survived the Great Fire of 1875 that burned 30 blocks; it was sold only three times in its 135 years—with all its original furnishings intact. A tour of the Castle will leave you panting after the priceless antique furniture and accouterments.

Also on B Street is **Piper's Opera House,** where the celebrated stars of the day entertained the Comstockers, some of whom paid $20 for proscenium box seats in a town where a fancy dinner for two cost 60 cents. The canvas walls, suspended balconies, dance floor (laid out on railroad springs), advertisements on the curtain, even the round-backed chairs are all original.

C Street separated the high life from the low. Down on D and E Streets were the miners' shacks and prostitutes' cribs. A portrait of the most famous of the "darlings of the desert," Julia Bulette, hangs with the other celebrities on the Ponderosa wall. There's also a **Julia Bulette Saloon,** one of the cleanest in town, which features the **Red Light Museum** in the basement; displays down here remind us that the current age has no monopoly on sex (check out the antique condoms and vibrators), drugs, and medical quackery—a must-see to get to the bottom, so to speak, of life in Virginia City during the boom.

The Chinese lived way down on I Street and the Paiute squatted below that, where no streets even existed. Later, two monumental churches were built on the lower, needier, side of town. **St. Mary's in the Mountains Catholic Church** was erected in 1875 with 100-foot-high vaulted ceilings and towering steeples; it remains one of the mining west's most beautiful religious buildings. The more modest **St. Paul's Episcopal Church,** built in 1876, is catty-corner to St. Mary's.

Along with its portraits symbolizing the early days of the Lode, the Ponderosa Saloon also represents the period of Virginia City's history between 1865 and 1872 when the Comstock came to be monopolized by San Francisco bankers. The

*Virginia City and mine tailings at sunrise. St. Mary's and St. Paul's rise in the background.*

bar itself is housed in the old Bank of California building, complete with the original vault—a half-inch steel-plate cage surrounded by two-foot-thick walls where William Sharon safeguarded his stash.

Sharon, the ruthless manager of the Bank of California's Virginia City branch, masterfully manipulated the Comstock's boom-bust economy until he controlled the local milling, lumber, freighting, banking, and insurance industries. He also had great influence in the stock market and owned all but one or two mining companies.

In 1869, with his grip firmly around the throat of the Comstock, Sharon undertook one of its great construction projects: a short line railroad to haul ore down to the stamp mills in the canyon south of the Lode, along the Carson River. **The Virginia & Truckee Railroad** shuttled so much paydirt down the tortuous track, dropping 1,600 feet in 13 miles, and so much bullion to the transcontinental main line in Reno, bound for San Francisco and points east, that in its time the V&T was among the richest short-line railroads in the west. Today, you can ride in restored passenger cars, pulled by a restored steam locomotive, a few miles down to Gold Hill, Virginia's sister town, along one of the steepest sections of the route and through Tunnel Number Four. Don't sit in the open car unless you're prepared to get steamed in the tunnel.

To make the most of the railroad, Sharon accelerated the mining. The history-packed **Ponderosa Saloon** is also the departure point for the **Underground Mine**

*Prior to the introduction of carbide lamps in 1920, miners used candles to light the tunnels where they worked. (photo courtesy Stanley W. Paher, Reno)*

*The Wells Fargo office and coach line in Virginia City, 1870. (Nevada Historical Society)*

**Tour,** the most authentic experience in Virginia City. A small section of tunnel snakes from the rear of the bar 315 feet into the bowels of the **Best and Belcher Mine.** In the deep dark guts of this nether world, you can see examples of the square-set timbering that held up the mountain as the miners hollowed it out (almost all the wood was provided by the virgin forests of Lake Tahoe). The heavy drills, rods, winches, and buckets used to muck the ore, and the myriad dangers that rendered death underground commonplace—cave-ins, fire, scalding steam and water, poison gas, lack of oxygen, explosions, falls—were all part of a world gone mad for silver.

Only one man stood between William Sharon and his complete control of the Comstock. John Mackay (pronounced "MACK-ee") started as a lowly miner in 1860 and worked his way up to become a mine superintendent by 1870. He and three partners owned the Kentuck, one of the last of the independent mines, where they located a low-grade vein, following the thread of silver into the Consolidated Virginia Mine next to it. Beating Sharon at his own game, Mackay managed to gain control of the Con. Virginia, and in 1872, at the 1,200-foot level, he hit the granddaddy of all Nevada ore bodies. This strike, known as the Big Bonanza, accounted for roughly $200 million of the $700 million in gold and silver (in 1870 dollars) extracted from the Comstock Lode, and finally crowned Virginia City the Silver Capital of the World.

The best symbol of this last and greatest Comstock boom is found today in the **Silver Queen Saloon**, home of a 16-foot-tall portrait of the fictional Queen herself, decked out in a low-cut dress made of 3,000 silver dollars, a belt of 28 gold pieces, a bracelet of dimes, and a 50-cent-piece ring.

*Bands often perform at the Bucket of Blood Saloon.*

You can also see portraits of John Mackay and his three partners, the Bonanza Kings, in the **Delta Saloon**, biggest and fanciest in town; the rest of the Delta is packed with historical photos and memorabilia, including the heavily hyped Suicide Table. And you can tour the **Mackay Mansion** on D Street, where John lived with his wife and ran his mining empire.

The Great Fire of 1875 destroyed nearly half the city, including the 10-block downtown. Some of the equipment used to fight that fire, and many others, is on display at the **Firehouse Museum** on C Street.

Big Bonanza wealth quickly rebuilt Virginia City; a year later, at the peak of the boom, the place claimed 23,000 residents, more than half of all the residents of Nevada. But by 1878, the Comstock mines were played out, Virginia City's heyday dead. The town survived, though barely, for the next 70 years, until tourists began to rediscover the well-preserved semi-ghost town after World War II.

Today, along with the Ponderosa, Mark Twain, and Silver Queen Saloons are the **Bucket of Blood,** which hosts live bands frequently through the year; the big **Bonanza Saloon;** and the **Red Dog,** which eschews local history for a rock 'n' roll theme, but still exudes local color.

**The Gambling Museum** has a large display that covers 150 years of gambling history in Nevada. Every town of this type has its own version of the **Wild West Museum;** its macabre and imaginative displays are almost a spoof on the genre. **The Fourth Ward School** was built in 1876 and educated students till 1936; many of the original furnishings are on display, along with the local branch of the Nevada State Museum. And **The Way It Was Museum** has a large and well-organized collection of Comstock and mining artifacts and memorabilia, as well as scale models of the mines and the mills.

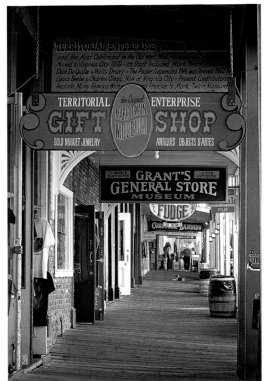

Otherwise, Virginia City is completely overrun with touristy shops—Comstock Rock Shop, Higgin's Diggins, Priscilla Pennyworth's Photograph Emporium, Red's Fudge Shop, Red Garter Gifts, Rotten Rowdy's Old-Time Photos, and Turquoise Kiva—to name a few.

A handful of coffee shops, public schools, the **Storey County Courthouse,** and the homes of roughly 800 residents round out the town.

*Tourist shops line the sidewalk outside the old* Territorial Enterprise.

US 395: RENO & SILVER COUNTRY

## ■ GOLD HILL AND SILVER CITY  *map page 192, B-3*

Continuing south on NV 341, you pass motels, a turnoff for the truck route down the mountain, and an open pit left over from some recent mining. You then come to Greiner's Bend. This double hairpin curve is the steepest and sharpest turn in Nevada's road system. Note the denuded hillside, also left over from some recent mining.

At the bottom of the grade is Gold Hill, a tiny settlement that predates Virginia City by about a year. The **Gold Hill Hotel** constitutes the entire action in town, but it's definitely worth a stop to poke in and stroll around the building, part of which dates back to 1859, making it one of the oldest standing structures in the state. The original wing consists of the Great Room, now a cozy lounge, complete with a fireplace and antique furnishings. (The bar itself was added in 1960, but made to look 100 years older.) There's also a restaurant on the main floor. Upstairs are the original four rooms and another seven in a newer wing; across the street are two self-contained guesthouses and a honeymoon cottage.

From Gold Hill, it's another couple of miles down the hill till you pass through **Devil's Gate,** an unmistakable cut in a jagged rock outcrop that separates Storey County from Lyon County. **Silver City** is just beyond the Gate. It's a larger settlement than Gold Hill, with a post office, some middle-class and some derelict homes, and a lot of for-sale signs.

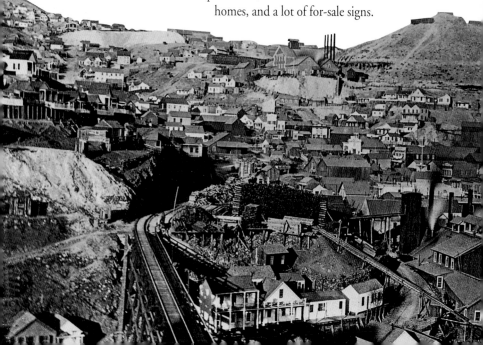

From Silver City, it's three miles down to the valley at the intersection with US 50. Go right and continue eight miles into Carson City.

■ CARSON CITY   *map page 192, A-4 (see inset)*

At the main intersection in downtown Carson City, US 50 west joins US 395 south and everyone—local traffic, through traffic, and visitor traffic—creeps along in a perpetual jam-up. For more than 20 years, Carsonites have been begging for a freeway bypass, to relieve the confounded congestion created by this confluence of conveyances. As I write, the road-building is about to begin: the Nevada Department of Transportation recently put out a request for bids on the first phase of the first part of the first bypass; the entire project is slated to cost $228 million and be completed sometime in 2007 or 2008. Of course, it's all on government contracts, so it's anybody's guess when the work will actually start (or end).

Speaking of government, did I mention that we're sitting in traffic, creeping past the Nevada Capitol, Legislature, Office of the Attorney General, old courthouse, and City Hall? Yes, Carson City is the Nevada state capital, one of the smallest in the nation (and one of the few that doesn't have scheduled air service), and has been since October 31, 1864, the day Nevada entered the Union as the 37th state. It was also the seat of territorial government for three years prior to statehood; in fact, it was the "capital" from the day it was founded, in 1858, by Abraham Curry.

Curry was one of Nevada's greatest visionaries. He foresaw a state capital where there wasn't a state yet. There wasn't even a territory. There was barely a settlement within 200 miles. But Curry did a Bugsy: standing in the middle of an ocean of sagebrush, in the shadow of the eastern Sierra, he envisioned his town site, with wide downtown streets, a government plaza, and small lots for homes. Five years later, the Comstock Lode had given rise to the state of Nevada, with "Curry's Folly" as the capital. Curry started up a business quarrying the local sandstone, with which he built the Carson City Mint (now the Nevada State Museum), the Ormsby Hotel, the original Legislature, and the first Supreme Court (all still standing).

Carson City will probably endure as the state capital for a long time, though its 52,000 residents are vastly overshadowed by Las Vegas's 1.3 million, many of whom, especially those who commute to the capital, yearn for the day when Las Vegas is not only the de facto capital of Nevada, but the official one as well.

*The Virginia & Truckee Railroad line carried supplies and bullion in and out of Gold Hill, circa 1870–90. (Nevada Historical Society)*

Thanks to its steady 140-year history, Carson City boasts more historic homes and stately old shade trees per square block than any other locale in the region. For a good walking tour, begin at the corner of Carson and Musser Streets, in front of the **Nevada Capitol,** built in 1871 of sandstone quarried nearby. On the second floor of the Capitol, in the old Senate chambers, is an elite collection of Nevada memorabilia, a must-see for anyone at all interested in local history. Walk two blocks north to Telegraph Street and the **Commission on Tourism** building, which dates back to 1891, the first federal office building in Nevada.

Now head two blocks west (toward the mountains) to the corner of Telegraph and Nevada and the **Abe Curry House,** built of Curry sandstone in 1871 by Uncle Abe himself. Another block west on Telegraph and Division is **St. Peter's Episcopal Church,** dating all the way back to 1868, when it was completed for $5,500; this church is an exceptionally fine example of the Gothic Revival style popular in the latter half of the 19th century.

A block and a half north at 502 North Division Street is the **Orion Clemens Home,** built in 1864 for Orion Clemens, first and only Secretary of Nevada Territory. Orion's brother Sam followed him to Nevada; the whole hilarious story of his many adventures, and many misadventures, is told in *Roughing It.* Up the block at

*The Nevada State Capitol in Carson City.*

*Gold bars stacked outside the Wells Fargo office in Virginia City, soon to be struck into coins at the Carson City Mint. (Nevada Historical Society)*

512 North Division is the **Henry Yerington House,** built in 1869 for the general manager of the Virginia & Truckee Railroad. The arched windows of the solarium were designed in the style of a railroad observation car.

Take a left on Robinson Street; at 503 West Robinson is the **William Stewart House,** built in 1887 for Nevada's first U.S. Senator. Three blocks west is the **Governor's Mansion,** built in 1909 in the Southern Colonial style; refurbished in the 1960s; Governor Kenny Guinn and his family live here today. A block south at 500 North Mountain Street is the **Krebs-Peterson House,** built in 1914. This home's claim to fame is that it served as the location of *The Shootist,* John Wayne's last, and some say best, movie.

Now stroll several blocks to King Street and take a left. At 449 West King is the **Carson Brewery Co.** (1864), which brewed Tahoe Beer for nearly 100 years and is now owned by Nevada Arts Alliance. Take a right on Minnesota and a left on Third Street for the **George Ferris House** (1869), 311 West Third; George Ferris the second invented the Ferris wheel. Continue on Third back to Carson Street; at the corner is the **St. Charles Hotel.** Built in 1862, it's one of the oldest commercial buildings in town; room 308 is reserved for Hank Monk, legendary Sierra stagecoach driver.

**The Nevada State Museum** is a few blocks north, housed in the old Carson City Mint, which coined Comstock silver from 1870 through 1893. As might be expected, this is the largest and most extensive historic museum in the state.

*Gold eagles ($20 pieces) with the Carson City stamp were minted only between 1870 and 1893.*

*The Wabuska Train Depot and water tower at the Nevada State Railroad Museum.*

Exhibits include coins and machines from the mint, a walk-through ghost town, authentic underground mine, and ecology, geology, archaeology, and changing galleries; there's also a gift shop with a large selection of local-interest books.

The big casino downtown is the **Carson Nugget,** with a jammin' pit, clanking slot machines, plus a good cheap snack bar, an oyster bar, a steakhouse, and a 24-hour coffee shop. Directly across the street are two slot houses, **Cactus Pete's** and the **Horseshoe,** both with excellent snack bars. Down and across the street is the 140-year-old **Ormsby House** (though it's been renovated and expanded so many times that nothing original remains). This casino is smaller and more sedate than the Nugget, with a half-pint pit, quiet slots, a coffee shop, and a steakhouse.

Two blocks down Carson Street is **Carson Station,** a small modern casino with the usual table games, slots, keno, sports book, snack bar, and coffee shop, which attracts both locals and passers-through. Carson Station management also runs **Pinion Plaza,** Carson City's full-service resort-casino about a mile east of downtown on US 50, with 64 Best Western rooms, 69-space RV· park, casino, sports book and bar, bowling alley, snack bar, and steakhouse. Another mile east on US 50 is Slot World Casino, a minor slot joint with lousy video poker and cigarette-clutching women huddled over the machines; I walked out singing the Beatles' lyric from "Day in the Life": "Local yokels choking smokers don't you think the joker laughs at you-hoo-hoo (hahaha heeheehee hohoho)."

If you took, or are planning to take, the Virginia & Truckee joyride from Virginia City to Gold Hill, you'll want to spend some time at the **Nevada State Railroad Museum,** at the south end of Carson City just north of the US 50 turnoff. This immaculate little museum houses more than 50 pieces of equipment from Nevada's railroading past (mostly from the V&T), including five steam locomotives and several restored passenger coaches and freight cars. During the summer, one of the steam engines does a slow one-mile loop around the museum grounds.

**Stewart Indian Museum** is one of many beautiful sandstone buildings on the 240-acre campus of the old Stewart Indian Boarding School, which operated from 1890 to 1980. This is as idyllic a spot as you'll find hereabouts (though most of the buildings are now the offices of the state prison administration). The museum, housing photos and baskets, is in the former superintendent's home. To get there

*"Susie," a Washoe Indian, beats pine nuts from cones she has harvested.*
*(Carson Valley Historical Society)*

head south on US 395; roughly three miles from downtown take a right on Snyder Avenue and drive a mile to the campus.

**Centennial Park** is just off US 50 a little east of town; one of the largest municipal parks in Nevada, it boasts several baseball and soccer fields, along with tennis courts, a public golf course, and picnic sites. **Mills Park** is also off US 50 (William Street) closer into town, with tennis courts, picnic sites, a one-mile kiddie choo-choo ride, and indoor and outdoor pools next door at the community center.

## ■ GENOA   *map page 192, A-5*

Carson City has spread a fer piece south over the past few years; driving down US 395 toward Minden and Gardnerville you pass a stretch of new subdivisions. But then the land opens up and you get the full vista of Carson Valley, one of the largest basins in Nevada, lying between the mighty Sierra Nevada on the west and the uprighty Pine Nut Range on the east. Beyond the tentacles of suburbia, the valley gets agricultural in a hurry: silos, fenced range, and rows and rows of alfalfa growing right up to the road, well-watered by the west fork of the Carson River. But it's also industrial on the east end, with some warehouses and small manufac-

*Alfalfa farming and cattle ranching flourish in the verdant Carson and Washoe Valleys.*

*Replica of the log cabin trading post at Mormon Station in Genoa, which is the oldest continually inhabited town in Nevada.*

turing plants around the Carson Valley Airport.

For a scenic detour along the pastoral west side of the valley, take a right onto **Jacks Valley Road** just beyond suburbia, which takes you into Genoa. Otherwise, a little less than 10 miles south of Carson is a turnoff that also takes you into Genoa.

Genoa (pronounced "ju-NO-ah") is the oldest town in Nevada, established in 1851, chosen by Mormon merchants and settlers for its striking beauty and named for Genoa, Italy. It managed to remain an idyllic, isolated, and independent little settlement up until, well, just the other day, but the area is too desirable, the town too picturesque, to escape notice by relocators and developers forever. Large new homes on big lots (even the garages are fancy), surrounded by white picket fences and big cottonwoods, coexist with cozy abodes inhabited by fifth-generation Genoans, big wooden barns and open sheds stuffed with bales of hay in the fall and winter, and a one-block downtown where most of the buildings are well over 100 years old.

Genoa also hosts of one of the oldest and the most renowned and successful annual events in the state. **The Genoa Candy Dance** is a crafts fair, homemade candy extravaganza, and dance that takes place over the last weekend of September. The 1999 event was the 80th annual, drawing 320 vendors and an estimated 10,000 attendees. It raised nearly $100,000—the proceeds account for the lion's share of Genoa's town budget.

Stop first at the museum, housed in one of Nevada's first courthouses (built in 1865): the original courtroom; the Virginia & Truckee Railroad; and Snowshoe Thompson, a legendary early letter carrier, are the focus of the exhibits. Across the street is **Mormon Station State Park,** site of the Mormon stockade and trading post; the fully reconstructed post houses the displays. Up the street is the **Genoa Bar,** which dates from 1863 and claims to be "the oldest continuously operated thirst parlor in Nevada." You won't be the first to hoist a whiskey at the Genoa Bar.

■ MINDEN AND GARDNERVILLE *map page 192, A-6*

Back on US 395 and a few miles south of Genoa is the bi-town Minden and Gardnerville area. Though the two are contiguous and nearly indistinguishable at first glance, they each have their own history and attractions. Gardnerville dates back to the 1880s when a hotel, saloon, and blacksmith shop were built to serve the various needs of the valley's homesteaders; in the early 1900s, an influx of Basque ranchers gave the town its enduring ambience. Minden was established in 1905 by the Virginia & Truckee Railroad to freight Carson Valley produce to market; it still has the feel of a company town, and it's the seat of Douglas County.

SWEET PROMISED LAND

*M*y father had married my mother when he was rich in sheep. She was Basque too, although raised more gently than my father in the soft lowlands of the French Pyrenees.

Both out of necessity and background, she was a practical woman. Her family had a small hotel and a travel agency in Bordeaux, and she had learned business there, and once she had even gone to cooking school in Paris. She came to America only to see her brother, who had been a French soldier and was dying from the poison gas he had breathed in the war. But, once here, she had loved America and its ways immediately, and never showed a desire to return to France.

She met and married my father in Reno, and after he had gone broke in sheep and she had had to bear children in rough camps and ghosted little towns, she had taken what little money they had and bought into a small hotel in Carson City. Later, as they prospered and my father went back into the hills with his own sheep, she had bought other business properties and the house in which we were to pass the rest of our childhood.

After that, I think our family spent half of its growing-up life looking for my father. We looked for him so much when we all lived at home that I used to dream about it. But this dream did not stem from fancy. It had it roots deep in reality, and it went something like this:

My brothers and I, Paul the older and John and Mick the younger, would be relaxing in the big dining room of our house in Carson City when my mother would come into the room in a high state of excitement. Either there were some business papers that needed my father's signature, or one of our two sisters, Suzanne or Marie, would be sick.

"We have to find your father," my mother would say.

My brothers and I would regard her in various postures of silence, but there was an awakening of something in our eyes.

"Go find him," my mother would say, a little irritated that we had not taken it up of our own free will.

"Oh sure," John would say. "Go find him."

Paul, who was the big brother, would be more constructive. "We don't know where he is." And Mick would add, "We haven't seen him in two months."

My mother would make a fluttering sweep of her hand, a gesture that covered an even one hundred miles of desert and Sierra Nevada. "He's in the hills," she would say easily.

"Oh sure," John, who had become a cynic at a very early age, would say. "He's in the hills."

"That's right," my mother would affirm with the finality of one whose word was law. "Go find him."

Then she would leave the room, and we would stare at each other in mute and hopeless contemplation of one thousand lost canyons of desert and mountains.

—Robert Laxalt, *Sweet Promised Land,* 1957

◆ MINDEN   *map page 192, A/B-6*

In Minden, the western of the two, check out the **C.O.D. Garage,** the oldest continuously operating car dealership in Nevada (dating back to 1910). Also stop by the excellent **Carson Valley Museum and Cultural Center,** in the old Douglas Valley High School, built in 1915, condemned in 1983, and reopened in 1995. You can easily kill an hour here. Wander through the natural history room, full of the heads of horned animals from around the world, plus bears, big cats, and moose; the telephone room, with lots of phones, a telephone timeline starting in 1876, a bunch of old switchboards, even a poster of "Hello Girls" from the early 1900s; an old print-shop exhibit; a Carson Valley agricultural exhibit, with black-and-white photographs and wooden farm implements; a Basque exhibit, complete with shepherd, tent, cot, campfire, Dutch oven, and bota; and the Washoe Cultural Room, with baskets, cradleboards, and a big winter house supplied by the Washoe, the Native American tribe that has lived in the area for the past thousand years or so.

Downtown Minden is dominated by the Carson Valley Motor Lodge, Carson Valley Market, Carson Valley RV Resort, Carson Valley Inn and Casino, and Fiona's fine dining, all built with the same distinctive dark brick.

◆ GARDNERVILLE   *map page 192, A/B-6*

Down the road, look closely at downtown Gardnerville to get a glimpse of its different flavor. The Basque influence is obvious in two downtown establishments, the **Overland Hotel,** opened in 1909, and **JT Basque Bar and Dining Room,** in a two-story wood building moved to Gardnerville from Virginia City in the late 1890s.

The Serbian influence is less obvious, but present nonetheless, at **Sharkey's Casino,** the only joint in Gardnerville. It's owned by Sharkey Begovich, noted for two main characteristics: his penchant for collecting memorabilia, and his annual Serbian Christmas dinner. Every inch of casino wall (and some ceiling) space is filled with Sharkey's stuff. Check out "Prizefighter Way" in the narrow hall to the restrooms, with historical photos of John L. Sullivan, Jack Dempsey, Bob Fitzsimmons, Gene Tunney, Rocky Marciano, etc., all posing in their underwear. A display room holds nearly 100 saddles, fancy or famous or both; another room has antique bicycles, sewing machines, old model trains, china, silver, pewter, mugs,

Tiffany lampshades, and slot machines. One section of the Rib Room restaurant is literally wallpapered in circus posters, while the other section displays more than 100 portraits of Native American chiefs.

Every January 7 or so, Sharkey's puts on a big pig and goat dinner to celebrate Serbian Christmas. It starts at 5 P.M., doesn't end till everyone's been fed, and—this is the God's honest truth—it's free to anyone who shows up. Thousands and thousands do.

Outside of Gardnerville, US 395 veers southeast, climbing out of Carson Valley and into the pinon and juniper forest of the Pine Nut Mountains. On the other side of the Pine Nuts the road cuts back south, heading directly toward the Sierra Nevada. At the head of a bucolic little ranching valley, you pass **Topaz Lake,** a reservoir on the West Fork of the Walker River that irrigates farms and ranches in Smith, Wellington, and Mason Valleys east of here. Topaz Lake Lodge has a casino, coffee shop, rooms, and RV park. Topaz Lake Campground is a big county park with camping right at water's edge and a mile of beachfront.

Just beyond Topaz Lake is that little-known state that borders Nevada to the west.

*The Sierra Nevada crest rises behind a barn in the Carson Valley.*

# I-80 & NORTHERN NEVADA

■ HIGHLIGHTS

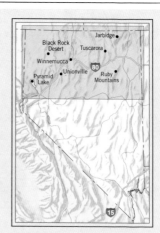

■ TRAVEL OVERVIEW

The Humboldt River was "discovered" in the 1820s; by the 1840s, emigrants were following it across most of northern Nevada. The railroad was laid next to it; in the 1920s the transcontinental Victory Highway was pushed through next to the railroad. The highway was later upgraded to US 40, and finally finished as Interstate 80. As such, this route was, and still is, and probably always will be the mother of all routes through Nevada.

Interstates, especially in the West, have a rhythm all their own: long monotonous stretches of four-lane white-line gas-guzzling travel, punctuated by fuel-pumping windshield-washing, junk-food-buying stops at exit ramps. In Nevada, the tempo is even more pronounced. The road—traversing a vast pale nothingness—is a narcotic, and the exit ramp—with its jarring neon and jangling slot machines—a psychosis.

The big towns along I-80, such as Wendover, Elko, Winnemucca, and Reno, diffuse the bizarre juxtaposition of road and ramp: the highway and its facilities are absorbed into the greater action. But it's in the small towns of Wells, Battle Mountain, Lovelock, and Fernley that the strangeness is especially magnified, where the casinos at the exit ramps are otherworldly.

Still, no matter how you feel about gambling, when you're traveling a casino can be your best friend. It's open 24 hours. It has restrooms, a coffee shop, a bar and, usually, a motel room. Other people are there. If you can weather the transition from highway to doorway, Nevada exit ramps are the perfect antidote to the interstate.

**Getting Around**

The widest road in the state, I-80 hosts every kind of vehicle. Oversized loads rumble down the highway, with pilot cars crawling along in front and behind. Big tractor-trailers roar through the desert, making deadlines and fudging logbooks. Greyhound buses haul passengers east and west. Automobiles, recreational vehicles, and motorcycles all share the pavement. Big freight and passenger trains clack along the track nearby.

Services aren't too far apart. Plenty of people are willing to stop and help in an emergency or with a breakdown; the Highway Patrol and a tow truck are just a cell-phone call away.

Still, there's no alternative to the interstate. You can get off in a town or city. You can take a side trip to the north or south on a connecting US highway or state road. But the nearest east-west arteries are US 50, 100 miles south, and Interstate 84, 100 miles north. You're stuck on 80, a totalitarian superhighway if there ever was one.

**Food and Lodging**

You'll find big hotel-casinos only at opposite ends of I-80 within Nevada, in Reno on the west and Wendover on the east. However, Winnemucca, Elko, and Wells have big motel-casinos; each town has at least one buffet, steakhouse, and lounge with live entertainment. Fernley, Lovelock, and Battle Mountain have casinos with coffee shops. At Carlin and the many little service and truck stops along the route are gas stations, fast-fooderies, convenience stores, and slot machines. Civilization is the order of the day, and night, on all 410 miles of Interstate 80.

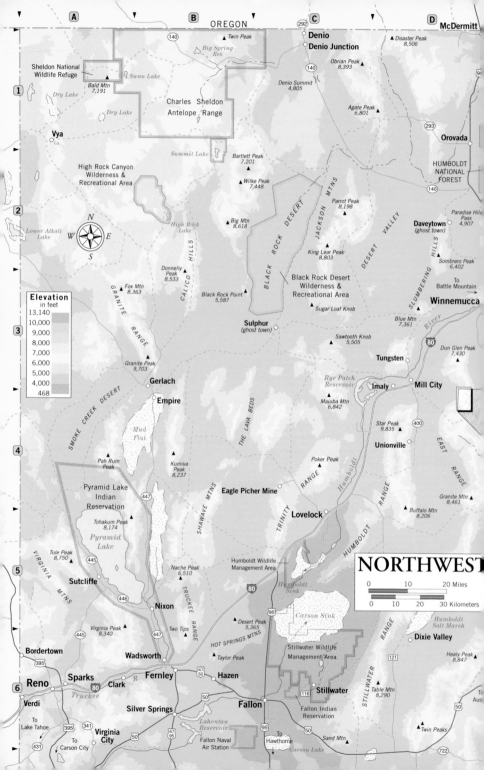

## ■ TRAVELING I-80

Say "Nevada" to most people and two images will come to mind. The first, if they're at all familiar with U.S. geography, is: Las Vegas. The second, especially if they've ever driven through the state on their way to or from California, is: mind-melting, anatomy-numbing, catalepsy-causing long flat stretches of... Interstate 80. And then, more often than not, they'll get drowsy at the mere memory of it.

Interstate 80 runs from downtown San Francisco nearly 3,000 miles to Hackensack, New Jersey. On the way, it crosses 410 miles of northern Nevada, from Verdi, on the California state line at mile one, all the way out to West Wendover, on the Utah.... Whoa! Sorry. Must've dozed off there. Where was I? Oh yeah... Utah state line at mile 410.

Even though I-80 runs from coast to coast, it plots a course through Nevada that's as much north and south as it is east and west. From Verdi all the way to east of Winnemucca, 190 miles, you travel due northeast. From there to east of Battle Mountain, another 40 miles, it's due southeast. The next 90 miles, to Wells, have a gentle northeast inclination, then the last 60 miles to Wendover are due southeast. As such, the road runs with the grain of the state—i.e., along endless tedious lengthwise stretches of basins, between distant drab dun ranges.

Part of the route of I-80 through Nevada is by design: it's much easier and less expensive to lay a road on a hardpan valley floor than it is to cut one into the side-long slopes of mountains. Still, part of the route is by default: For nearly 300 miles, from west of Lovelock to east of Wells, I-80 follows the circuitous and tortuous meanderings of the Humboldt River.

The Humboldt is the river that Jedediah Smith, famed mountain man and explorer, discovered in 1825, making him the first white man to whom the river made its presence known. The California Trail, chosen by more 1850s and '60s emigrants than any other, followed the Humboldt through northeastern Nevada. The Central Pacific, first transcontinental railroad, laid its tracks next to the Humboldt in 1869; those tracks haven't moved since, and it's still a busy route for freights and Amtrak. US 40, the first transcontinental highway, was paved parallel to the tracks; the highway was eventually replaced by the interstate. It took nearly 30 years to complete I-80 in Nevada; the final section wasn't opened until 1983.

How is it that the banks of a 300-mile-long river have been the best route to tramp, chug, and drive across Nevada? Well, for 300 miles the Humboldt flows sluggishly, little more than a long puddle, a few feet below the sand and sage of the high desert. Although you travel next to it for hours on end, you rarely see it. If

*The Southern Pacific and I-80 follow the path of the lazy Humboldt River.*

you didn't know it was there, you wouldn't learn of it by looking out the car window. You only cross it three times on the whole route. The Humboldt doesn't, to be sure, relieve the humdrum of the interstate.

That's not to say that the whole Nevada stretch of I-80 is entirely monotonous. Just almost so. Beyond Reno and Fernley, it nears only seven towns of any consequence. It climbs over three mountain summits, one at nearly 7,000 feet, the others at less than 6,000. It twists and turns through a single river canyon (the Truckee, not the Humboldt) and passes through one tunnel.

No doubt about it. Interstate 80 isn't exotic: two-lane US 50, a hundred miles south, is a much more interesting and enjoyable east-west route across Nevada. But "the I" is fast: 75 miles per hour is the speed limit on the four-lane superhighway across most of Nevada. Which means you're pretty safe going up to 85, unless some highway patrolman is having a very bad day. And as long as you're making up so much time on the road, you might as well stop in a town or two or three along the way—if only to wake up.

*(opposite) A primitive road follows a wagon route through sagebrush on the Emigrant Trail.*

I-80 & NORTHERN NEVADA

## SAGE AND SAGEBRUSH

*D*uring most of my time in the Great Basin I admit to having taken sagebrush for granted. It is always there; from its matrix rise the island mountain ranges, below it the rings of salt desert spiral toward barren playas. Its sharp scent, laced with dust and wind and sometimes a trace of rain, becomes so familiar that it no longer registers—until you leave this country and miss it.

Sagebrush indeed forms an ocean from which all other Great Basin places depart. If you picked the right line, you could move through the entire length and breadth of the desert from north to south, from west to east, always walking through aromatic gray-green sagebrush.

A single species, "sagebrush," does not dominate the Great Basin. Twelve sagebrush species (big sagebrush, *Artemisia tridentata,* and its allies) grow in the West, and several of these have distinct subspecies. Numerous other members of the genus occur (e.g., bud sagebrush) but are more distantly related to big sagebrush and thus not official sagebrushes. Most travelers through the Basin have not only lumped all sagebrush, but in their expansiveness have included shadscale and other shrubs unrelated to sagebrush.

Sagebrush has become a brand-name generic—like Kleenex and Scotch tape.

Further confusing its identity, sagebrush is not a true sage; it is a sagebrush. True sages of the genus *Salvia* belong to the mint family and give personality to many a western image: "riders of the purple sage" ride through *Salvia,* not *Artemisia.* Woe to the creative camp cook who adds a few sagebrush leaves to the cookpot, again mistaking bitter *Artemisia* for the *Salvia* that flavors Thanksgiving turkey.

—Stephen Trimble, *The Sagebrush Ocean*

■ TRUCKEE RIVER  *map page 216, A/B-6*

I remember clearly the moment I fell in love with Nevada. It was a dark and rainy day. I was driving east over the Sierra, windshield wipers whipping, from my home in northern California. The Silver State's siren song had been summoning me for a few weeks and I was answering its call. I'd just completed my first travel book, a 500-page guide to Alaska and the Yukon, and a sort of personal manifest destiny was flowing through my veins; I was now looking to claim another geopolitical chunk of territory to extend my growing guidebook empire. There was but a single requirement: it had to be close. Four days of hard travel, overland, were required to get to my Alaska beat, and I wanted something a little more accessible. One glance at a U.S. map showed me that Nevada was a mere three-hour commute from my house—up and over the hill and I'd be at work.

So there I was, driving white-knuckled through the Sierra, tractor-trailers blinding me with highway spray as they blew by. I'd crested Donner Pass and left the mountain town of Truckee behind, when suddenly the rain tapered off. Fifteen minutes later I emerged from the mountains and the storm; fluffy white clouds flew lazily east amidst patches of blue sky. As I crossed the Nevada state line, the sun broke through. Finally, I laid eyes on Reno, rays reflecting off the hotel-tower windows. It was the most numinous skyline I'd ever seen. It was more magical than Oz. It was my own Cibola, city of gold.

That feeling has never faded. I still love Reno, my hometown for the past decade. It's not too tough having the Sierra Nevada, hemming in the west side of the Truckee Meadows, providing the backdrop to the city. But the hidden charm of the area resides along the Truckee River.

One John Fulton, waxing eloquent in an old issue of the *Nevada Historical Society Papers,* said of the river,

> The Truckee River has but few associations and a short history. It has no legends, no ruins, no relics, no classic battlefields. No Washington made it sacred by crossing its swollen and ice-choked current in the face of an overwhelming force. No gentle Irving embalmed its name in literature. Long years after our other rivers were famous in song and story it lay neglected in the wilderness. No man can guess the ages it took the glaciers to hollow out its giant cradle, Tahoe, and Pyramid, its grave.

*The Truckee River flows out of the Sierra Nevada and into Nevada's desert before eventually terminating in Pyramid Lake.*

The source of the Truckee is Lake Tahoe. It flows over a dam (in good water years) at Tahoe City and begins its precipitous fall northward through a narrow steep-walled gorge, dropping 1,300 feet in its first 40 miles, draining a gigantic volume of mountain runoff, making a beeline for the basin.

As it emerges from the mountains behind it and approaches the desert ahead, the Truckee turns sharply eastward. There, Interstate 80 follows it through Upper Truckee Canyon. The road curves along and above the river, crossing it several times, until the canyon yields to a broad and fairly flat valley, Truckee Meadows. Here, the road veers a bit north while the river turns a little south. At the widest part of the valley, near its eastern end, the river channel also widens, turning slightly marshy—the swampy flare of a floodwater funnel.

The funnel narrows into the Lower Truckee Canyon through the Virginia Range. The road meets up with the river again here; together they pick a winding path through the intervening hills. Once more the river emerges from mountains into a valley and makes a big bend, this time northward again. Interstate 80 continues purposefully east, taking its leave after having followed the Truckee for more than 50 miles.

We're going to stay with the river and take a long detour north, into the remote northwest corner of Nevada. Interstate 80 will be there when we get back in a day or so.

## ■ PYRAMID LAKE *map page 216, A-5*

Exit 43 takes you into and through **Wadsworth**, a tiny old railroad town, one of the dozen railroad towns, big and small, strung all the way along this route. Wadsworth hosted the Central Pacific's maintenance plant from 1869 till 1905, when the railroad moved the shops, and most of the houses, 30 miles west to the new town of Sparks. Today, the old town is pretty much gone; the high school still stands, but it's been abandoned since 1951. An old footbridge across the Truckee is a local landmark. The new elementary school doubles as the town's social center. There's also an inn, a market, a picturesque church, huge cottonwoods, the Pyramid Lake Paiute campground and smoke shop, and the Nevada Cement Company.

At the junction of NV 447, hang a left and start heading north. In a mile you enter the Pyramid Lake Paiute Reservation. Drive 15 miles, paralleling the river again, to Nixon, the small reservation community. Just north of Nixon the Truckee abandons the strict definition of a river, seeping out into a wide quicksandy delta before emptying into Pyramid Lake, one of the world's most beautiful desert lakes.

You have to see this aqua apparition to believe that any body of water, let alone one this big, could exist in such an arid and desolate land. Except for a few stickimuh trees hither and yon, there's nary anything tall and green in the whole picture. More amazing yet, there aren't any lakeside villages, inns, condos, casinos, parking lots, mansions, sternwheelers, seafood restaurants, outdoor stores, or Sea Doo rentals. There aren't even any beach volleyball or soft-drink stands under umbrellas. No bikini-clad babes, no macho muscle-heads.

What is there here? You've got houses, offices, the reservation school, and the **Pyramid Lake Paiute Cultural Center** in Nixon. You'll see a few farms at the southeast edge of the lake, **Anaho Island National Wildlife Refuge** partway up the east side, and the eponymous pyramid just north of there. There's a lodge and marina at Sutcliffe, opposite the pyramid part way up the west side. A few primitive beaches are strung along the lake between Sutcliffe and Nixon. Otherwise, this is a typical Nevada basin, in between the northern end of the Virginia Range to the west and the southern end of the Lake Range to the east. A typical, sparsely inhabited, Nevada basin—except for the fact that it's full of fresh warm water.

*(above) The Pyramid Lake Paiute Cultural Center in Nixon.*
*(following pages) Anaho Island rises 600 feet out of Pyramid Lake. For scale, note the vehicle parked on the isthmus to the right of the island.*

Pyramid Lake, like Walker Lake, is one of the last remnants of mighty Lake La-hontan, the inland sea that covered most of northwestern Nevada 20,000 years ago. It's 27 miles long, nine miles wide, and a little more than 300 feet deep at its deepest. It's inhabited, primarily, by Lahontan cutthroat trout, which can grow to 10 or 12 pounds, and the indigenous cui-ui. Like the desert pupfish in the pools at Death Valley National Monument outside Pahrump, the bottom-feeding cui-ui sucker fish are direct descendants of a prehistoric species that filled Lake Lahontan; as the huge inland sea disappeared, the cui-ui managed to survive at the bottom of the Pyramid puddle. **Anaho Island**, the 600-foot-tall rock just off the lower east side of the lake, is the nesting grounds for the American white pelican, among other shorebirds. Seeing pelicans over Pyramid is phenomenal and preposterous at the same time, but there you are.

**Sutcliffe** is where the action is, the little of it that's visible, anyway. **Crosby's Lodge** has a bar, rooms, a store, a gas station, campsites, and showers. Closer to the water is **Pyramid Lake Marina**, run by the Paiute. Pay your $5 day-use fee (plus your camping and fishing fees if you're staying here and not heading north with me) at the ranger station, then wander around the convenience store, boat dock, and RV park; also be sure to allot plenty of time to explore the museum here for a good solid lesson in the unique natural plumbing of western Nevada, as well as the unusual science of desert limnology. Up the hill from Sutcliffe is the **Dunn Hatchery**, which stocks Pyramid and Walker Lakes with a million trout every year.

The rest of the action hereabouts is invisible. This lake, and the half-million acre reservation, have been the province of the *Kuyui Dokado* ("Cui-Ui Eaters") and their ancestors for probably 10,000 years. The spirits are very strong: camp out on the east side near the pyramid and the Great Stone Mother, who filled the lake with tears of grief over her wayward children, and you'll have no trouble getting in touch with them.

## ■ GERLACH AND BEYOND

Back on NV 447 heading north out of Nixon, you skirt unmistakable **Marble Bluff** and head for the east side of the Lake Range, behind which Pyramid disappears. It's a ruler-straight 60-mile shot up NV 447 to Empire and Gerlach, the only settlements in a huge wild hunk of northwestern Nevada.

◆ EMPIRE  *map page 216, A/B-4*

Empire is an orderly four-square-block company town for the workers at the gypsum plant, which manufactures drywall. If, by some strange coincidence, you happen to have your golf clubs with you, you can play a round at Empire's nine-hole, par-32, 2,000-yard **Burning Sands Golf Course,** which is free to anyone who shows up. On the outskirts of town is Empire Farms, an amazing little garlic-geothermal operation that ships 11,000 tons of garlic seed to growers worldwide and produces enough geothermal power to sell it to Sierra Pacific, the northern Nevada utility company.

◆ GERLACH  *map page 216, B-3/4*

From garlic to Gerlach, a small town with a big presence. Barely 250 people live up here, on the pavement but nearly off the planet, the largest settlement in an area that's roughly equivalent to the size of Maryland. Founded by Western Pacific, the second transcontinental railroad, in 1906, Gerlach chugged along as a typical outback wide-spot-in-the-tracks for 70 years, until the railroad company, tired of fixing it, sold Gerlach's water system, throwing in all the land under the town, to the residents for $18,000. Today, Gerlach boasts four-score houses, a school, a Texaco station, and four bars, including **Bruno's Country Club,** famous for its homemade raviolis; check in at the bar for Bruno's Motel, next to the gas station.

Eight miles north of Gerlach on NV 447 is **Planet X,** a 200-acre solar-pottery ranch owned by unreconstructed hippies John and Rachel Bogard; stop in to see the Bogard's desert dishes (that's *desert,* though you could use them for dessert) and panorama pottery.

◆ BLACK ROCK DESERT  *map page 216, B/C-2/3*

Every place can be considered a gateway to another place, and Gerlach is the gateway to the Black Rock Desert. The Black Rock is a million-acre playa, the largest in North America—a vast cracked-mud plain, flat as a mackerel, far-out as the moon. It's a cosmic blank canvas, the arid earth as easel, ready and waiting for anything anyone cares to paint, project, or produce on it. It's one of the most forbidding and at the same time inviting places on the planet, a majestic, magnetic, romantic—in short, magic—milieu, where mirages are material and substance is, yes, an illusion. And that doesn't even come close to describing it.

There are many ways to experience the Black Rock Desert. You can just come up here in your Saturn or Suburu or Suburban and, if it's dry enough, drive forever, as fast as you want, bothering neither to steer nor even watch where you're going. (But make sure it's dry on the playa: when it's wet, the unprepared get bogged down in the mud and die.) You can arrive with your landsailer, a sort of windsurfer on wheels, catch a cross wind, and never be heard from again. You can bring your metal detector or telescope and stare at the ground or the sky. You can even bring your golf clubs and play on **Lucifer's Anvil** golf course in the **Black Rock Desert Classic,** a makeshift, self-invitational, free-form tournament held every June.

Speedsters also show up from time to time with jet cars to set land-speed records. For example, in the summer of 1997, Craig Breedlove carted his 44-foot-long 48,000-horsepower rocket on wheels up to the Black Rock to face off against Richard Noble, with his 54-foot-long 110,000-horsepower turbo-jet bad boy.

*(above) These geysers in the Black Rock Desert were created around 1925, when a rancher drilling for water inadvertently pierced an underground thermal chamber.*

*(opposite) Cracked curled playa designs on the Black Rock Desert at sunset.*

*This first known photo of a shock wave on the ground shows dust being churned up as a transsonic car reaches 728 miles an hour. The sound barrier was broken the following day. (photo by Marilyn Newton)*

They set up 15-mile tracks and let 'em rip; Andy Green, the driver (pilot?) of Noble's horizontal cruise missile cranked it up to the supersonic speed of 764 miles per hour, breaking the sound barrier on the ground for the first time in history. Just another day on the Black Rock.

◆ BURNING MAN

But the best way to experience this surreal sucker is the psychedelic way. The Black Rock is the home of the renowned Burning Man Art Festival—indeed, this event could happen no other place on Earth. It's a post-apocalyptic hippie hoedown, Mardi Gras on acid. In the sparkling words of my tinsel-tongued friend Bruce Van Dyke, boss jock of Reno's KTHX (100.1), the best radio station in Nevada if not the solar system, "It's a wild weird festival of art and alternica, set in a mercurial munici-pality, which inspires nightly celebrations that never fail to provide brain-boggling surprise after brain-boggling surprise." And that doesn't begin to describe it. The event lasts a week, culminating on the Saturday night of Labor Day weekend, and tickets can cost up to several hundred dollars.

## GALACTIC TRAVEL ON THE PLAYA

*F*ollowing the caravan of mutant vehicles past the gates of time Ellen and I tuned into 99.5 Radio Free Burning Man as we converged on the bizarre scene ahead of us. A growing number of strange figures—resembling human beings in size and shape but uniquely different in color and attitude—appeared. A yellow wind surfer whizzed by us at a good clip creating a 500-foot white cloud of dust behind him. On a 400 square mile alkaline slab in the middle of the Black Rock Desert in northern Nevada the biggest and most chaos-driven art event of the 20th century clearly was well underway. Over 23,500 people joined together here to form a massive temporary city built on the ideals of creative hedonism and free artistic expression. A Chinese anarchist long ago once wrote, "We shape clay into a pot, but it is the emptiness inside that holds what we want." In this sense an empty desert was transformed into a surreal postmodern festival of excess and abandon.

Passing the expanse between Pluto and Neptune and entering the orbit of Uranus we were faced with our first decision of going right into the past, or left into the future. After a moment's hesitation we merged left and soon landed up at our new

*The Burning Man goes up in a blaze of glory on the final night of the event.*
*(photo by Mark Downey)*

address: 6:45 Uranus, slightly in the future and just the other side of reality. Swimming pools, trampolines, pleasure rides, putting greens and bowling alleys dotted the landscape as did spiritual temples, great pyramids, live camels, radio towers, lighthouses, mazes, fire waterfalls, and geodesic domes. We grabbed our portable keg and headed out on foot into the vast mysterious new city that lay before us.

As we passed Unconditional Love Camp, the primal rhythms grew louder surrounding us from all directions. Brilliantly painted sculptures towered over us like dinosaurs and theme camps grew larger and larger to incredible proportions. Mobile smoking lounges and traveling tropical beach bars carrying 40 or 50 passengers passed before us as if floating on air, while neon kangaroos hopped evenly through the darkened moonless landscape. Thirty-foot stacks of 300-watt amplifiers and a half-dozen huge synchronized video screens formed the boundaries of the playa, and from where we stood the four-story-tall stick Man was a glowing firefly.

The inner circle began with the orbit of Mercury, with the Man at its center and a circumference I would estimate at over two miles. The sea of humanity inside, wildly dancing and seemingly possessed by the jungle beats, reminded me of some of the street festivals I'd witnessed years ago in Bombay and Katmandu (of course Burning Man had a distinctly more theatrical and high-tech character). The audience was the event and the desert the stage. No one was in control of the production. Fireworks and rockets split the starry sky as synchronized green lasers pulsed digital rays across the expanse. All over the playa communal bonfires seemed to spontaneously erupt. Around a fire near us naked savages pounded on twisted pieces of metal with sticks and crow bars. Past these possessed tribesmen came a school of 12 blue and orange neon clown fish floating 10 feet off the ground. They were followed by some jumping blue dolphins in a stunning oceanic display. Cultural road warriors on bicycles with flame jets behind them shot past us as the crowd worked itself deeper into a millennium fever. Rastafarians passed me on the left and pink ballerinas on the right as I continued on into the new universe of shapes, sounds, and colors. From above the city lights stretched in a circle around me as far as the eye could see. Strange alien spaceships blinked across the desert towards Area 51 camp and orange electrical currents streaked along the desert floor toward specified targets at incredible speeds. Many were sucked into the mouth of a 30-foot tall Darth Vader helmet with red eyes beckoning all to enter his mouth as high energy dance music raged inside. This was where I lost Ellen.

—David Rodrigues, 2000

◆  SHELDON NATIONAL WILDLIFE REFUGE  *map page 216, A-1*

Meanwhile, back in the mundane travel guide, you can continue on the "high" (paved) road, NV 447, into that other author's state to the west, cruising through Eagleville and Cedarville. At Cedarville, you head east (right) on CA 299; the pavement ends at the border, where you roll onto NV 8A, which takes you into the Sheldon National Wildlife Refuge. Or you can take the "low" (gravel) road a mere 110 miles up through aptly named Long Valley to the entrance of the NWR.

The Sheldon National Wildlife Refuge is one of the finest places in the world to see pronghorn antelope. A few thousand of these flighty antlered critters, along with the occasional deer, burro, and bighorn sheep, roam the half-million-acre refuge, just this side of the Oregon line. The Sheldon is almost entirely undeveloped, with just a cozy stone headquarters house, a few primitive campsites at the edge of small reservoirs, and 75 miles of unpaved roads; you won't bump into too many other people hereabouts.

*Rhyolite cliffs in Sheldon National Wildlife Refuge in the northwestern corner of the state.*

Halfway through the park, the gravel roads converge and merge with US 140, paved, which runs 25 miles to the eastern end of the refuge, then another 15 miles to Denio Junction, where there's a typical, though extremely welcome, service stop, complete with bar, cafe, gas station, motel, and showers. Three miles north of the junction is Denio itself, a tiny border town right on the Oregon state line. US 140 continues southeast for 65 miles till it deadends at US 95 at the south end of the Santa Rosa Range; from that intersection, it's another 30 miles due south into Winnemucca, where you can connect back up with I-80.

## ■ LOVELOCK   *map page 216, C-4/5*

But before we get to Winnemucca, we have to continue on the interstate from Wadsworth, where we last saw it, another 65 Morpheus-muddled miles to Lovelock. Wadsworth is only a mile or so west of Fernley *(covered on page 171)*. East of these, though you might not notice them even if you're looking, two Nevada river systems reach their final rancid resting places along this stretch. The Carson River

*Seven Troughs was a mining town that existed about 30 miles northwest of Lovelock. This photograph was probably taken around 1910. (photo courtesy of Stanley W. Paher)*

expires in the extensive alkali flats south of the freeway, and east of US 95 at exit 83, in a topographical area known as the **Carson Sink**. Nearby, the Humboldt River disappears in its own stinky sink. Rivers swallowed by the desert are one of the hallmarks of the Great Basin Desert, which was named by explorer John C. Frémont for just that phenomenon: internal drainage. All rivers that arise in or flow into the Great Basin die there as well; none flows out.

Just beyond the area that's defined as the Humboldt Sink is Lovelock, both the town and the irrigation district. Lovelock has two main claims to fame. The seat of Pershing County, Lovelock is the proud possessor of a one-of-a-kind **circular courthouse**, designed in 1920 by the most famous Nevada architect, Frederick De Longchamps, and modeled, it's believed by some, after the Pantheon. The courtroom is round; the jury box sits in the middle of the room, between the judge and the spectators. Also, Lovelock was the last town to be bypassed along the entire Interstate 80 route; I-80 wasn't finished until 1983 when the Lovelock freeway and exits were built.

**The Marzen House Museum**, right off Lovelock's west exit, is the place to catch exhibits on the local history and industry, and to pick up visitor information. **Sturgeon's** is the main joint in town, at the east exit, recently expanded in the continuing process of the Lovelock business district's reorientation to the interstate; it has a good little coffee shop, a sports bar, a casino, and something Lovelockian usually going on. You can tool around the original railroad downtown, one block east of Cornell Street on Broadway; one of the old hotels and a couple of the bars are still operating.

■ RYE PATCH DAM AND RESERVOIR  *map page 216, C–3/4*

Twenty-four miles east on I-80 (but actually north) is Exit 129 for **Rye Patch Dam and Reservoir**. Rye Patch dams up the lower Humboldt here and supplies water for the Lovelock Irrigation District, which provides as much continuity and stability as possible for Lovelock's tenuous alfalfa economy. On the highway side of the dam is the entrance to the **Rye Patch State Recreation Area**, where you pay your fee to use the place. Drive across the 800-foot-long dam and take your first right for the main lakeside picnic area, or left for the main riverbank campground (44 well-shaded sites, with drinking water). Continue driving past these two turnoffs on the access road to get to the north picnic area, campground, and a small sandy beach.

*Flattened cattails at the Great Meadows in Rye Patch State Recreation Area.*

The cabins, lodge, and offices on the highway side of the dam comprise a private resort area for owners of property at **Humboldt River Ranch,** a 10,000-acre development, the largest rural subdivision in the state; the one- to ten-acre lots are across I-80 on the flats and in the foothills of the large Humboldt Range.

## ■ UNIONVILLE   *map page 216, D–4*

The Rye Patch Reservoir is 22 miles long; you drive alongside it as you head east (north) on the interstate. Thirty miles from the recreation area is the Mill City exit (149), gateway to an interesting side trip. Twenty miles back south on NV 400 (17 paved, the last three gravel) is Unionville, a semi-ghost town clinging to either side of steep and narrow Buena Vista Canyon on the east side of the Humboldts. Unionville saw some minor mining in the early 1860s; a hilarious account of Unionville's early boom was recorded for posterity by Mark Twain in *Roughing It.* Though the silver excitement ended 130 years ago, a handful of hangers-on, attracted by the beauty and remoteness of the surroundings, have kept the town alive ever since.

## MEN OF MICA

*I* confess, without shame, that I expected to find masses of silver lying all about the ground. I expected to see it glittering in the sun on the mountain summits. I said nothing about this, for some instinct told me that I might possibly have an exaggerated idea about it, and if I betrayed my thought, I might bring derision upon myself. Yet I was as perfectly satisfied in my own mind, as I could be of anything, that I was going to gather up, in a day or two, silver enough to make me satisfactorily wealthy— and so my fancy was already busy with plans for spending this money.... Then I began my search with a feverish excitement that was brimful of expectation—almost of certainty. I crawled about the ground, seizing and examining bits of stone, blowing the dust from them and rubbing them on my clothes, and then peering at them with anxious hope. Presently I found a bright fragment and my heart bounded! I hid behind a boulder and polished it and scrutinized it with a nervous eagerness and a delight that was more pronounced than absolute certainty itself could have afforded. The more I examined the fragment, the more I was convinced that I had found the door to fortune. I marked the spot and carried away the specimen. Up and down the rugged mountainside I searched, with always increasing interest and always augmenting gratitude that I had come to Humboldt and come in time. Of all the experiences of my life, this secret search among the hidden treasures of silver land was the nearest to unmarred ecstasy. It was a delirious revel. By and by, in the bed of a shallow rivulet, I found a deposit of shining yellow scales, and my breath almost forsook me! A gold mine, and in my simplicity I had been content with vulgar silver! I was so excited that I half believed my overwrought imagination was deceiving me... I set about scooping them out, and for an hour I toiled down the windings of the stream and robbed its bed. But at last the descending sun warned me to give up the quest, and I turned homeward laden with wealth....

"Gentlemen," said I, "I don't say anything— I haven't been around, you know, and of course don't know anything—but all I ask of you is to cast your eye on that, for instance and tell me what you think of it!" and I tossed my treasure before them.                    *(continues)*

*Mark Twain's cabin in Unionville, where he supposedly lived in the early 1860s.*

> There was an eager scramble for it, and a closing of heads together over it under the candlelight. Then old Ballou said:
>
> "Think of it? I think it is nothing but a lot of granite rubbish and nasty glittering mica that isn't worth ten cents an acre!"
>
> So vanished my dream. So melted my wealth away. So toppled my airy castle to the earth and left me stricken and forlorn.
>
> Moralizing, I observed, then, that "all that glitters is not gold."
>
> Mr. Ballou said I could go further than that, and lay it up among my treasures of knowledge, that nothing that glitters is gold. So I learned then, once and for all, that gold in its native state is but dull, unornamental stuff, and that only lowborn metals excite the admiration of the ignorant with an ostentatious glitter. However, like the rest of the world, I still go on underrating men of gold and glorying men of mica. Commonplace human nature can't rise above that.
>
> —Mark Twain, *Roughing It*

It's worth an hour's detour just to get an eyeful of the old town's stone ruins, the new town's cozy homes, and the trees that shade both. There's a "thrift store," selling a little bit of everything, and a gorgeous bed-and-breakfast in renovated 19th-century buildings. It all sits in the shadow of Star Peak, rising to nearly 10,000 feet; you can park at the edge of town and be standing on the peak in 20 minutes—if you've brought along your jet backpack.

Back on I-80 at Mill City, it's another 27 miles to Winnemucca.

■ WINNEMUCCA  *map page 239, A–2/3*

It starts to sound like a broken record after a while: a stopping point on the Emigrant Trail in the 1850s; a mining settlement spawned by Virginia City prospectors in the 1860s; a whistlestop emplaced by the railroad, taking advantage of the population center, in the 1870s; the US and interstate highways delivering a steady stream of passers-through and settlers-down; and gold in them thar nearby hills ensuring that the local economy will enjoy booms and suffer busts. But if it gets to be repetitious, well, too bad: it describes Winnemucca, Battle Mountain, Carlin, Elko, and Wells.

But first, Winnemucca. On Bridge Street just this side of the highway stands the **Winnemucca Hotel,** where it's stood since 1863. That's old anywhere west of the Rockies; in Nevada, it ranks in the top five oldest buildings extant, and the

Elevation
in feet
13,140
10,000
9,000
8,000
7,000
6,000
5,000
4,000
468

**1**  **2**  **3**  **4**

Goshute Indian
Reservation

Montello

West Wendover
Wendover
Ferguson
Springs

Oasis
Shafter

To Salt Lake City,
UT

80

Flowery
Lake

White Peak
8,270

PEQUOP    MOUNTAINS

Contact

Mineral Hot
Springs

Lages
Station

To Ely

93

Victoria

Currie

Mt Taylor

CROW RANGE

White Elephant
Butte

93

Bishop Creek
Reservoir

Pequop Summit
6,967

Spruce Mtn
10,263

Snow Water
Lake

93

Wells

Ward Creek
Ranch

Marys River

232

Jarbidge

Copper
Mtn

230

Hole in the Mtn Pk

229

Humboldt
Pk

Humboldt
Wilderness Area

229

Ruby Mountains
Wilderness Area

Ruby Valley

Franklin
Lake

RUBY  VALLEY

Ruby
Lake

Wild Horse

Wild Horse
State Park

Wild Horse
8,199

Deeth

Halleck

Humboldt
Wilderness Area

Verdi Pk

Lamoille

Lee

Wines
Peak

Jiggs

Pearl Peak
10,847

Humboldt
National
Forest

Humboldt
National
Forest

225

Mountain
City

Taylor Canyon

226

South Fork
Indian Reservation

Wild Horse Res

Elko

227

Spring
Creek

228

Te Moak
Indian Res

Robinson Mtn
8,740

ALKALI  FLAT

Owyhee

Indian
Reservation

South Fork Owyhee
Wilderness and Recreation
Area

Dry Lake

Jack Creek

Chicken Creek Summit
6,436

Tuscarora

Willow Creek Res

Table Peak

Beaver
Peak

Leeville

766

Emigrant Summit
6,114

Adobe Summit
6,548

80

Carlin

Palisade
(ghost town)

South Fork
State Park

S Fork
Res

278

Bald Mtn
8,359

Watts Hot
Springs

Midas

Dunphy

Beowawe

Twin
Summit

Humboldt

Crescent
Valley

Gold
Acres

CORTEZ  MOUNTAINS

306

CALICO LAKE VALLEY

McDermitt

Cordero
Mine

95

Capitol Pk
8,255

Granite Pk
9,728

Orovada

Santa Rosa Pk
9,701

Paradise
Valley

290

Paradise Hill
Pass 4,907

Granite Pk
7,835

293

140

95

Winnemucca

To
Reno

Golconda

789

Golconda Summit
5,145

Little Humboldt River

Humboldt    River

Adam Pk
8,678

OSGOOD   MTNS

Valmy

80

North Pk

Battle
Mountain

305

SHOSHONE  MOUNTAINS

305

AUGUSTA  FLAT

Mt Tobin
9,779

AUGUSTA  MTNS

Needle Pk
7,618

Table Mtn
7,390

EAST  RANGE

Granite Mtn
8,461

**NORTHEAST**

0       15       30 Miles
0    15    30    45 Kilometers

*Sarah Winnemucca, daughter of the famous Paiute chief. (Nevada Historical Society)*

second oldest hotel. You can get a Basque lunch or dinner here, or just drink at the bar under all the foreign currency. The cash register is probably as old as the building. **The Martin Hotel,** at Melarkey and Railroad in the old downtown, is the other still-operating Basque bar and restaurant.

Across the highway and up the hill on US 95 (which leaves I-80 in Winnemucca and heads north), take a left on Jungo Road for the **Humboldt Historical Museum,** housed in a 1900s church building and a 1990s museum building; check out the exhibits of local interest and the antique car collection. Downtown in the Winnemucca Convention Center (Bridge Street and Winnemucca Boulevard) is the **Buckaroo Hall of Fame and Western Heritage Museum,** whose name is almost as extensive as the displays of art and artifacts of the local *vaquero* population.

Winnemucca has three main (Winners, Red Lion Inn, and Parker's Model T) and two minor (Sundance and Legends) casinos, all strung along Winnemucca Boulevard, along with all the motels and gas stations, most of the restaurants, and a fair number of shops; the rest of the business district is downtown on Bridge and Melarkey Streets. Winnemucca is also the seat of Humboldt County and has the courthouse.

By the way, if you're wondering just who the hell this guy Humboldt was, after whom nearly every river, mountain, national forest, county, and museum are named, he was Alexander Von Humboldt (1769–1859), a German scientist, world traveler, writer, and diplomat admired by John C. Frémont, who explored Nevada thoroughly in the 1840s and named everything he saw.

And while we're on the subject, if you're wondering what's a Winnemucca, it's the name of an influential Pauite chief who worked tirelessly to establish peace for his people with his white brothers. Chief Winnemucca's daughter, Sarah Winnemucca, is also remembered for *her* tireless efforts to achieve equality for her people with her white brothers.

## ■ PARADISE VALLEY AND THE SANTA ROSA RANGE

*map page 239, A–1/2*

Bridge Street, north of downtown, turns into our old friend US 95. It travels a ruler-straight line north, passing solitary **Winnemucca Mountain**—the one with the big whitewashed "W" on the side of it—presiding over the town at 6,700 feet.

Twenty-two miles north of the interstate is the turnoff onto NV 290 for a bucolic valley that, unlike the Eagles' valley in "The Last Resort," is called Paradise

but never had to be kissed goodbye. It's still as paradisal a valley as can be found in a state that's chock-full of valleys. Strung with ranches all the way into the little semi-ghost town of the same name, Paradise Valley sits in the late afternoon shadows cast by 9,400-foot Paradise Peak.

**Paradise Valley,** the town, is near the top of Paradise Valley, the valley, 18 miles northeast of US 95. There's a ranger station, a funky bar, and an eclectic mercantile with a a couple thousand videos to rent (it's

*A May morning in the town of Paradise Valley.*

also the hang-out for the region's kids and a gathering place for residents.

Around town are a number of photogenic skeletons, carcasses, rattletraps, and other wrecks and ruins—of abandoned wooden buildings, that is.

If you don't want to backtrack to the main highway, there's only one other way out of Paradise Valley: up and into the towering Santa Rosa Range on a steep and serpentine dirt road, over Hinckey Summit at 7,800 feet, around Windy Gap, and down again to the highway, a 40-mile rock-and-roll that dumps you off on US 95, 37 miles north of where you turned off on NV 290. One of the prettiest campgrounds in Nevada, **Lye Creek,** is up near Hinckey Summit; you'll think you hit a space warp and were transported to the Olympic Peninsula or the Amazon Basin, that's how flourishingly foliaged, florid, and forestal it is up here.

From the junction of gravel and asphalt, it's another 14 miles into **McDermitt,** an unexpectedly bustling burg right on the Oregon state line, but not so surprising when you consider that it's one of two settlements servicing the huge and wild southeast swath of the Beaver State. Stop by the **Say When Casino** for some action; there are also a few historic buildings (dating back to the late 1800s), a couple of motels and bars, a service station and snack shop, and a library. Outside of town is the Fort McDermitt Indian Reservation, strung along a scenic 13-mile road.

*(above) Sand dunes at sunrise in the Santa Rosa Range.*
*(opposite) A lichen-covered basalt boulder on the rim of High Rock Canyon.*

*Dunes and snow-dusted peaks in the Osgood Mountains of the Santa Rosa Range.*

■ GOLCONDA TO VALMY   *map page 239, A–2/3*

From Winnemucca, it's 18 miles east on I-80 to **Golconda**, founded by the railroad and sustained, on and off, by mining. Nevada 789 runs northeast out of Golconda into the old Getchell Mining District, which has produced gold, silver, and tungsten, on and off, for the past 70 years. The pavement ends after 16 miles, but the road, unpaved, continues for another 70 miles, all the way to Tuscarora *(see page 253)*. Twenty-eight miles along the gravel is **Midas**, another semi-ghost mining town that has survived since the early 1900s. It has a couple of bars, a handful of occupied singlewides, doublewides, and real houses, some ritzy (for Midas) summer homes, and tall shade trees lining the graded streets.

Twenty-three miles from Golconda east on I-80 is **Valmy**, a small roadside settlement with a motel, cafe, trailer park, and the Valmy Power Plant, which supplies electricity to most of north-central Nevada. From Valmy, it's 13 miles to Battle Mountain.

I-80 & NORTHERN NEVADA

■ BATTLE MOUNTAIN *map page 239, B–3*

Battle Mountain is an Emigrant Trail–railroad-mining-highway town of several thousand souls. The emphasis, however, is on mining—so Battle Mountain has been in somewhat dire straits since gold hit a 20-year low of $255 an ounce in mid-1999. Most of the nearby mines, which roared day and night only a few years ago, are closed; the venerable Owl Club downtown is closed; Dale's Drugs is closed. One business that's brisk is in for-sale signs.

Still, Battle Mountain isn't exactly in danger of drying up and blowing away. It's the seat of Lander County, so it performs the local administrative duties. It has a hospital, a civic center, a couple of big truck stops, a string of motels along Front Street, the Nevada Club casino (with a big restaurant and a mineral exhibit), Lemaire's old-time grocery store, and the **Trail of '49ers Interpretive Center.**

The museum (take a left on Front and another left on Second) has an interesting variety of displays, including local Native American and Overland Trail history; some antique handguns and rifles; an exhibit that answers the question, "what is an ox?"; and a big Conestoga wagon (ask someone to explain all the mechanisms, especially how the whole thing can be taken apart in five minutes). There's also a small bookstore here.

*Interstate 80 at the west entrance of the Carlin Tunnel at dusk.*

Nevada 305 heads south from Battle Mountain for 90 miles along the Reese River Valley to Austin, at the south end of Lander County. I-80 continues east for 36 miles to the exit (261) for NV 306, which heads down to **Beowawe,** a tiny railroad village in the middle of gorgeous **Whirlwind Valley,** long known for the presence of one of the largest active geyser systems in the world. Unfortunately, geothermal explorations in the early 1960s deactivated the geysers and today only a few tame puffs of steam escape through vents in the area; a large geothermal power plant shunts electricity into the Sierra Pacific grid.

Back on I-80, from exit 261, you climb into the southern Tuscarora Mountains and crest Emigrant Pass at 6,100 feet.

From there it's another 10 miles into Carlin.

■ CARLIN  *map page 239, C–3*

Carlin is a small railroad-mining-highway town—what else is new? It has an old downtown by the railroad tracks, where there are two bars, an old hotel, and a footbridge over the switching yard (the only one of its kind accessible to the public in Nevada). It has a less-old commercial district along Bush Street (on old US 40), with a Chinese restaurant, a motel, and a brothel (actually, Sharon's is outside of town near the west exit of the interstate). And it has an expanding commercial district at the east exit of the interstate, with fast food and a motel.

Scattered around town are a supermarket, ball fields, a big school complex, and a few stray eateries. Also, like Winnemucca and Battle Mountain to the east, and Elko to the west, Carlin expanded noticeably during the gold-mining boom of the early and mid-'90s; lots of new houses mushroomed up in a new subdivision west of the older houses of Carlin.

Because what Carlin is really known for is the fact that it sits at the south edge of the **Carlin Trend,** one of the most productive gold-mining locales in the world. Annual production along the trend has exceeded 1.5 million ounces for each of the last seven years. It's responsible for a large part of the $2.6 billion worth of gold mined in Nevada (1998), which adds up to three-quarters of all the gold produced in the United States, the third largest gold-producing country in the world (behind South Africa and Russia). Nevada single-handedly mines and refines one-tenth of the yearly gold production worldwide.

Nevada mines pioneered heap-leaching, where you spread your gold-bearing ore out on a pad atop an impervious plastic sheet. You heap sodium cyanide on it to leach out the gold. Then you pick up the plastic and carry it to the refinery.

Your conditions have to be hot and dry, which is why Nevada mines can produce an ounce of gold for as little as $200. Of course, that's for the most efficient and well-capitalized companies, such as Newmont and Barrick, which have a number of major mines on the Trend, both open pit and hard rock (or underground).

Most of the smaller operations working deposits along the Trend have been crushed by the recent bear market in the yellow metal, with the spot (cash) price of an ounce of gold dropping below $260 in 1999. And as we've seen, that's hurt the mining towns along I-80. But the price of gold will go up again; after all, gold has been the ultimate standard of value for thousands of years. Indeed, paper money, or fiat currency, started out as a receipt for gold; national fiat currencies have only been in wide usage for the past 100 years or so, and most of them have either changed dramatically, or disappeared, since they were introduced.

As recently as 1972, the value of the dollar was still based on the price of gold; it's only been since Richard Nixon unceremoniously dumped the gold standard that the dollar, and the rest of the world's national currencies, have floated in free space, keyed to nothing but confidence. I've heard it said that if the unit of American fiat currency were pegged to the price of gold today, one dollar would be worth around three cents, and an ounce of gold would sell for $3,500. So when the price of gold goes up, happy days will be here again for northeastern Nevada, which lives today under the same boom-bust cycle it has for a century and a half.

■ PALISADE  *map page 239, C-3*

Meanwhile, back in the travel guide, 10 miles southeast of Carlin on NV 278 is Palisade, where you'll find the remnants of an old railroad town at the one-time junction between the main transcontinental line and the Eureka & Palisade shortline. Most of the town is long gone, but what's still here is a dramatic canyon through which the river and the railroad pass, along with a tunnel or two and a trestle thrown in for good (photogenic) measure.

Back at the east exit (282) of I-80, it's another 20 miles to Elko. On this stretch the highway crosses the Humboldt River, then immediately passes through the aforementioned tunnel, cutting through the bottom of one of the Independence Mountains for a quarter-mile (thereby bestowing independence from having to go around it). This is one of three tunnels in Nevada; another runs through Cave Rock at Lake Tahoe, the third under the eastern runways of McCarran International Airport in Las Vegas (McCarran also claims the only "subway" in the state: the mile-long tube out to the new D terminal).

# ■ ELKO  *map page 239, D–2/3*

If Elko were in California, it would be that state's 216th largest town (out of 500 or so towns with populations greater than 5,000). Being in Nevada, however, Elko, with a whopping 23,000 residents, is the largest small town in the state, seventh out of 85 (towns with populations of 100 or more, that is). In fact, Elko is the largest town in an area—including northern Nevada, southwestern Idaho, southeastern Oregon, and northwestern Utah—that's roughly equivalent in size to Pennsylvania.

So on the one hand, Elko is halfway between nothing and nowhere. On the other hand, this town isn't too big for its britches. In fact, Elko fits into its britches perfectly. You might even call it the biggest little city in the state—though Renoites might raise their eyebrows. Elkoans might be surprised to hear it, but the biggest little city in Nevada is similar to the biggest big city: destined to dance to its own tune, to take its own steps toward creating its future as an important commercial center in the midst of cattle and gold, a magnetic town offering the amenities of a city five times its size.

## ◆ ELKO HISTORY

It had a head start. In the 1860s, the homesteading and mining country of the vast four-state high desert awaited the arrival of the transcontinental railroad, somewhere around Elko, with bated breath. And as soon as Elko arrived, by way of the Central Pacific in 1869, it turned into a bustling transshipment and supply center for the whole huge chunk of the central intermountain west. At the same time, it assumed municipal responsibility for half of northern Nevada as the seat of Elko

*Elko in 1876. (Nevada
Historical Society)*

*Elko County Courthouse.*

County. (It's been whittled down since, but the county still comprises the 17,000-square-mile corner of northeastern Nevada—a little smaller than West Virginia.)

Of course, being so remote, if it intended to grow, it had to do it all on its own. Good thing Elko has had a strong streak of self-reliance since its inception. When land-grant state-university charters came up for grabs, Elko got the University of Nevada. (Couldn't hold onto it, but took it first.) In the early 1900s, it grew to meet with adequate facilities the swelling passenger counts coming through on the railroad; grew some more in the 1920s when the Victory Highway, and through automobile traffic, started showing up; and even grew to service the first commercial airplanes flying around the west.

Elko then embraced wide-open gambling when it became law in 1931; the magnetism from that was magic. A few years later, Elko went into the entertainment business: bright lights, 24-hour casinos, plentiful brothels, even big-name live acts. In the 1980s, when the railroad was getting in the way of downtown traffic, Elko up and moved the tracks to the edge of town, right next to the Humboldt River. No other railroad town in Nevada has ever pulled that off, and the railroad is still in the way of downtown traffic in all of the other towns along the main line.

I-80 & NORTHERN NEVADA

### ◆ ELKO TODAY

Elko has a 900-seat convention center, community college, downhill ski slope, major regional museum, orchestra, and theater company. It has hotel-casinos, motels with indoor swimming pools, Basque restaurants galore, the Cowboy Poetry Gathering, Wal-Mart, four brothels, and traffic jams. It's headquarters for one of the biggest mining districts in the world, so big that even the depressed state of gold-mining hasn't dampened the local boom.

What's more, Elko is the gateway to an incomparably vast, rugged, and remote part of the state. The big outdoors hereabouts is in the heart of Elko, since Elko is at the heart of it. The remote ranches and mines. The Ruby Mountains, just southeast of town, the most gorgeous and grand of all the ranges in the state. Ruby Valley's 38,000-acre national wildlife refuge, a full-scale bulrush marsh. The big Independence Range north of town, and the heartbreakingly beautiful Independence Valley. The Jarbidge wilderness area, and the Owyhee River, which drains north, out of the Great Basin, into the Snake River.

After all that, it's plain to see why Elko has a streak of independence as wide as, well, the distance between it and a couple of capital cities. Elko has been known to be at odds with Carson City officials and policies and judicial rulings and the like. But more importantly, Elko is the birthplace, the spiritual home, of the Sagebrush Rebellion, rural Nevada's antagonism toward Washington, D.C. Two state senators from around Elko County enflamed the 1979 Nevada Legislature to approve a legal battle to force the feds to return the 60 million acres of Nevada it claimed it owned. This turned out be a symbolic gesture in the end, as little Nevada gave up when faced with the threat of a fight to the finish by U.S. attorneys, financed by U.S. taxpayers. Unexpectedly, Nevada also found itself lined up against the sportsmen and environmental lobbies, which claimed that if Nevada controlled all its own land, the state would be taken over by special interests.

But damned if that Sagebrush Rebellion doesn't endure—even grow—and flare up every now and again hereabouts. Lately, Elko County has been into it big time with the National Forest Service. It's a typical disagreement over the Forest Service refusing to repair a flood-damaged road up near Jarbidge, to restore long-standing public access to fishing, hunting, and camping. It got heated for a while in 1999 and *almost* escalated into a good old-fashioned confrontation. The Sagebrush Rebellion is alive in the hearts of the people, where municipal rebellions against the central authorities always hit the same bullseye: regional rights, and by extension, individual rights.

## ◆ SIGHTS IN ELKO

First stop in Elko should be at the **Northeastern Nevada Museum,** on Idaho Street on the east side of town. This city-caliber facility is spacious, professional, fascinating. Displays include wildlife, gold, the Basques, buckaroos, the railroad, even a Chinese exhibit from the railroad-building days. After spending an hour in the museum, you'll be ready to buy a book or poster or piece of art in the gift shop.

Also be sure to stop by **J. M. Capriola's** buckaroo outfitters and saddlemakers, corner of Commercial and Fifth right downtown. Not outfitters for "cowboys," mind you, those ranch hands down in Texas and out in Montana who don't know how to do things in style. These accessories are strictly for buckaroos, the elite ranch hands from Nevada, Idaho, and Washington who want custom saddles and silver bridles, who want to rope and ride with grace; who want to take showers every couple of days. Anyway, downstairs Capriola's sells ranch and Western wear; upstairs is the saddlery, where you can watch artisans hand-produce them.

From there, cross the square (Commercial and Railroad Streets, which seem oddly arranged until you remember that what's missing are the railroad tracks) to the **Western Folklore Center,** home of the **Cowboy Poetry Gathering.** Poke around the gift shop for Western books and music, and posters of the various

*Many of the Basques who settled in northern Nevada continued the sheepherding tradition of their ancestors in the Pyrenees. (Northeastern Nevada Museum, Elko)*

*A poet recites his work at the annual Cowboy Poetry Gathering in Elko. (photo by Penn Jensen)*

Gatherings. The Cowboy Poetry Gathering is Elko's biggest event of the year; taking place in January (the 16th annual was in 2000), it's also northern Nevada's biggest event of the winter. This weekend of poetry recitals, Western music, art exhibits, seminars on ranching issues, and private get-togethers takes over the entire town, no less than Hot August Nights does Reno or Comdex does Vegas. The big summer event is the **National Basque Festival** held over Fourth of July weekend. Elko doesn't do anything in a small way.

For casinos, Elko has the ancient **Commercial Hotel,** which hearkens all the way back to year one: 1869. The Commercial was one of Nevada's first major casinos, along with Harold's Club (Reno), the Las Vegas Club, and the Silver Smith (Wendover). The Commercial's first casino boss added a 200-seat lounge to the joint and booked national acts—Ted Lewis, Sophie Tucker, Chico Marx—into Elko. Thus began the casino tradition of headliners in the showrooms. It's dinky and a little dingy, but check out the White King, a one-ton polar bear, on display.

Across the square is **Stockmen's,** the Commercial's brother hotel-casino: a big pit, slots, a sports bar, and a popular coffee shop. On the eastern, more recently developed end of Idaho Street is the **Red Lion Inn**—the biggest casino outside of Reno and Las Vegas, with a pit that fits two crap tables, tons of slots and video poker, buffet, gourmet room, disco, and bona fide hotel (rather than motel) rooms.

## ■ NORTH OF ELKO: TAYLOR CANYON TO JARBIDGE CANYON

Only two paved, and two unpaved, main roads pierce the northern heart of Elko County. Nevada 225, a.k.a the Mountain City Highway, runs east, up and over the minor Adobe Range, then turns north, paralleling the major Independence Mountains. Twenty-seven miles from town, you come to the junction with NV 226 to Tuscarora. **Taylor Canyon Resort** is here, famous locally for its annual "game feed and dance." Hunters and anglers bring whatever meat they have left over from last season—deer, elk, wild boar, bobcat, sage grouse, duck, and all kinds of fish; the resort barbecues it up and serves 500 or so partygoers. There's a bar, store, rec room, laundromat showers, RV hookups, and cabins.

### ◆ TUSCARORA   *map page 239, C–2*

You pass through Taylor Canyon, a narrow wash in the hills, then drive another 15 miles to the turnoff (left) onto a graded gravel road to Tuscarora. This near-ghost town was the site of a 15-year boom in the 1870s and early '80s; at the peak of the boom, Tuscarora was larger than Elko. At the nadir of the bust, less than 10 people kept the town alive. Then, in the 1960s, Dennis Parks, a potter from southern California, stumbled across Tuscarora, moved in, set up a pottery shop and school, and proceeded not only to put Tuscarora back on the map, but to transform it into an imperative pilgrimage for potters internationally. In so doing, Parks added a new designation to the long list of different kinds of Nevada towns: art town. The pottery studio is in the old hotel, behind the post office. A few other artists call Tuscarora home; anyone you bump into here will show you around if they have time. But remember: this isn't a ghost town. It's people's property. Show some consideration.

From Tuscarora, the gravel road runs 42 miles west to Midas *(see page 244)*.

Back on NV 226, you continue north up Independence Valley, stunning ranch country occupying the well-watered bottomlands at the base of the Independences. Around 20 miles from the Tuscarora turnoff, the pavement ends; from there it's another 40 or so rugged back-route miles into Owyhee, the small reservation town for the Duck Valley Shoshone-Paiute Reservation.

You can also take a winding road through the Independences by going right at a fork at Jack Creek and driving through the shadow of 10,000-foot Jacks Peak back to the pavement of NV 225. Another right-hand fork in five miles at Deep Creek also leads to pavement, a lower and longer route through the Bull Run Hills.

I-80 & NORTHERN
NEVADA

◆ WILDHORSE STATE
RECREATION SITE
*map page 239, D–1/2*

Whichever way you go, make sure you get to Wildhorse State Recreation Site, roughly 70 miles north of Elko on NV 225. This large reservoir impounds Owyhee River water; you can boat, fish, camp, and shower here. Across the road from the park entrance is the turnoff to Jarbidge; we'll be returning here in a couple of paragraphs. A bit north is the **Wildhorse Dam,** and the **Wildhorse Crossing Forest Service campground,** with 17 sites on the densely vegetated riverbank.

Heading north, you meander through spectacular **Owyhee Canyon.**

*Since very little wood was available, the mill site and smelter (above) at Tuscarora was fueled by sagebrush. (below) Sagebrush is fed into the mill's boiler. (courtesy Stanley W. Paher)*

The Owyhee River runs northwest into Oregon and eventually empties into the Snake River west of Nampa, Idaho. You emerge from the canyon into flat ranchland, then come into **Mountain City**, a small town left over from a copper-mining boom of the 1930s and '40s; here you'll find a big service station, a jam-packed general store, a Forest Service ranger station, a few motels, bars, and a steakhouse.

Twelve miles north of Mountain City, just south of the Idaho state line, is **Owyhee**, the reservation village. Check out the stone architecture—administrative buildings, church, community center. There's also a school, a big hospital, motel, and general store.

◆ JARBIDGE  *map page 239, D–1*

Back on NV 225 at Wildhorse State Recreation Area is the turnoff to the road to Jarbidge. This is 60 miles of graded (you hope recently) dirt, passing through ranchland, canyonland, gorgeland, plateauland, and bottomland. Finally you come to the Jarbidge River and a T-junction: Take a right (south) to get to Jarbidge, one of the most remote towns—by the time you get here you'll swear it's *the most* remote town—on the continent.

Pop quiz, true or false: Jarbidge is an old mining semi-ghost town that produced for a couple of decades in the early 1900s and has since been kept alive by a handful of die-hards and recluses. (The answer will appear in the second edition of this guide.)

Jarbidge claims a couple dozen year-round residents, friendly folk who are happy you made it there. It has a small store, a couple of bars (the Outdoor Inn burned to the ground in November 1999, but it's on track to be rebuilt), a service station, a bed-and-breakfast, and a bunch of campgrounds. (The washed-out road to the more remote campgrounds is the one in contention between the feds and Elko County.) Also peek into the old jailhouse, the community hall, and schoolhouse. Mostly, though, if you've come this far, you just want to kick back and really leave it all behind.

You can backtrack all the way to Wildhorse on the dirt road if you're so inclined, but you don't have to. By returning to the T-junction and continuing north on the access road, you pass **Desert Hot Springs**, a remote resort with hot tubs, warm swimming pool, and cafe, bar, cabins, and a campground. From there the road climbs up and out of **Jarbidge Canyon**, crosses the state line into Idaho, and hits pavement. From there it's about 30 miles to the tiny town of Rogerson on US 93; take a right and head back south 18 miles to Jackpot and Nevada.

## A NIGHT OUT IN JARBIDGE

*My Hammond World Atlas* lists Jarbidge, NV, as having a population of 11. But I know better. There must be 50 or more souls, maybe fewer in the dead of winter. It was a Saturday afternoon in early September that we rode into town. Our group of riders from the Cottonwood Ranch, four of us paying customers and three cowboys, led by Aggie, had just spent five days and four nights crossing the Jarbidge Wilderness. Some people rode out in a jeep and met us with a few beers about three miles from town. We rested ourselves and our mounts—and, of course, drank the beer. We came up with the idea that Banjo Bob, one of our group, should play his banjo as we ambled into town, but Aggie was afraid that the banjo playing might spook the horse and that Bob would be thrown flat on his face. (This could've been true, but also Bob had consumed a lot of beer, and maybe would have fallen on his own.) So Aggie started tying Banjo Bob onto his horse and saddle. This entrance was a big event for the Cottonwood group, and for Bob as well, because Jarbidge was his adopted home town. At night when we'd sit around the campfire, Bob would get kind of dreamy and say, "I'm just so glad I found Jarbidge." And he was, too.

So down the road we went, with Bob leading the pack. The horses were feisty. This was the end of the trail and they knew there was alfalfa at the other end of town. And Bob, he played his heart out, and his horse jumped around, but Bob kept playing. And the townspeople came to their front doors and gates and yelled "whoopie," and cried out, "Look it's Bob, on horseback!" or "Good for you, Bob!" They all clapped, too, as we passed. It was as if we were cavalry home from patrol, or cowboys home from the drive. We *were* proud. The townsfolk knew that Aggie could call a mean Virginia Reel, and that Banjo Bob could strum that music for an hour, minimum. So it was that Saturday night, at a bar called the Outdoor Inn, that I'll never forget.

The place was packed with townfolk who'd gathered to dance (not that drink wasn't flowing mightily, too). Aggie stood up, donning his weathered Stetson with the eagle feather poking up high, and called out, "Ladies and Gents, choose your partners for the Virginia Reel." Linda, who'd ridden over the mountains with us, and I quickly partnered up. So did 30 or 40 others. Folks pushing 80 years or more, and boys and girls just shy of teenage. Wearing cowboy hats, bill caps, boots, heels, bare feet, jeans, flouncy skirts.

Lance, a 20-odd-year-old itinerant piano player (with ever so many teeth missing, but smiling just the same) started up like a house afire, and Banjo Bob joined in, just strumming away to beat all. And Aggie was calling, "Promenade, and swing your partners, do si do." And after every progression, a new partner, a new do-si-do. The sweat poured down and sometimes in the promenade a man would fall down—especially one fellow also called Bob, the much loved town mechanic, I think. "Get up Bob," and "Look where you're going, Bob," the others chided. And Bob, drunk and good-natured, would get up and start whirling again.

Relentless was the music. The steps, at first easy, became a struggle as our bodies tired. And we couldn't stop laughing. I think everyone was laughing. Here we were, the gathering of a tribe, dancing away in a dimly lighted saloon in the middle of 100 square miles of wilderness. Far removed, and the better for it. That night Jarbidge was the Old West in all its glory.

—E. Roger Thompson, 2000

*Marys River Peak at 10,565 feet looms over Emerald Lake in the Jarbidge Wilderness Area.*

### ■ SOUTH OF ELKO: RUBY MOUNTAINS *map page 239, D–3/4*

Stand anywhere above Idaho Street in Elko and look south: you see such gloriously jagged scenery that you'll be itching to don hiking boots and head for the hills. It's easy. Just head out NV 227, a good four-lane commuter road to Spring Creek, Elko's sprawling suburb (in case you were wondering where all the people lived). In another 10 miles, you'll come to a turnoff that takes you into Lamoille Canyon and up to Ruby Mountain Scenic Area. First, though, drive a mile past the intersection to tool around **Lamoille**, a picturesque little village tucked into an idyllic location at the foot of the mighty Rubies, with a general store, bar and grill, dinner house, bed-and-breakfast, and central park.

Then head back to, and up, **Lamoille Canyon Road**, which runs 12 miles between the two towering metamorphic walls cut down over the eons by glaciers and Thomas Creek. Halfway up is **Thomas Creek Campground**, so lush with tall conifers, aspens, willow shrubs, and fireweed (blooming in late July) that you

might think you're in south central Alaska. The creek roars right through the middle of it all.

Back on Lamoille Canyon Road, waterfalls tumble down the steep canyon walls. At the back of the canyon the road ends at a big parking lot, where hikers jump out of their minivans, SUVs, and pickups and hit the trails. The Liberty Pass Trail heads a mile and a half up the mountain; there's so much monkshood, lupine, willow, and Mormon tea that you might think you're in south*eastern* Alaska. You pass a couple of kettles before reaching **Liberty Pass**, at 10,500 feet, with more lakes, and the **Ruby Crest Trail** continuing 40 miles south along the ridgetops.

Another trip into the wilderness south of Elko starts at the intersection of NV 227 and 228, just before you get to Spring Creek. Nevada 228 heads due south for 30 miles, running through the tiny village of **Jiggs**, then crossing the Rubies at Harrison Pass (7,247 feet), the south terminus of the Ruby Crest Trail. Ruby Valley and the Ruby Lake National Wildlife Refuge await at the eastern foot of the

*Haystacks and grazing cattle along Highway 228 in Elko County.*

*(previous pages) The spectacular Ruby Mountains as seen from near the historic Hastings Cutoff along the Emigrant Trail.*

*The bucolic town of Lamoille rests in a lush valley at the foot of the Ruby Mountains just southeast of Elko.*

mountains. Here you'll find refuge headquarters, a campground, and the extensive riparian habitat for hundreds of species of birds and fish.

■ WELLS   *map page 239, E-2*

Fifty miles east of Elko on I-80 is Wells, an Emigrant Trail–railroad-highway-mining-ranching town with a west and east exit off the interstate, not unlike—which won't come as any surprise—Battle Mountain, Winnemucca, and Lovelock. It has a historic (the polite way of saying derelict) railroad downtown on Seventh Street. Sixth Street is old US 40, with the motels, gas stations, and bars. At the east exit is the junction with US 93; the 4-Way casino and Lucky J's truck-stop casino are on either side of the interstate.

Just outside of Wells is what's left of **Metropolis**, an ill-fated reclamations experiment, the only agricultural ghost town in Nevada. The front wall of the old school is all that's left (head out Eighth Street and follow it into the desert about 10 miles).

I-80 & NORTHERN
NEVADA

South of town (take Humboldt Ave. under the west exit, then follow the sign to the right) is the route to Clover Valley and Hole in the Mountain Peak *(covered in the US 93 chapter)* and up into the **East Humboldt Range**. The mountain road climbs 11 miles straight toward Grey's Peak (10,674 feet). Seven miles up is Angel Creek Campground: 18 sites in a small arroyo with shade trees and drinking water. Four miles up from there is Angel Lake Campground: 26 sites in an open bowl at 8,400 feet with the small mountain kettle good for some fishing and small motorless boating.

### ■ EAST TO WENDOVER   *map page 239, F–3*

From Wells, it's 60 miles to West Wendover on the Utah line. About 35 miles east of Wells, you crest **Silver Zone Pass** (5,940 feet) in the Toana Range, then drop into **Pilot Peak Valley,** with the eponymous peak standing proudly and symmetrically to the north. The base of Pilot Peak provided the emigrants on the California trail with their first fluids and forage in a three-day sinus-scorching, retina-roasting trudge across the Great Salt Lake Desert.

Nearing Wendover, you climb a minor rise, round a bend, and get the whole view east—of West Wendover in Nevada, Wendover in Utah, and the blinding Bonneville Salt Flats to the east, crossed by the gunmetal-gray belt of the interstate. If you view the salt flats through binoculars, you can actually see the dark road bow as it crosses the broad expanse of level white plain. How can the road arc on a flat surface? Is it a mirage? An optical illusion? The concrete contractor's nightmare? None of the above. This is simply one of the few places on the planet from which you can readily discern the curvature of the Earth.

### ■ WEST WENDOVER   *map page 239, F–3*

Like Stateline at Lake Tahoe, Wendover is a good-sized border town with a split personality—the exciting half in Nevada, the prosaic half in Utah (big surprise). Wendover's environment is otherworldly, mostly surrounded by the Bonneville Salt Flats, the heavily mineralized bottom of mighty Lake Bonneville (of which Utah's Great Salt Lake is a mud-puddle remnant). Wendover's 100-year history is no less quirky, encompassing the railroad, mining, land-speed records, casino gambling, and the atom bomb.

The town was founded in 1900 by the Western Pacific as a service stop, the water piped ten miles from Pilot Peak. A decade later, speed freaks discovered that conditions on the salt flats were perfect for cranking cars up to breakneck speeds, and land-speed records were set here well into the 1970s. In the 1920s, a desert rat named Jim Smith opened a service station on the new Highway 40, which he expanded into the Silver Smith casino. During World War II, the U.S. Army built a three-million-acre air force training range; five years later, the crew of *Enola Gay* trained here before dropping one of the atom bombs on Japan.

Today, West Wendover has a **Nevada Welcome Center,** where you can pick up area and statewide information. Five major casinos include the original (though greatly expanded) Silver Smith, the adjoining State Line (fronted by the neon Wendover Will), Peppermill, Rainbow, and Red Garter. **Wendover, Utah,** has the **Speedway Museum,** full of exhibits on the fast cars and their drivers, the sprawling concrete apron of the old air base, and the salt flats themselves, stretching east and curving, visibly, over the horizon.

*Nevada greets you at West Wendover on the Utah border.*

# US 50: LAKE TAHOE &
## C E N T R A L   N E V A D A

**■ HIGHLIGHTS**   *page*

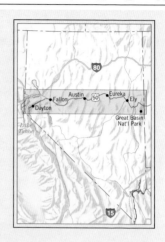

**■ TRAVEL OVERVIEW**

US Highway 50 is a 415-mile roller coaster of a road that cuts a curvy and bobbing swath right across the waist of Nevada. Climbing over mountain passes and traversing wide basins, US 50 follows the route of the Overland Stage and Pony Express operations of the 1850s and '60s; the transcontinental telegraph was also laid along this right-of-way. The transcontinental Lincoln Highway was surveyed in the 1920s and was later upgraded to US Highway status. But it always played second fiddle to the northern route across Nevada—the Emigrant Trail–Central Pacific–Victory Highway–US 40–Interstate 80 right-of-way—and it still does.

In other words, the vast majority of Nevada passers-through blow across the state at 75 m.p.h. on I-80. Still, a daredevil minority takes the rollicking ride on what's been called "the Loneliest Road in America." It's several hundred miles shorter than the epic north-south US highways through Nevada, but no less of an adventure: In the 250 miles between the large towns of Fallon and Ely, for example, there are only two settlements—two gas stations and no fast food between them.

If you're traveling across Nevada on US 50, that means you're starting at Lake Tahoe and ending at Great Basin National Park, or vice versa. Talk about spectacular bookends to a ten-hour drive in the country.

**Getting Around**

You're on your own out here. It's essentially cars, RVs, SUV, PU, and the occasional service vehicle; even the Highway Patrol barely exists. You might see some cyclists: US 50 has become something of a destination for two-wheel human-powered road rallyers.

Because US 50 cuts the state in half, a number of roads peel off to the north and south: US 395 in Carson City, Alternate 95 in Silver Springs, US 95 in Fallon, NV 361 to Gabbs, NV 305 to Battle Mountain, NV 376 to Tonopah, NV 278 to Carlin, and US 93 in Ely. You're even more on your own on most of these.

**Food and Lodging**

Lake Tahoe has a ton of both, as does Carson City. Dayton has a little of the former and none of the latter. In Fallon you have a choice of nearly 500 rooms, though there's not much difference between a Comfort Inn and a Budget Inn. Fallon is similar in the food department: Would you prefer a Happy Meal or a Smiley Meal?

I once spent the night in Austin in a room where I could sit on the toilet, shave at the sink, and wash my hair under the shower all at the same time. The other 38 rooms in town are similar. And if you stop to eat in one of Austin's coffee shops, make sure you have a lot of time.

Eureka actually has some lodging variety, with a beautifully restored inn, a 100-year-old hotel, and a brand new Best Western. The food is similar, with a great restaurant at the inn and a couple local institutions.

Ely has the Nevada Hotel, Holiday Inn, and a couple of upscale motels, plus enough fast food to get by. Baker has a motel and, amazingly, both a bar and grill and a diner, right next to each other. But bring all your food and lodging with you to Great Basin National Park.

# ■ "THE LONELIEST ROAD IN AMERICA"

US 50 cuts across the wide middle of the United States, starting gloriously from Ocean City, Maryland, and ending abruptly in Sacramento, California. (In the early 1970s as a reckless young hippie, I hitchhiked the entire length of US 50, walking through most of St. Louis and Kansas City to avoid the interstates, catching a ride with a Colorado State Trooper to get past a prison near Canon City, and finally getting busted by a CHPman on an entrance ramp to I-80 in Sacramento, where I then spent four hours in jail on account of a bench warrant on a guy from Stockton with my exact name, age, and description before it all got straightened out and I was shuttled to the Trailways depot and told to get outta town.)

US 50 is one of the oldest, longest, and most intact of all the old US highways, stretching 3,200 miles across the "backbone of America." In the process, it stretches 415 miles across the backbone of Nevada, from Stateline at South Lake Tahoe to just east of Great Basin National Park. The topography it crosses can best be described as corrugated, shaped by tectonic forces into parallel ridges and grooves; you crest a dozen different mountain summits and cruise another dozen valley floors along the way.

The road passes the towering temples of treasure just over the California state line and travels briefly through the massive granite Sierra Nevada before descending, literally and figuratively, to the hallowed halls of government at the state capital, Carson City. Then it settles down to the serious business of traversing Nevada's desert basins and ranges, pausing for a handful of remote but well-spaced towns, four having to do with mining, two with farming.

Though no one in the state department of tourism has ever been able to cite chapter and verse from the *LIFE* magazine that supposedly named it "the loneliest road in America" (in fact, it was probably *TRAILER LIFE* magazine that did so), and though many roads in Nevada are much more solitary and forsaken than this rollicking route, you'll notice a few remnants of a well-worn "I Survived The Loneliest Road" promotional campaign as you travel along US 50 in outback Nevada.

## ■ THE Y JUNCTION AND WEST SHORE  *map page 268, B&C–6*

In California, US 50 heads east from Sacramento, winds through the Sierra south of Lake Tahoe, climbs over Echo Summit (elevation 7,382 feet), then turns north at the small settlement of **Meyers** (a.k.a. Tahoe Paradise). Five miles north of Meyers is the fork in the road known as the **Y** Junction: Highway 89 bears left, hugging

# BASIN AND RANGE

*B*asin. Fault. Range. Basin. Fault. Range. A mile of relief between basin and range. Stillwater Range. Pleasant Valley. Tobin Range. Jersey Valley. Sonoma Range. Pumpernickel Valley. Shoshone Range. Reese River Valley. Pequot Mountains. Steptoe Valley. Ondographic rhythms of the Basin and Range. We are maybe forty miles off the interstate, in the Pleasant Valley Basin, looking up at the Tobin Range....

We are looking at a new seismic scar that runs as far as we can see. It runs along the foot of the mountains, along the fault where the basin meets the range. From out in the valley, it looks like a long, buff-painted, essentially horizontal stripe. Up close, it is a gap in the vegetation, where plants growing side by side were suddenly separated by several meters, where, one October evening, the basin and the range—Pleasant Valley, Tobin Range—moved, all in an instant, apart. They jumped sixteen feet. The erosion rate at which the mountains were coming down was an inch a century. So in the mountains' contest with erosion they gained in one moment about twenty-thousand years. These mountains do not rise like bread. They sit still for a long time and build up tension, and then suddenly jump. Passively, they are eroded for millennia, and then they jump again. They have been doing this for about eight million years. This fault, which jumped in 1915, opened like a zipper far up the valley, and, exploding into the silence, tore along the mountain base for upward of twenty miles with a sound that suggested a runaway locomotive.

—John McPhee, *Basin and Range*

the west lakeshore up to Tahoe City, while US 50 veers right, heading straight for the craziness of South Lake Tahoe and Stateline. Factory outlet stores and Tahoe Valley Campground (a huge RV resort) are right at the intersection.

I wanted to launch right into the epic journey on US 50 through Nevada, but my editor prevailed upon me to take a quick detour around the lake.

"But that's the other state," I argued, "the liberal one, with all the victim-disarmament laws, where I'd be a hardened felon just for having my Russian military-surplus SKS semi-automatic carbine in my gun safe."

"Please?" she said.

That did it. I mean, if you knew my editor, who's talented, patient, and gorgeous, you'd be happy to oblige too. And I'll just leave my guns at home.

### ◆ CAMP RICHARDSON

Anyway, roughly five miles north of the **Y** on Hwy. 89 is **Camp Richardson,** one of the two largest and most diverse full-service resorts (along with Zephyr Cove on the Nevada side) on the lake; the highway runs right through the middle of it. Camp Richardson boasts a string of fantastic white-sand beaches; a huge campground under the pines, cabins, restaurant, and convenience store; marina and pier (with boat launch, repair shops, rentals, and kayaking, waterskiing, parasailing, windsurfing, and Sea Dooing); bike repair shop, rentals, and trails; equestrian center, stables, and trails; volleyball and other beach activities; and cross-country skiing and snowshoeing (right on the beach) in winter.

### ◆ POPE-BALDWIN RECREATION AREA AND TALLAC HISTORIC SITE

Next door to Camp Richardson is the Pope-Baldwin Recreation Area and Tallac Historic Site. Stop in for a stroll around the 150-acre grounds of three summer homes remaining from Tahoe's early 1900s "Era of Opulence." **The Baldwin House,** built in 1921, represents the estate of Elias "Lucky" Baldwin (read about his incredible life story in the museum inside), who built and operated the Tallac Resort, known as the "greatest casino in America" in its day (late 1800s). Next door, the **Pope House** is the most luxurious of the old mansions on this side of the lake; check out the honeymoon cabin and the boathouses (with railroad tracks leading into the water to float the cabin cruisers). Various historic and artistic programs are presented here during the summer, including the Great Gatsby Days festival. **The Heller House,** also known as Valhalla, is the youngest and smallest of the three, used for community and private events.

Trails criss-cross the grounds. One leads down to the Forest Service's small **Taylor Creek Visitor Center,** featuring various exhibits, interpretive programs, and nature walks. You can also pick up stinkin' permits to hike and camp on land claimed by Washington, D.C. overseers, and browse the books, maps, and posters for sale. **The Rainbow Trail** leads from the visitors center to the **Stream Profile Chamber,** which offers a look below the surface of Taylor Creek (as it runs from Fallen Leaf Lake into Lake Tahoe). Floor-to-ceiling picture windows give a trout's-eye view of the ecosystem; other exhibits inform about the greater ecology of the area.

◆ EMERALD BAY   *map page 268, B–5/6*

Four miles west of Tallac along Hwy. 89 is Emerald Bay, a three-mile-long and one-mile-wide mini-fjord, gouged out by massive glaciers in the mists of history and famed for its symmetry and serenity. Smack dab in the middle of Emerald Bay is Fannette, Tahoe's only island; atop Fannette's 150-foot rocky peak are the ruins of a stone Tea House, built in 1928. The road makes a U high above the bay, curving around Emerald Bay State Park. Check out the whole eye-popping panorama from the Emerald Bay overlook, if you can find a parking place.

A steep mile-long trail from the lookout leads down to **Vikingsholm,** a 38-room replica of a 1,000-year-old Viking castle, built out of materials native to the area, in 1929. You can tour the castle to see the furnishings—Scandinavian antiques and custom period reproductions; the sod roof sprouts wildflowers each spring. Carry down a snack or picnic lunch to fortify, at picnic tables along the

*A recreational steamer—the* Tahoe—*crosses the lake, circa 1920. (Nevada Historical Society)*

gray-sand beach, for the clutch climb back to the car. If you're wondering why you're panting so hard on the hike up, it's either that daily pack of Pall Malls or the 6,200-foot elevation. To avoid a coronary infarction, make use of the strategically placed benches and stone culverts to rest on—if you can find a parking place.

◆ D. L. BLISS STATE PARK  *map page 268, B–5*

Next stop is D. L. Bliss State Park, the last large chunk of the vast local holdings of Duane LeRoy Bliss, a 19th-century lumber, shipping, and banking magnate who once owned most of the Tahoe Basin. The Bliss family deeded the land, including three miles of shoreline, as a park to the state 70 years ago. Bliss is a favorite family camping area, with 170 wooded secluded sites just up from the water, striking rock formations (including enormous **Balancing Rock,** which rests on a fist of gneiss), and hiking trails. One leads to the promontory (complete with lighthouse ruins) at the end of **Rubicon Point,** the lake's deepest dropoff from the shoreline; another heads five miles along the shore back to Vikingsholm Castle.

◆ SUGAR PINE POINT STATE PARK  *map page 268, B–4*

Eight miles north of Bliss State Park is 2,000-acre Sugar Pine Point State Park. The main attraction here is the Ehrman Mansion, a three-story stone-and-shingle summer home built in 1903; you can explore the mansion, along with a number of surrounding structures. General Phipps's log cabin, nearby, was built in the 1860s. A number of trails meander through the park, including a nature trail through a preserve and a five-mile stroll along General Creek. Here also starts the 10-mile biking trail to Tahoe City.

Within those 10 miles you'll pass Meeks Bay Resort, the tiny settlement of Tahoma, the popular ski and snowboard resort town of Homewood (look left to see the ski slope, which runs almost all the way down to the highway), and the small Tahoe City suburb of Sunnyside.

■ CALIFORNIA NORTH SHORE  *map page 268, A&B–1-3*

Even though Tahoe City sits only a few miles north of the middle of Tahoe's *west* shore, it's always categorized as a north-shore town. Regardless of the eccentricities of its geographical categorization, Tahoe City is the oldest, and second largest, settlement on the California side of the lake, established in 1863, with a population of 6,000 or so crammed into less than a dozen residential streets and a teeming little commercial district.

*(following pages) Mule ears bloom on the slopes above Lake Tahoe in summer.*

# TAHOE AREA SKI RESORTS

| SKI RESORT TOWN/LOCATION | INFO: GENERAL *LODGING* | VERT. RISE | TRAILS | LIFTS | RIDES/ HOUR | SKIING ACRES | SNOW MAKING | X-C |
|---|---|---|---|---|---|---|---|---|
| **Alpine Meadows** Tahoe City, CA | 530-583-4232 *800-441-4423* | 1,802' | 100 | 12 | 16,000 | 2,000 | 7% | NO |
| **Boreal Mountain** Donner Summit, CA | 530-426-3666 | 500' | 41 | 10 | 13,200 | 380 | 75% | NO |
| **Diamond Peak** Incline Village, NV | 775-832-1177 | 1,840' | 30 | 6 | 7,900 | 655 | 75% | 35k |
| **Donner Ski Ranch** Donner Summit, CA | 530-426-3635 | 750' | 50 | 6 | 7,800 | 400 | 15% | NO |
| **Granlibakken Ski Res.** Tahoe City, CA | 530-583-4242 | 300' | 1 | 2 | 500 | 10 | 0% | 3k |
| **Heavenly Ski Resort** Stateline, NV | 775-586-7000 | 3,500' | 82 | 27 | 29,000 | 4,800 | 69% | NO |
| **Homewood Mt. Res.** Homewood, CA | 530-525-2992 | 1,650' | 56 | 8 | 8,500 | 1,260 | 10% | 40k |
| **Kirkwood** Kirkwood, CA | 209-258-6000 *800-967-7500* | 2,000' | 65 | 12 | 15,600 | 2,300 | 2% | 80k |
| **Mt. Rose Ski Area** Tahoe Meadows, NV | 702-849-0704 | 1,440' | 43 | 5 | 10,000 | 900 | 5% | NO |
| **Northstar-at-Tahoe** Truckee, CA | 530-582-1010 *800-GO NORTH* | 2,280' | 63 | 13 | 19,400 | 2,420 | 50% | 65k |
| **Sierra-at-Tahoe** Phillips, CA | 530-659-7453 | 2,212' | 46 | 12 | 14,920 | 2000 | 4% | NO |
| **Soda Springs** Soda Springs, CA | 530-426-1010 | 652' | 16 | 2 | 1,800 | 200 | 0% | NO |
| **Squaw Valley** USA Tahoe City, CA | 530-583-6985 | 2,850' | 100 | 30 | 49,000 | 4,000 | 12% | 18k |
| **Sugar Bowl Ski Res.** Norden, CA | 530-426-3651 | 1,500' | 84 | 13 | 15,188 | 1,500 | 27% | 328k |
| **Tahoe-Donner Dnhl.** Truckee, CA | 530-587-9400 | 600' | 14 | 4 | 2,500 | 120 | 0% | 100k |

◆ TAHOE CITY  *map page 268, A–2/3*

Tahoe City is home to numerous shops, restaurants, marinas, and historic attractions. The central spot in town is Fanny Bridge, nicknamed for the keisters of the visitors leaning over the railing to view the giant rainbow trout amassed in the deep pool beneath the bridge. A half-block from Fanny is the **Gatekeeper's Log Cabin Museum;** check out the historic exhibits and memorabilia, the research library and archives, and the extensive basket and doll collection from local and North American tribes.

A couple of blocks from Gatekeeper's, in the center of town, is the **Watson Cabin Museum,** built in 1909 as a honeymoon cottage; docents in historical costumes lead tours of the oldest building in Tahoe City; check out the indoor bathroom, one of the first at the lake. Behind the cabin is Tahoe City Commons and beach.

◆ UPPER TRUCKEE CANYON  *map page 268, A–2*

Tahoe City is the site of Lake Tahoe's only outlet, a weak and porous volcanic ledge in the rim of the lake where the Truckee River spills over the edge and begins its journey to Pyramid Lake. Tahoe is dammed here; the outlet gates control the surface level of the lake, the top six feet of which are a reservoir for the Tahoe-Reno-Pyramid-Fernley-Fallon water system. Highway 89 forks off to the west and north, following the river down Upper Truckee Canyon, past Squaw Valley, a half-dozen 8,000-plus-foot peaks, and Donner Lake (pull off here for a quick dip at the recreation area) into the town of Truckee, where it hooks up with Interstate 80. Highway 28 continues northeast around the lake to Kings Beach and Nevada.

◆ KINGS BEACH  *map page 268, B/C–1/2*

Heading northeast on Hwy. 28, you encounter the small wooded subdivisions of Lake Forest, Carnelian Bay, and Tahoe Vista, before coming into the bustling burg of Kings Beach, with its jumble of motels, shops, restaurants, and service centers strung along both sides of the road, two lanes in each direction hereabouts. Kings Beach State Recreation Area boasts one of the longest, sandiest, and busiest stretches of beach on the lake, with a profusion of water-sports concessions and volleyball courts, along with a picnic area and playground. Also here is the **North Tahoe Beach Center,** which has a beach with an enclosed swimming area, windsurfing, nonmotorized boat rentals, four volleyball courts in the sand, a 26-foot

*Sunset over Lake Tahoe.*

hot tub, barbecue and picnic area, a fitness center, a snack bar, and a clubhouse.

On the west side of town is the intersection with Hwy. 267, which cuts north for 13 miles into Truckee. On the east side of town the road climbs up Brockway Hill to the Nevada boundary; you won't need the border sign to let you know you've left behind the state where the legislators meet all year long, coming up with new and creative ways to intrude into people's lives and tinkering with (read: raising) the state income tax, and happily have entered the state with legal gambling and prostitution, and no income tax.

## ■ CRYSTAL BAY  *map page 268, B/C–1/2*

Contiguous to Kings Beach is Crystal Bay, a small border town with four casinos, a couple of restaurants, a post office, a tiny residential area, and little else. The historic **Cal-Neva** is situated on a spit of land that juts into Crystal Bay; opened in 1926, it's the only true casino-lodge in Nevada (though the casino's been shrinking and the lodge has been growing for the past decade or so). The large wood-and-stone lobby is known as the **Indian Room,** for its display on the indigenous Washoe tribe; a white stripe down the middle of it (and continuing outside through the middle of the pool) designates the California-Nevada state line. The **Tahoe Biltmore** across the street is where you'll find the real casino action in Crystal Bay, along with a sports bar (pool tables), a lounge that rocks on the weekends, and a good coffee shop (try the bargain breakfast). **Jim Kelly's Nugget** across the street is Nevada's only brick casino, and the only one that ever closes, shutting down annually each winter.

### ■ INCLINE VILLAGE

*map page 268, B/C–1/2*

From Crystal Bay it's three miles around the top end of the lake into Incline Village, one of the youngest, richest, and municipally oddest towns in Nevada. Incline dates back to the early 1960s, when an Oklahoma developer bought 5,000 acres for $5 million, master-planned a town, and began selling homesites. A one-acre lakeshore lot fetched $15,000; today, you couldn't touch such a parcel for less than several million—and that's without the 8,000-square-foot mansion on it.

*The Incline tramway carried timber from trees felled on Lake Tahoe's south shore, then transported by flume to Virginia City.*

If you're in Incline and find yourself wondering just where the village is, it's spread across nine square miles of real estate; in addition, it was laid out without a central commercial district, to prevent congestion and to preserve a natural feel. It's still privately owned: the "government company" is called the Incline Village General Improvement District, and it owns and operates the infrastructure, two golf courses, two beaches, a ski resort, and a recreation center.

Over the past 40 years, Incline has turned into Nevada's only classic alpine resort town, with more condos, real estate agents, vacation rentals, property managers, and outdoors outfitters than the rest of the state combined (at least it seems that way). But that's pretty much the whole story right there. Unless Incline is your ultimate destination—other than a cruise along Lakeshore Drive to see how the other half lives, a pit stop at the Hyatt Regency Lake Tahoe Hotel-Casino (corner of Lakeshore and Country Club Drives), a quick cruise through the shopping centers to see if any of the restaurants look inviting, or a stop at the library or visitors bureau—there's little more to occupy your time in Income Village.

■ PONDEROSA RANCH  *map page 268, C/D–1/2*

Then again, there *is* one time-gobbler hereabouts, but it's more apart *from,* rather than a part *of,* Incline. In fact, it's an entire privately owned "village" of its own. The Ponderosa Ranch is a Western theme park based on the old TV series "Bonanza." It's the kind of place in which travel writers are loathe not only to invest the price of admission (close to 10 clams), but even to set foot; the brief and vague descriptions that one guidebook scribe lifts from another (who lifted it from a third) are a dead giveaway.

But your faithful travelogue servant is here to tell you that visiting the Ponderosa Ranch is one of the coolest things to do around the whole lake—with or without kids.

The centerpiece is the log home of the television show's Cartwright family. Many of the indoor scenes during the later years of the program were taped here; tours are conducted every hour. From there, you can wander for more hours around the extensive grounds, taking in the exhibits of antique firearms, vintage coaches and carriages, and classic cars in the museum; sitting down to a meal in the cafe, snacking on a Hossburger or chop suey from Hop Sing's Kitchen, and drinking in the saloon; taking in the blacksmith shop and metal-working demonstrations, the roping-cum-comedy acts, and the wild west gunfight and stunt shows; visiting the petting zoo or putting your kids on a pony; watching a (real) wedding in the quaint chapel; panning for gold or hiking the nature trail; marveling over the huge mining machines littering the neighborhood; and trying to stay upright in the anti-gravity Mystery Mine. You can also come for breakfast: tractors pull haywagons a couple of miles up the mountain for an all-you-can-eat open-air bacon-eggs-and-pancake feed (for a few bucks tacked onto the price of admission). Work it off by strolling back down the hill to the ranch.

## ■ THE EAST SHORE: LAKE TAHOE–NEVADA STATE PARK

### ◆ SAND HARBOR *map page 268, D–2*

Four miles south of Incline Village is Sand Harbor, the main public area of Lake Tahoe–Nevada State Park. Two sides to the beach are separated by a long thin peninsula: On the south side is a sandy crescent beach; on the north side a rocky cove where you can climb, snorkel, catch crawdads, and sit in the shade of big pine trees. A half-mile boardwalk meanders around the spit; interpretive signs impart a good brief lesson in the local ecology. Since there are no concessions or services, you must bring everything you'll need (and take what's left of it home with you when you leave, please).

Six miles south of Sand Harbor is the intersection with US 50 near **Spooner Summit**. No, we're not heading east on US 50 yet, I'm sorry to write. First we have to cover the last 15 miles of Tahoe for my editor, so we'll travel west on US 50 for a few miles, then swing south for several more, finish up in Stateline and South Lake Tahoe, then (sigh) backtrack to this spot and carry on eastward. But believe me, if you knew her, you'd do it too.

### ◆ CAVE ROCK *map page 268, C–4/5*

About seven miles south of the junction, you come to Cave Rock, a solid stone promontory at the southern end of Lake Tahoe–Nevada State Park. Two tunnels, one (sorta) natural and one man-made, pierce this throat of an extinct volcano for the two-way traffic on NV 28 to pass through. Rock climbers scaled this cliff for years, insulting the Washoe Indians in the process, who consider it sacred; climbing is now prohibited. Tahoe Tessie, the lake's version of the Loch Ness monster, is reputed to live in a cavern below the outcrop. Cave Rock towers over a parking lot, lakefront picnic ground, boat launch, and rest area, which provides the best vantage point of the big formation.

◆ ZEPHYR COVE   *map page 268, C–5*

A couple of miles south of Cave Rock is Zephyr Cove, the only settlement of any size between Incline Village and Stateline and the second largest full-service family resort on the lake (after Camp Richardson). It has a lodge, eateries, cabins, a beach, a marina, an RV park and campground, a picnic area, horseback riding, boat and jet-ski rentals, parasailing, and a general store. Also here is where you catch the 550-passenger **MS *Dixie II*** sternwheeler for its sightseeing and dinner cruises to Emerald Bay, as well as the glass-bottom trimaran ***Woodwind*** for its sightseeing and champagne excursions around the lake. Note that Zephyr Cove is one of Tahoe's most congested attractions. Arrive early for anything you plan to do, to ensure a parking place and to beat the lines (also, be prepared for the pain of paying for parking).

From Zephyr Cove, it's another four miles to the turnoff for NV 207, a.k.a. Kingsbury Grade, which climbs up and over Daggett Pass (7,334 feet), then drops into Carson Valley and connects up with US 395 at Minden-Gardnerville. Less than a mile south of the intersection is Stateline.

*Fishing in Lake Tahoe from Nevada State Park. The park is also a favored location for photographing sunsets (opposite).*

■ STATELINE AND SOUTH LAKE TAHOE  *map page 268, C–5/6*

Stateline (Nevada) and South Lake Tahoe (California) are contiguous towns at the southern tip of the lake. Deke Castleman, author of *Nevada Handbook,* described it thus:

> South Lake Tahoe could be the quintessential California-Nevada border-town, a representation not only of the strange glue that binds the two together, but also of the discrete elements that differentiate each from the other. The California side of town is an elephantine freeway exit ramp, taffy-pulled into an elongated frontage road. Literally hundreds of low-rise motels, fast fooderies, service stations, shopping centers, and apartment, condo, and professional complexes all jut up like warts from one continuous Brobdingnagian asphalt parking lot, cars crawling all over it like so many Lilliputians. On the Nevada side of the border are the half-dozen or so pleasure palaces, as contained and vertical as the California side is sprawling and horizontal. These temples of temptation engorge themselves with the offerings and sacrifices of the vast hedonistic polyglot, who are then disgorged, most of them empty-handed, to sweep back across the border, regroup, and return to pay homage another day. Beyond the high-rises north along Nevada's east shore is the wilderness, naturally—the cathedrals are all that stand between the masses and the great unknown.

Couldn't've said it better myself.

◆ STATELINE RESORT-CASINOS  *map page 268, C–5/6*

Stateline has four big resort-casinos and two small low-roller joints. **Harvey's** is the oldest, dating back to the 1940s, and largest, with 740 rooms. Its lobby is a level below the casino, though the 40-foot chandelier spans both. The casino is huge, and has the best slot club of the four, if you're of a mind to feed the machines. There are also eight restaurants, health club, spa, and pool, and a hand-tooled leather mural hanging on the wall of the poker room.

**Harrah's** is one of two Nevada hotels ever to earn the coveted five-star (AAA) and five-diamond (Mobil) designations. That was a few years ago and it's now a four-star/diamond kinda place, but it's still about as good as it gets. The rooms all have two baths (phone and TV in each), a minibar, and great views. The buffet and steakhouse are on the 16th floor and the Summit gourmet room is on the 18th. The pool is indoors, the kids' arcade is huge, and a tunnel runs under the highway to connect with Harvey's.

**Caesars** (now owned by Park Place Entertainment, the gaming arm of Hilton) is the newest; it opened in 1980, which tells you something about the state of development around here. It has 440 rooms, five restaurants, including Planet Hollywood, a rockin' casino, and an indoor pool; unlike Harrah's, there's an Italian restaurant poolside (you're not allowed to dine in your swimwear, but you could, presumably, swim in your diningwear). The Circus Maximus Showroom hosts the likes of Willie Nelson, David Copperfield, George Carlin, and Tom Jones.

The 539-room **Horizon** has a cozy casino, a small buffet, and a gourmet restaurant. **Bill's** is a low-roller joint with a casual atmosphere, McDonald's, free popcorn, and a popular coffee shop. The **Lakeside Inn** is a low-rise motel-casino a half-mile from casino center at Kingsbury Grade, with a light and airy casino and a coffee shop.

◆ SOUTH LAKE TAHOE   *map page 268, C–6*

South Lake Tahoe is a sprawling mini-city that occupies 26 square miles of lakeshore, marshland, valley, and hills. US 50 runs for miles through the commercial center, lined with beaches, marinas, docks, bike trails, campgrounds, and countless motels, restaurants, souvenir shops, outfitters, and the like. Houses are crammed into subdivisions in every other available spot, from the affluent waterfront inlets of Tahoe Keys all the way up to the condos that huddle around the edges of the vast Heavenly Valley ski resort.

For a great overview of the area, ride the 50-passenger **Heavenly Tram**, which runs, year-round, 2,000 feet up the ski-resort slopes. At the top (8,200 feet) are a restaurant, cafeteria, and several trails around the mountainside. Back on the lake, the 500-passenger Hornblower's *Tahoe Queen,* a glass-bottom paddlewheeler, offers a line-up of cruises similar to those of the MS *Dixie II* out of Zephyr Cove: 90-minute happy-hour cruises, two-hour sightseeing cruises, and three-hour dinner-dance cruises. In winter the boat becomes the only waterborne ski shuttle in the world, transferring skiers from South Lake Tahoe across the lake to Squaw Valley and back.

## ■ EAST ON US 50 (FINALLY) *map this page*

Head northeast out of South Lake Tahoe, by way of Stateline, past Zephyr Cove, through Cave Rock, and up to the intersection with NV 28. Bear right at the intersection. There's a pull-out on either side of the highway at Spooner Summit (7,140 feet), where you can park your trusty steed and access the **Tahoe Rim Trail**, a 150-mile path that circles the lake along the ridgelines, at elevations between 6,300 and 9,500 feet. Nearly 20 years in the making, Tahoe Rim has six trailheads, passes through six counties and three national forests in two states, and has been all but completed.

From the summit, it's 10 S-curving miles on the four-lane highway down to the valley floor at the south end of the capital city of Carson City. *(Carson City is covered in the US 395 chapter; see pages XX).* Go left on Business 50 (a.k.a. Business 395, a.k.a. Carson Street) and creep through town (you'll get up to 25 m.p.h. if you're lucky). Watch for the signs and take a right on US 50 (a.k.a. Williams Street), where you'll leave the local and 395 traffic behind and pick up a little speed as US 50 gets outta town. Still, it's another five miles to the outskirts of the capital; two miles beyond is the intersection with NV 341 to Virginia City, and two miles beyond that is the little village of Dayton.

## ■ DAYTON AND BEYOND *map this page, A/B–1/2*

Dayton grew up in the 1850s, at the base of Gold Creek, a little rivulet that flowed down the east slope of the Virginia Range and emptied into the Carson River a few miles east of the base of the Sierra. Prospectors, a few hopeful ones on their way to the Mother Lode but mostly disappointed ones on their way back

# FORT CHURCHILL STATE HISTORIC PARK
*map page 284, B–1/2*

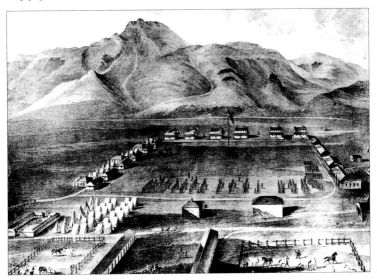

Fort Churchill, Nevada's first and largest permanent Army base, was established in 1860 (above) to protect Overland Route travelers as well as miners from Paiute Indian attack. Later, the fort served as a recruitment center for soldiers during the Civil War; it also protected Pony Express riders.

The fort became obsolete upon completion of the transcontinental railroad. It was auctioned for $750 in 1871, and later briefly served as an Indian school. The ruins today stand 26 miles east of Dayton on Fort Churchill Road. *(top image, Nevada Historical Society)*

from it, discovered gold along Gold Creek in 1849. Over the next several years, miners followed the indications up Gold Creek into Gold Canyon in the Virginia Range, settling Gold Hill in the process. Finally, in 1859, two Irish prospectors stuck a pickax right into Sun Mountain and unearthed the fabled Comstock Lode.

Recently, Dayton's promoters have claimed it to be the oldest settlement in Nevada. So does Genoa down the road, site of the territory's first Mormon trading post and agricultural settlement. It's an interesting controversy, extravagantly described by Guy Rocha, the state archivist, as a "classic dispute [that] pits those who embrace the Jeffersonian ideal of the yeoman farmer and the primacy of agrarian frontier settlement patterns against the proponents of dynamic mining camps as the archetype settlement in the West." Though the evidence leans toward Genoa as older, it's so close (mere months apart) that, in my book, it's your call.

The west side of Dayton falls within the Comstock Historic District, and it remains—you guessed it—a historic district. Take a left off US 50 onto Main Street at the traffic light. In old downtown are the Old Corner Bar and Steak House and the Wild Horse Saloon and Gold Canyon Steakhouse, along with Butcher Block Antiques, the Union Hotel, the old firehouse and jail, and the restored Bluestone Building. Odeon Hall, the town's one-time concert hall, is now **Mia's Swiss Restaurant.** The owner entertains patrons by yodeling during dinner. No kidding. The schoolhouse downtown is Nevada's second oldest, built in 1865; it's now the **Dayton Historic Society Museum** (open weekend afternoons in the summer). Next door to the museum is **St. Anne's Roman Catholic** (crackerbox) **Church,** one of the oldest and certainly one of the tiniest houses of worship in the state.

Four miles east of downtown Dayton is **Dayton State Park,** a small campground between the Carson River and the highway. Dayton has been spreading east, along the north side of US 50 and the south side of the Carson River. New subdivisions, a golf course, an industrial park, and a shopping center have all burst forth from the brush, outside the historic district, over the past five years or so.

US 50 and the Carson River keep company for 10 or so miles east of Dayton; then the river continues east while the road veers northeast. **Silver Springs** is a small crossroads settlement 27 miles east of Dayton, where US 50 and Alternate 395 intersect, 14 miles south of Fernley. At the junction are a mini-mart, gas station, and **Piper's,** a venerable bar and slot joint.

For the next eight miles, US 50 runs parallel to the north shore of Lahontan

*Lahontan Reservoir in autumn.*

Reservoir, created by Lahontan Dam, which impounds Carson River water for the agricultural area around Fallon. The dam is the focal point for the **Lahontan State Recreation Area**, with picnicking and camping on the beaches, and boating and fishing on the lake.

Nine miles east of the dam is the junction of US 50 and Alternate 50, where the latter cuts off to the northwest, heading 18 miles into Fernley, and the former continues east, another nine miles into Fallon.

■ FALLON  *map page 284, B-1*

Black-necked stilts and white-faced ibises wade in a marsh on the edge of a lush field where a group of cows and calves graze on verdant alfalfa, while overhead, two F-14s hit the after-burners and climb straight up from Earth, bullying the blue sky. It's a typical moment in Fallon, yet another one-of-a-kind town in a state where almost every town is one of a kind.

Just how out of the ordinary is Fallon? First, it's big and brash: the population of nearly 10,000 puts it on a par with Ely and Winnemucca, though it's much more modern than the former, and much more boisterous than the latter. Fallon's

US 50: LAKE TAHOE
& CENTRAL NEVADA

*At the 1915 Nevada State Fair, the formal dance was held at The Alfalfa Palace, which was built of 44 tons of hay bales. (Nevada Historical Society)*

casinos, shopping centers, fast-food and small-business franchises, gas stations, motels, used-car lots, and traffic are strung along the two US highways, 50 and 95, that cross at the main intersection downtown.

### ◆ NEVADA'S "OASIS"

In addition, a thin slice of suburbia separates the bustling commercial strips from the verdant farmlands that surround town—the farmlands that are responsible for Fallon's moniker as the "Oasis of Nevada." Fallon has been the state's largest agricultural area since the early 1900s, when dams on the Truckee and Carson Rivers —the Federal Bureau of Reclamation's earliest projects—diverted irrigation water to Fallon's farms, which a hardy breed of agricultural pioneers had hacked out of the desert with hand tools.

Today, upwards of 60,000 acres are planted in alfalfa, onions, garlic, and the regionally famous Heart o' Gold cantaloupes. But that's slowly shrinking, as more and more reclaimed desert is reclaimed from farmland by developers and as Fallon's irrigation lifeline shrinks. These farms are at the tail end of the western Nevada water system, to which numerous powerful special interests, such as Sierra Pacific (the Reno-Sparks water utility), the U.S. Fish and Wildlife Service (representing the Stillwater National Wildlife Refuge, which we'll get to anon), the Pyramid Lake and Stillwater Paiute tribes, and the Nature Conservancy and other environmental lobbies all lay claim. Both the urbanization of the rural West and the new political incorrectness of sharing finite water supplies to grow alfalfa are taking their toll on Fallon's traditional lifestyle.

◆ NAVY BASE   *map page B–1&2*

Finally, Fallon is unusual in that it's home to a major Navy base. The Navy? In sand-and-sagebrush Nevada? The U.S. Naval Air Station occupies a sizable chunk of Fallon real estate and accounts for a sizable chunk (estimates run as high as 33 percent) of the employment in Churchill County, of which Fallon is the seat—and the only town to speak of. The Navy's famous Top Gun air-combat school is based here, where hotshot aviators dogfight in F-14 Tomcats and F-18 Hornets.

The **Churchill County Museum,** which occupies an old Safeway supermarket building, boasts a huge collection of local and historical exhibits: everything from quilts to vaults, from duck decoys to player pianos. If you do one thing in Fallon,

*Top Gun pilots walk to F-18s on the runway at the Navy's Van Voorhis Field.*

visit this museum. Fallon also has the requisite three casinos: the **Nugget** is the big sawdust joint right downtown; the **Depot** is the slot joint nearby; and **Stockmen's** is the modern casino on the west end of town on US 50.

## ■ STILLWATER NATIONAL WILDLIFE REFUGE  *map page 284, B-1*

Five miles east of Fallon on US 50 and another 10 miles east on NV 116 brings you to Stillwater National Wildlife Refuge. At the west end of Stillwater, the Carson River (or what's left of it after being dammed and diverted) fans out into a marsh; at the east end of the marsh the water disappears into the "dead flats" of the Carson Sink. In between, Stillwater supports an enormous variety of waterfowl and vegetation—in wet years, anyway. In dry years (such as after the prolonged drought, which ended in the early 1990s) Stillwater practically disappears. Inquire at the museum as to the condition of the marsh; if it's thriving, this unexpected riparian paradise is a worthwhile sight to see.

*Rider Dustin Clark rides Baron during a Pony Express reenactment.*

*Timothy Sullivan took this silver print of the Carson Desert sand dunes in 1867.*
*(Library of Congress)*

■ EAST FROM FALLON   *map page 284, B&C&D–1/2*

Ten miles east of Fallon and only 100 yards from US 50 is **Grimes Point,** site of more than 150 prehistoric rock-art petroglyphs, etched into basalt boulders for ritualistic purposes roughly 2,000 to 5,000 years ago. Across the highway is the end of one of the runways of the airbase.

Fifteen miles east of Grimes Point is **Sand Mountain,** a 200-foot-tall "seif" (sword-edged) sand dune backed up against a minor hillock of the Stillwater Range. When wind and sand conditions are just so, Sand Mountain is said to make a deep booming sound—though I've been here a dozen times and have yet to hear it. You're more likely to hear the buzzing of dirt bikes and dune buggies, especially on the weekends when off-road speed demons and noise freaks come here to play. Nearby (signposted) is **Sand Springs Desert Study Area;** take the self-guided nature walk, which brings you to the ruins of an 1860s stone stationhouse used by the Overland mail riders, whose route across Nevada US 50 follows.

Twenty miles east of Sand Mountain is the intersection of US 50 and NV 361.

*The interior of the Berlin stamp mill, which stands in one of the best preserved ghost towns in Nevada.*

A 30-mile detour south on the state road takes you to **Gabbs,** a mining settlement (motel, cafe, grocery store, gas station) at the base of the Paradise Range, founded in the 1940s to mine brucite and magnesite for Basic Magnesium, the giant metals factory in Henderson.

A mile north of Gabbs, NV 844 heads east over the Paradise Range and across Ione Valley, arriving in 20 miles at the appropriately named **Berlin-Ichthyosaur State Park** (by the time you get there from US 50, your ichthyo will be suitably saur). Berlin is a true mining ghost town that boomed briefly in the 1860s and again in the 1910s; since 1955, it's been preserved as a state park. You can wander among the ruins of houses, shops, offices, and halls; the big stamp mill is the best-preserved such relic in the state.

Continue along the park road to the 14-site campground, with running water and outhouses, then farther to the ichthyosaur fossil site. These marine dinosaurs (60 feet long, 50 tons, with foot-long incisors) terrorized their Mesozoic prey—right here, where the fossilized skeletons of up to 40 bathysmal bruisers were buried 100 million years ago, uncovered in the mid-1950s, and now displayed in the fossil shelter of the state park. It's a surreal sensation to stand among the sage and sand of these desert foothills and imagine the entire scene drowned under 500 feet of water, with boxcar-sized leviathans loose in the seascape.

Back on US 50, from the turnoff for Gabbs, it's another 64 miles to Austin.

■ AUSTIN    *map page A–1*

In *Stories From the Sagebrush,* author Don Cox, a reporter for the *Reno Gazette-Journal,* quotes an ex-long-haired biker type who settled in Austin years ago and says about his adopted town, "It's a place where you can be different. It's accepted and allowed, sometimes even encouraged." Still, he adds, Austinites are protective of each other, and he gives a personal example. When he started dating a local woman, he was "pulled aside, literally, and told, 'You treat that woman right or we'll dump you down a mine shaft.' They were dead serious."

Austin, one of Nevada's first mining boomtowns, prides itself on its laissez-faire and close-knit way of life. That, and a glorious past, are about all it's got going for it. The silver boom lasted a decade (1863–73), and Austin went into an inexorable decline for about, oh, 106 years, bottoming out in 1979 when Battle Mountain, the other town in Lander County, appropriated the county seat. Since then, the little settlement has survived on the lonely highway, which brings an infrequent lorry or jalopy through.

Still, there's a palpable spell cast by a village that seems to exist in a different time and place. The very idea that there's nothing to do in Austin can keep visitors occupied for a good long while, and residents busy for a lifetime. To add to the contrariness of the place, Austin is situated at 6,000 feet, high up at the north end of the mighty Toiyabe Mountains, so its winters are long and its summers short. And it sits at the bottom of a tiny canyon, with steep slopes on both sides, so even the sun seems to withhold its benevolent brightness the better part of the day.

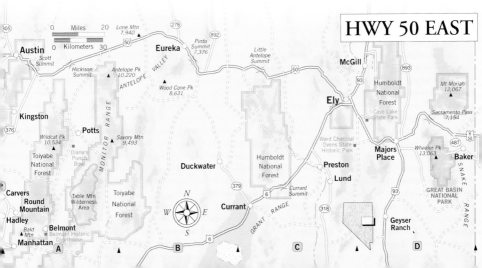

HWY 50 EAST

Fewer than 400 people live here, manning three motels (a total of 39 rooms in town), a few cafes and bars, a gas station, a corner store, the "loneliest bike store in the country," and the only Baptist Church–RV park combo I know of anywhere.

Austin does claim some sites of historical interest. **The International Hotel** was moved to Austin from Virginia City in 1863; a bar and restaurant occupy the ground floor. Also in 1863, the **Gridley Store** opened; the proprietor earned his 15 days of fame (time moved more slowly back then) by carrying a 50-pound sack of flour around the far West and raising a quarter-million dollars for charity. **St. Augustine's Catholic Church** is the oldest in the state, completed in 1866. The ex-county courthouse was built in 1871.

On the west side of town, Castle Road cuts off US 50, winds around a hill, and dead-ends at the ruins of a three-story stone ruin known locally as **Stokes Castle**. The Stokes in question was a mining and railroad magnate who built the Castle in the 1890s out of local granite and lived here for two months total. It's been abandoned ever since—a good place to get out of the car and commune with an apt symbol of Austin.

East of Austin, US 50 climbs into the Toiyabe Mountains, the central range of central Nevada. Twelve miles east of town is the junction of US 50 and NV 376, a spectacularly scenic byway that runs along the eastern base of the Toiyabes, with the near-equal Toquima Range on the east, the two ramparts hemming in Big Smoky Valley for nearly 80 miles, almost all the way to Tonopah.

*Stokes Castle, as photographed in the 1920s. (Nevada Historical Society)*

## ■ BIG SMOKY VALLEY

*map page 293, A–1/2*

Just after turning right onto NV 376, a dirt road heads off to the left, cutting across Big Smoky Valley toward the Toquimas. About halfway across the valley, a left turn takes you to **Spencer Hot Springs,** a semi-developed hot pool that you'll practically own if you make it this far.

Seven peaks in the Toiyabes rise above 10,000 feet, including Arc Dome (11,788 feet), the centerpiece of the 115,000-acre **Arc Dome Wilderness Area,** largest of the 13 Forest Service wildernesses in the state. Across the valley from Arc Dome is **Mount Jefferson** of the Toquimas at 11,949 feet. If you love mountain views, you'll never want to leave.

Forty-seven miles south of US 50 on NV 376 is the small town of **Carver's,** which services the Round Mountain open-pit gold mine eight miles southeast on NV 378. A mile south, on the west side of NV 376, is **Hadley,** the company town for the mine, complete with a school, heated pool, grocery, and golf course.

Eleven miles south of the junction with NV 378 is NV 377. A left turn and seven miles bring you to **Manhattan,** a tiny old mining town of 50 or so souls in the shadow of 9,274-foot Bald Mountain. Here you'll find a couple of bars, two dozen occupied houses (some seasonally), and the Manhattan Public Library.

At the far end of Manhattan, at the top of the Toquima Range gulch where the village squats, the NV 377 pavement ends; from there it's another dozen miles to **Belmont,** as close to a ghost town that isn't entirely dead as you'll find in Nevada. People (even though there are only eight or nine of them) live here, so don't trespass. Belmont was the seat of Nye County from 1867 to 1905; a two-story boarded-up courthouse is the big deal here. **The Belmont Saloon** is the other big deal, open on weekends.

Back on US 50 east of Austin, it's a straight and level shot across Antelope Valley for nearly 50 miles. Then you climb into the Mountain Boy Range and pass through Devil's Gate. From there, you drop down into Diamond Valley, turn southeast, and head into Eureka, at the north edge of the Fish Creek Range.

## MICHAEL HEIZER:
## A SCULPTOR'S COLOSSUS IN THE DESERT

*M*ichael Heizer doesn't want you to know where he lives, just that he's in the middle of nowhere in the middle of Nevada. His ranch is an isolated copse of trees and low buildings in an immense, flat, otherwise bone-dry valley—a desert ringed by mountains, 40 miles, more or less, from the nearest neighbor, up to two hours' drive to the closest paved road. Beside the house is what looks from a distance like a low, U-shaped enclosure, an odd though not particularly dramatic bump in the land. Scale is deceptive in the desert. Up close, the bump turns into Heizer's sculpture "City," or, to be precise, the first phase of it, which he has just finished. The sculpture consists of three rectangular structures around a curved, sunken gravel-coated court or pit.

The structures—which he calls "complexes," a term archaeologists use for buildings at ancient sites—are immense concrete and dirt mastabas, rectangles with sloped sides. "Complex 2" is by itself more than a quarter-mile long. Its irregular surface incorporates two projections, one triangular and one rectangular, and several upright slabs that poke up over the top like mountain peaks. The slabs (Heizer calls them "steles") rise as much as 70 feet and weigh up to a thousand tons each. Altogether, what exists of "City" has got to be one of the most massive modern sculptures ever built. After nearly 30 years, Heizer has passed the first stage toward completing what is essentially his own Chichen Itza in the desert. There are four more stages to go.

Heizer came up with the idea for "City" in 1970, when he was in the Yucatan studying the serpent motif in the ball court at Chichen Itza. He was 24. The previous year he finished "Double Negative," a spectacular 1,500-foot-long, 50-foot-deep, 30-foot-wide gash cut onto facing slopes of an obscure mesa in Nevada, a project that required blasting 240,000 tons of rock. It was quickly recognized as the archetype of what people were beginning to call Land Art or Earth Art or Environmental Art. It made a huge impact. His next plan, for "City," was to build a suite of giant, variously shaped abstract sculptures over an area that covered more than a mile end to end — modern art turned into monumental abstract architecture, with ancient ruins as the model. Heizer's goal with "City" was to link contemporary American art and Pollock's legacy with the grandeur of the Olmecs, Mayans, Incas and Aztecs. "I was just doing what had already been done for centuries, but not in a while," he says. "City" was a very American kind of dream: big, brash, maverick, optimistic and a little loopy.

With money, Heizer was able to hire outside help. Decades of pent-up desire combined with the inexperience of the construction crew to make the situation sometimes rocky at first. Heizer can be warm and solicitous, but also touchy, anxious and strong willed. The men had never worked on a project like this, which involved unusual materials, gigantic forms in odd shapes and tricky conditions. Storms would sweep across the valley and, in minutes, wipe out $30,000 of labor on one of the steles. This happened four or five times. The surfaces of the complexes required constant readjustment. Heizer would become upset when the shape of one of the forms he had drawn was not reproduced as he wanted. He wanted everything to be just right. At one point, he asked that hundreds of thousands of yards of dirt be moved 27 inches to align Complexes 2 and 3.

"I'm not a dogmatic, purist psychopath," he insists. "There's an unfair image of me — mean, crazy, hostile. I'm really a very gentle person." But part of the experience of being in the "City" inevitably involves the isolation of the valley, the light and the weather, which are aspects of the environment. From 80 degrees the previous afternoon, the temperature plummeted to 15 overnight, causing an efflorescence, like frost, to coat parts of the complexes, whose masses were shimmering gray silhouettes in the half-light. When the sun rose, daylight fell gradually over different parts of the complexes. They were so big that the sun didn't seem to strike them equally all at once, which was part of Heizer's intent. Time is an element, as it is in other projects in the land, like "Lightning Field" and James Turrell's "Roden Crater," in Arizona, another long-delayed sculpture lately revived with help from the Lannan Foundation.

Does he feel isolated in the desert, working on his sculpture decade after decade? "Nevada is the only place for me that's home," he says, then adds: "I'm a committed professional, and I would go anywhere to pursue this line of work... for a sculptor like me it's impossible to build big works in New York. It's too expensive. I need cranes. I operate in the 20-ton minimum range. "I don't work with scale," he adds. "I work with size. Scale is an effete art term. If I screw up out here," he says, "I know it will be big time. I'm going to go down in flames."

*—Excerpted from an article by Michael Kimmelman which appeared in the* New York Times *entitled "A Sculptor's Colossus in the Desert"—December 12, 1999*

## ■ EUREKA   *map page 293, B-1*

A quick 70 miles from Austin, Eureka is a world apart. As derelict and desperate and dark as Austin is, that's how prosperous and propitious and perky Eureka is. You'll notice it the moment you breeze into town: the beautifully restored redbrick **Eureka County Courthouse** (1879), the beautifully restored redbrick **Eureka Opera House** (1880), and the beautifully restored redbrick **Jackson House** (1877) next door. (You'll also notice the new all-brick Best Western Eureka Inn, the new all-brick Tru-Value hardware store, and the new all-brick—and blue-tin-roofed— Eureka County Medical Clinic.) If you don't fall in love with Eureka in the first two minutes, then maybe you belong in Austin.

Be sure to stop in for a look around the **Eureka Sentinel Museum** on Ruby Hill Street one block above US 50, with its exhibits on Eureka's history: the silver-lead discovered by Austin prospectors in 1863, the smoky smelters that cast a Pittsburgh-like pall over the town, and the Eureka & Palisade Railroad that operated for 63 years. (Taxes collected from the recent 10-year boom in gold mining at the north end of Eureka County outside of Carlin financed the resurrection of Eure-

*The restored stage screen of the Eureka Opera House, which was built in 1880.*

ka.) Also, don't miss the room full of old printing machines left over from the *Eureka Sentinel* (1870-1960).

On Main Street, peek into the **Eureka Opera House,** the cultural center for all of central Nevada, which hosts a concert, theater performance, school dance, or some community event nearly every week of the year. Next door is the **Jackson House,** a stunningly restored inn with a bar and restaurant below and guest rooms above.

Also on Main Street are **Tommyknockers** stained-glass shop, crafts, antiques, and art stores, and **Raines,** a general store with a few dozen hunting trophies mounted on the walls

*The original architectural plans for the Eureka County Courthouse.*

(most were taken down by store matriarch Lee Raines). A block off Main Street is the **Colonnade Hotel,** built in 1880. It's 77 miles from Eureka to Ely, where US 50 and US 93 cross, and the two US highways meet up with a third, US 6.

■ ELY  *map page 293, C/D–1*

**Hotel Nevada,** located at the corner of Aultman and Fourth, the main intersection in downtown Ely, is nearly 75 years old, which is so old around here that it's among the state's five oldest lodging houses; it was also briefly the tallest building in Nevada. You can read the whole story in an article posted on the wall by the cashier. Afterwards, feel free to wander around the casino, staring at the walls, where every available space is occupied by some kind of display: guns, swords, snakes, wagons, casino chips, a ton of photographs (from boxers to lounge acts), even two walls actually branded with hot irons from local ranches. Then head over to the coffee shop for the famous 24-hour steak-and-eggs special. Now you're in the right frame of mind to look around the rest of eclectic Ely.

Cross the street and take a left for the **White Pine Convention Center.** In the lobby is a framed display of the cross-section of a nearly 5,000-year-old bristlecone pine tree named Prometheus. Prometheus is believed to have been the oldest tree (thus the oldest living thing) on Earth, when it was cut down in the bristlecone pine forest high up on Wheeler Peak, 60 miles east of Ely, back in 1964.

Ely has two museums. **White Pine Public Museum** is home to a collection typical for a small Nevada town: there are dolls and minerals, a county map and a cannon, a schematic of Ely's big open-pit copper mine, and a petrified dinosaur footprint. No doubt about it, Ely is eccentric.

But the second museum is even more intrinsically Nevadan. **The Nevada Northern Railway Museum** is nothing if not authentic. It was a hard-working mining shortline for most of the century, shuttling countless billions of tons of ore from the big copper mine in Ruth, five miles northwest of Ely, to the big smelter in McGill, 12 miles north of Ely, then on to the transcontinental railroad in Cobre (Spanish for "copper"), 100 miles north of Ely. In the late 1970s, the Nevada Northern shut down suddenly, leaving everything as it was. Luckily, the railroad started up again only six years later, as a tourist attraction.

And a fine one it is. There's a 45-minute tour of the sprawling railyard: engine house, rip-track shop (home of the 1910 Baldwin steamer or "Ghost Train"—fascinating story!), roundhouse, and transportation building. You'll see a snowplow train, diesel locomotives, cabooses, endless flat cars, passenger coaches, and plenty of tools, machines, and parts. If there's no tour, you can wander around (outside) on your own.

Weekends during the summer, retired train crews fire up the steamer and diesel, pull out the passenger cars, and roll visitors along the tracks up to Ruth and McGill. By the time you're chugging up the mountain to the open-pit mine or across the flats to the smelter town, you'll be a believer in the uniqueness of Ely.

But there's more. Take a half-hour drive into the desert south of town to the **Ward Charcoal Ovens State Historical Monument,** six brick duncecaps that would fit a team of cyclopes—and I don't mean your standard cyclops, but giants among them. These kilns, used to produce hot-burning charcoal for refining lead from a short-lived mine nearby, are 30 feet high and 25 wide at the base, and can fit 35 cords of wood. Leave it to Ely to claim one of the finest examples in the American West of this 2,000-year-old technology.

Finally, there's **Cave Lake State Park,** a half-hour drive from Ely high up in the big Schell Creek Range (at 7,300 feet). The setting couldn't be more stunning for a big reservoir: giant rock outcroppings, forested slopes, backcountry and big sky as far as the eye can see. A five-mile trail disappears into the mountains. Two campgrounds combine for 36 sites, with flush toilets and great showers. Just the place to remind yourself of how lucky you were to stumble across Ely.

■ EAST TO BAKER  *map page 293, C/D–1/2*

Continuing east out of Ely, US 50, 93, and 6 run together southeast for another 27 miles to Major's Place, where US 93 parts company.

At **Major's Place**, US 50 and 6 cut east across long, thin Spring Valley, a straight shot to the base of the Snake Range. There, the highway veers northeast, then makes a hard turn southeast and climbs over a saddle in the Snakes called Sacramento Pass (7,154 feet). At the bottom of the pass is a **Y** junction, where US 50 and 6 continue east into Utah, and NV 487 turns southeast. Five miles from the **Y** on NV 487 is Baker.

**Baker** is a tiny village that sits in the lush valley at the eastern base of the Snake Range, surrounded by alfalfa fields with cattle grazing contentedly and 100-year-old trees circling big ranch houses. **The Outlaw** is Baker's bar and grill; **T&D's** is the cafe (nice little sunroom to eat in) and country store. **Silver Jack Motel** has seven rooms and an amazing little gift shop next door, selling eclectic art and crafts handmade by local artisans. In the middle of town is the access road, NV 488, to Great Basin National Park.

■ GREAT BASIN NATIONAL PARK  *map page 303*

Great Basin is young, small, remote, and undeveloped, as national parks go. Those four fortuitous factors combine to render it a lot less circus-like than the older, larger, more accessible, and more developed national parks in the Lower 48. However, that's not to say Great Basin isn't comfortable. Far from it. **Wheeler Peak campground,** for example, has a paved loop with raised curbs painted black, freshly painted clean outhouses, and lots of running water from hand pumps. Each campsite has a level concrete slab supporting a long picnic table, a firepit that you could use for a hot tub, and a barbecue grill. All at 10,000 feet.

That's also not to say, however, that the campground is *over*developed. Far from it. The 40 sites are a quarter-mile apart (well, maybe a sixth of a mile), many of them right on the edge of **Lehman Creek,** in the midst of a healthy virgin forest of Engelmann spruce, limber pine, Douglas fir, and gnarly aspen trees all around.

*Many bristlecone pines live for thousands of years.*

Great Basin basically preserves the upper half of the east side of a massive mountain, **Wheeler Peak.** From the valley you climb up to the visitors center at a little less than 7,000 feet; here you'll find a few exhibits of local interest, a bookstore, a theater (hosting a movie about Lehman Caves and a slide show about the park), snack shop, gift shop, and restrooms. Outside is the entrance to the caves, a self-guided nature trail (after a half-hour you'll be an expert on mountain mahogany, cliffrose, Utah juniper, single-leaf piñon pine, Mormon tea, prickly pear, and sage), and 120-year-old fruit trees planted by Ab Lehman, an early homesteader in the area.

◆ LEHMAN CAVES   *map page 303*

Sign up for the next available guided tour of Lehman Caves at the cashier in the visitors center. The tour takes you through several rooms and along long passageways full of limestone formations that have been taking shape for tens of millions of years. The Park Service naturalist explains a little about the history and geology of the maze of caves, pointing out the noteworthy stalagmites, stalactites, helictites, aragonites, dynamites, suburbanites, and israelites. These are the only public caves in Nevada, and the tour of them alone is worth the trip to Great Basin.

*(following pages) Ridges and snowpatches on Wheeler Peak, which at 13,063 feet, is just 80 feet shorter than Boundary Peak, the state's highest peak.*

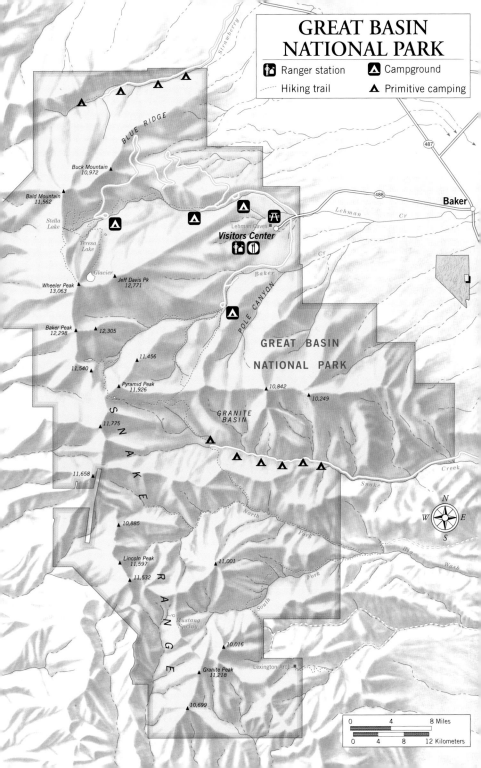

# GREAT BASIN
# NATIONAL PARK

Ranger station    Campground

Hiking trail    Primitive camping

Baker

487

488

Lehman Cr

Lehman Caves

**Visitors Center**

Baker

Cr

POLE CANYON

BLUE RIDGE

Buck Mountain
10,972

Bald Mountain
11,562

Stella
Lake

Teresa
Lake

Glacier

Wheeler Peak
13,063

Jeff Davis Pk
12,771

Baker Peak
12,298

12,305

11,540

11,456

Pyramid Peak
11,926

11,775

11,658

**GREAT BASIN**

**NATIONAL PARK**

10,842

10,249

*GRANITE BASIN*

Snake

Creek

North Fork

Big

Wash

S
N
A
K
E

R
A
N
G
E

10,885

Lincoln Peak
11,597

11,532

11,001

South Fork

Mustang Spring

10,016

Granite Peak
11,218

Lexington Arch

10,699

N
W    E
S

0        4        8 Miles

0    4    8    12 Kilometers

◆ GREAT BASIN PARK CAMPGROUNDS  *map page 303*

From the visitors center, Baker Creek Road, a well-maintained gravel road, leads three miles to **Baker Creek Campground,** in a little draw along the creek under tall conifers. At the far end of the road is the trailhead for the 12-mile Baker Creek loop trail, which passes **Baker** and **Johnson Lakes.** You can also bushwhack off the loop trail into the ultra-remote south end of the park. Another way to get there is via jeep tracks off Hwy. 21 in Utah (NV 487 continues southeast of Baker to the tiny Utah border village of Garrison, turning into UT 21 there). One high-clearance-vehicle road four miles south of Garrison leads to **Lexington Arch,** a big hole in a sandstone wall.

Meanwhile, back at the visitors center, the paved park road continues climbing up the side of Wheeler Peak at a steep and winding eight-percent grade. You pass **Lower Lehman Creek Campground,** with 11 sites (six pull-throughs) at 7,500 feet; **Upper Lehman Creek Campground** is 300 feet higher, with 24 sites for car campers (not advised for trailers). Lehman Creek runs right through both.

The road climbs and climbs. It's 13 miles from the visitors center to the top of the pavement, which deadends at **Wheeler Peak Campground** at a nose-bleeding 10,000 feet. The last time I was there, in July 1999, it rained for three days straight. The locals loved it—it hadn't rained for two solid months—but never in my wildest dreams did I imagine it would rain three days straight in Nevada in July. Finally the sun came out, and then it turned really cold, dropping into the 20s the third night. The moral of this story is to be prepared: the weather is changeable at 10,000 feet.

◆ BRISTLECONE PINES

From the campground, two short trails lead to **Theresa** and **Stella Lakes,** two lovely alpine kettles that you'll usually have all to yourself. Also from the campground, one long trail leads to a veritable forest of bristlecone pines, the most amazing trees you'll ever see. To survive in such a harsh environment, bristlecones *(Pinus longaeva)* have evolved one of the hardiest constitutions of any living creature, and they're almost immortal. Many of the trees you see in this stand are more than 3,000 years old. Rub your hands over the exposed barkless trunks of these trees to feel the smoothness that comes from thousands of years of polishing by wind, rain, grit, and sun.

From the bristlecone forest, the trail continues to a viewpoint overlooking the spectacular cirque, a mountain bowl with sheer thousand-foot walls all around, Wheeler Peak towering above. Within the cirque is the southernmost permanent icefield on the continent. Take it slow—crawl on your hands and knees if you have to—but don't leave the park without hiking up to the bristlecones and the peak overlook.

◆ WHEELER PEAK TRAIL  *map page 303*

Just before the campground on the park road is the trailhead for the Wheeler Peak trail, a five-mile hike one way, much of it along an exposed ridgeline, past craggy outcroppings, on the edge of sheer thousand-foot cliffs, up to the wind-blown peak at 13,063 feet. When you get to the top, you're standing higher than anyone else in the state (save some lone sole who's braved the utterly inaccessible Boundary Peak at the other end of the state, which is 80 feet higher, but he's probably looking the other way into California).

I dragged my six- and seven-year-old sons onto the peak trail during our July 1999 trip to Great Basin. Five minutes along, my six-year-old, big for his age, started complaining that he felt sick and didn't want to hike. There was only one thing to do: pick him up and give him a piggy-back ride.

Humming, "He ain't heavy, he's my son," didn't ease the 60-pound burden, so I tried pretending he was a backpack. It wasn't easy, because a backpack doesn't strangle you to hold on. A backpack doesn't squirm. And a backpack doesn't whine:

"I don't *waaanna* hike!"

"I just wanna go *hoooome!*"

"I think I'm gonna *baarrrrf!*"

Someone ought to invent a fidgeting, crying, 50-pound backpack so first-timers can prepare for parenthood.

If you come down from the park, blow through Baker, return to the **Y** junction, and continue east on US 50, in seven miles you'll come to the Utah border. The Border Inn is right there, with Sinclair gas, eight motel rooms, a coffee shop, a bar, gift shop, sundries, a pool table, slots and video poker, and a jukebox (half-country, half-rock). The border runs along the east wall of the building.

The speed limit drops from 70 m.p.h. in Nevada to 65 in Utah; meanwhile, the hour skips ahead from 6:00 Pacific Time to 7:00 Mountain Time.

# FOOD & LODGING

> ⛏ *Lodging rates, per room, double occupancy*
> $ = under $50;  $$ = $50-$100;  $$$ = $100-$150;  $$$$ = over $150
>
> ✗ *Restaurant prices, per person, excluding drinks, tax, tip:*
> $ = under $10;  $$ = $10-$20;  $$$ = $20-$30;  $$$$ = over $30

For information regarding camping in Nevada's recreation areas, contact the **Division of State Parks**, 1300 Curry St., Carson City, NV 89710; 775-687-4384.

## Austin  *map B/C-2*

⛏ **Lincoln Motel**. 728 Main St.; 775-964-2698 $
With 17 rooms, this is the largest motel in Austin. The rooms are small and utilitarian, but have satellite TV. The International Cafe is adjacent.

⛏ **Pony Express House**. 115 NW Main St. (PO Box 28); 775-964-2306 $-$$
Austin's little B&B, the Pony Express is a two-bedroom house built in 1865; you can rent one or both bedrooms. You fix your own breakfast.

✗ **International Cafe**. 801 Main St.; no phone $-$$
Moved board by board from Virginia City in 1863, this is the second oldest hotel building in Nevada; the upstairs rooms are said to be haunted. Road food prevails: burgers, potatoes, and steak.

## Baker  *map D-3*

⛏ **Silverjack Motel**. Main St.; 775-234-7323 $

Closest indoor lodging to Great Basin National Park (five miles from the visitor center), the Silverjack has eight rooms and is open April through October. Check out the gift shop, one of the most eclectic in the state, next door.

✗ **The Outlaw**. 100 Main St.; 775-234-7302 $-$$
The social center for the park, the town, and the region, the Outlaw has a bar, pool table, slot machines, and a basic American menu: buffalo burgers, pasta, steak, ribs.

## Battle Mountain  *map C-2*

⛏ **Best Western-Big Chief Motel**. 434 W. Front St; 775-635-2416 or 800-528-1234. $$
The most modern motel in Battle Mountain, the Big Chief has 58 recently renovated rooms, indoor hot tubs, and kitchenettes, plus an outdoor pool. Pets are allowed.

⛏ **Broadway Colt Motel**. 650 W. Front St.; 775-635-5424 or 800-343-0085 $-$$

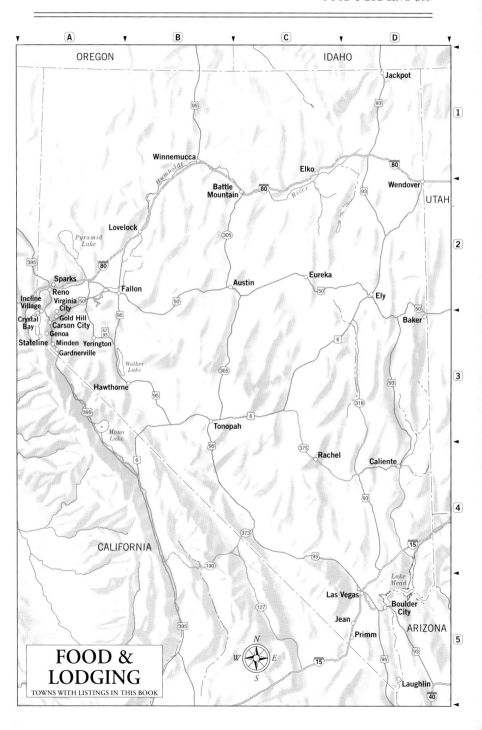

OREGON      IDAHO

Jackpot

UTAH

Winnemucca

Elko

Battle
Mountain

Wendover

Lovelock

*Pyramid
Lake*

Sparks
Reno
Incline
Village
Virginia
City
Crystal
Bay
Gold Hill
Carson City
Genoa
Stateline
Minden
Gardnerville
Yerington

Fallon

Austin

Eureka

Ely

Baker

*Walker
Lake*

Hawthorne

*Mono
Lake*

Tonopah

Rachel

Caliente

CALIFORNIA

Las Vegas

*Lake
Mead*

Boulder
City

Jean

ARIZONA

Primm

Laughlin

FOOD &
LODGING
TOWNS WITH LISTINGS IN THIS BOOK

FOOD & LODGING

This is the largest travelers complex in town, with 72 rooms, mini-mart, truck stop, RV park, and 24-hour coffee shop. Jacuzzis and waterbeds in some rooms, along with mini-fridges and microwaves.

⊞ **Comfort Inn.** 521 E. Front St.; 775-635-5880. $-$$
The newest motel in town, this three-story Holiday Inn was built in 1991. There's a heated pool and whirlpool; daily complimentary continental breakfasts. Some rooms have refrigerators.

✕ **El Aguila Real.** 254 E. Front St., 775-635-8390 $
A good Mexican restaurant right at the main intersection downtown. The lunch specials are an especially good deal.

✕ **Mama's Pizza and Deli.** 515 E. Front St., 775-635-9211 $-$$
This is a homegrown pizza place, serving pizzas, subs, deli sandwiches, and pasta.

## Boulder City *map D-5*

⊞ **El Rancho Boulder.** 725 Nevada Hwy.; 702-293-1085 $$-$$$
One of the more historic motels along the main drag in Boulder City: 39 rooms, cable TV, pool, complimentary coffee in lobby, some refrigerators.

⊞ **Super 8.** 704 Nevada Hwy; 702-294-8888 $
The 114 rooms are no different from any other Super 8 anywhere else in the country, but there's an indoor pool, whirlpool, and game room.

✕ **Happy Days Diner.** 512 Nevada Hwy.; 702-293-4637 $
You can't miss this *American Graffiti* eatery: Just look for the big neon sign with an arrow. Inside, it's full of Coke memorabilia (napkin holders, glasses, signs), with some classic car and Marilyn Monroe stuff thrown in. Burgers include vegie and turkey; daily specials are on the order of meatloaf, chopped sirloin, and beef stroganoff.

✕ **Tiffany's.** 1305 Arizona St.; 702-294-1666 $$
On the main floor of the Boulder Dam Hotel, directly off the original lobby, Tiffany's serves Italian-American fare—pasta, chicken, veal, steak, and seafood—in elegant historic surroundings.

## Caliente *map D-4*

⊞ **Caliente Hot Springs Motel.** US 93N, 775-726-3777 or 800-726-3777 $-$$
The 18 rooms are ordinary and small, but they come with the use of the Roman baths: oversized hot tubs in private rooms in a separate wing; fire-hydrant faucets fill them with sulphur-free 105-degree water in three minutes flat.

✕ **Pioneer Pizza.** US 93, 775-726-3300 $
This little storefront, just north of the big turn downtown, has a great selection of pizzas-try the Hawaiian pesto-build your own sandwiches and subs, and Italian breads.

## Carson City *map A-3*

⌕ **Carson Station Hotel-Casino.** 900 S. Carson St.; 775-883-0900 or 800-528-1234. $$-$$$
This is a clean, well-run, 100-room, Best Western hotel, with a full-service casino, 24-hour coffee shop, lounge entertainment, snack bar, pool and spa, and game room. Some refrigerators available.

⌕ **City Center Motel.** 800 N. Carson St.; 775-882-5535 or 800-338-7760 $-$$
Recently renovated, the City Center is the motel that goes with the Carson Nugget Casino across the street. The location is ideal (if a little noisy) for taking a walking tour of downtown Carson City.

⌕ **Days Inn.** 3103 N. Carson St.; 775-883-3343or 800-DAYS INN $-$$$
The 61 rooms in this branch of the national chain are large and well-appointed; they come with a complimentary continental breakfast.

⌕ **Deer Run Bed and Breakfast.** 5440 Eastlake Blvd., Washoe Valley; 775-883-3643 $$
This B&B is scenically situated 10 miles north of Carson City, with a view of Washoe Lake, valley ranches, and Sierra Nevada foothills and mountain peaks. It's a working alfalfa ranch with a natural pond, gardens, and orchard, even a potter's studio. The two bedrooms share a bath; there's also a cozy sitting room. Full complimentary breakfast is served.

⌕ **Ormsby House.** 600 S. Carson St.; 775-882-1890 or 800-662-1890 $-$$$
This is Carson's big (200-room) historic hotel, which has been around in one of many incarnations since the 1860s. The casino is relatively quiet, and there's a 24-hour coffee shop and buffet.

✕ **Dominique's Supper Club.** Ormsby House, 600 S. Carson St.; 775-882-1890 or 800-662-1890 $$-$$$
The steakhouse at the Ormsby serves fine food in an opulent room. Specialties are veal (oscar, marsala, picatta, scallopine), seafood linguine, and macadamia-crusted halibut. The king crab and steak-and-lobster dinners are reasonable.

✕ **Heiss' Dinner House.** 107 E. Telegraph, 775-882-9012 $$-$$$
Since 1970, Heiss' has been dishing up excellent salads, pasta, and burgers for lunch; and steaks, prime rib, and seafood for dinner, in an unbeatable location downtown across from the old federal building. Try the hot spinach salad for lunch or the seafood casserole (prawns, scallops, crab) for dinner.

✕ **Horseshoe Snack Bar.** 480 N. Carson St.; 775-883-2211 $
One of the great snack bars in Nevada, the little counter at the little Horseshoe serves burgers, bacon and eggs, fish and chips, and a top sirloin—each for less than five bucks.

✕ **Nugget Oyster Bar.** 507 N. Carson St.; 775-882-1626 $-$$
Chowders, louies, stews, pan roasts,

cioppino, fish and chips, and catch of the day are all served with a nautical flair in this small oyster bar at the big downtown grind joint.

✗ **Whiskey Saloon and Steakhouse.** Pinion Plaza Hotel-Casino, 2111 E. Hwy. 50, 775-885-9000 $-$$
This is a popular eatery with the locals, who like the rustic wood decor and the reasonable prices. For lunch, there's Caesar salad, chicken quesadilla, chili burger, and shrimp and mushroom fettucine; dinner offerings include steak, prime rib, salmon, pasta, chicken, and pork chops.

## Crystal Bay  *map A-2/3*

⌷ **Cal-Neva Resort.** 2 Stateline Rd.; 775-832-4000 or 800 800-CALNEVA $$-$$$$
Cal-Neva is the oldest lodging (1926) on the Nevada side of Lake Tahoe. Situated at the edge of an isthmus that juts into Crystal Bay, every room has a fantastic view; most have balconies. The gorgeous lodge lobby is in California, while the casino is in Nevada. Coffee shop, restaurant, heated pool, tennis courts, spa, game room, and wedding chapels round out the amenities.

⌷ **Tahoe Biltmore.** NV 28; 775-831-0660 or 800 800-BILTMORE $-$$
Popular with younger skiers and meal-deal hounds, the 92 utilitarian rooms go for generally bargain prices. A complimentary full breakfast comes with the rate.

✗ **Soule Domain.** Cove St., across from Tahoe Biltmore; 530-546-7529 $$-$$$
A romantic 1927 pine-log cabin with a stone fireplace is the setting for some of Lake Tahoe's most creative and delicious dinners. Chef-owner Charles Edward Soule IV's specialties include grilled tuna with papaya-mango salsa, and filet mignon with shiitake mushrooms, Gorgonzola, and brandy.

✗ **Tahoe Biltmore.** NV 28; 775-832-4000 $
The 24-hour coffee shop here is famous for its two-dollar breakfast special, along with cheap lunch and dinner specials.

## Elko  *map C-1*

⌷ **Best Western Ameritel Inn Elko.** 1930 Idaho St.; 775-738-8787 or 800-600-6001 $$-$$$
This motel has two heated pools, one indoors—just the thing for high-desert winter afternoons. A complimentary continental breakfast is served.

⌷ **Centre Motel.** 475 Third St.; 775-738-3226 $-$$
This 22-room motel has a great location right downtown, with a view of the neon of the Commercial and Stockman's. But it's a block off Idaho St., so it's relatively quiet. Pool and non-smoking rooms.

⌷ **Holiday Inn.** 3015 E. Idaho St.; 775-738-8425 or 800-HOLIDAY $$
This typical Holiday Inn is the second-largest lodging in Elko, with 170 rooms.

It has a fine indoor pool and whirlpool, coffee shop and room service, coin laundry, and exercise equipment.

⊞ **Red Lion Inn.** 2065 E. Idaho St.; 775-738-2111 or 800-545-0044 $$-$$$$
This is the largest and fanciest hotel-casino in town. The rooms are big and comfortable. There's a 24-hour casino and coffee shop (with buffet), a showroom, lounge, gourmet restaurant, beauty shop, and game room.

⊞ **Shilo Inn.** 2401 Mountain City Hwy.; 775-738-5522 or 800-222-2244 $$-$$$
Located in the newer northwest side of town, the Shilo is the only all-suite lodging in Elko. It has an indoor pool, whirlpool, steam room, and exercise equipment, as well as some refrigerators, microwaves, and wet bars. A complimentary continental breakfast is served.

✕ **Machi's.** 450 Commercial St.; 775-738-9772 $$
For a taste of some urban sophistication in rural Nevada, not to mention one of the best steamed-clam appetizers (in Elko!) and prime rib dinners I've ever had, head right for Machi's bar and grill downtown.

✕ **Misty's.** Red Lion Inn, 2065 E. Idaho St.; 775-738-2111 or 800-545-0044 $$-$$$
Elko's hotel-casino fine dining, Misty's is like an old-fashioned Las Vegas gourmet room, with its high-backed booths and crystal chandelier. The menu features Peking duck, pasta pescatore, and filet mignon.

✕ **Nine Beans and a Burrito.** 5503 Mountain City Hwy. (Raley's Shopping Center); 775-738-7898 $
Good Mexican fast food, with homemade tortillas and salsa, and a good selection of beer.

✕ **Star.** 246 Silver St.; 775-753-8696 $$
Elko is a Basque food kind of town, and the Star has been serving up family-style dinners since 1910. After bread, soup, salad, beans, french fries, and lamb, steak, cod, or pork for dinner, you probably won't be able to eat another bite till dinner the next day.

## Ely *map D-2*

⊞ **Holiday Inn & Prospector Casino.** 1501 E. Aultman St.; 775-289-8900 or 800-HOLIDAY $$
The newest and fanciest accommodation in Ely, this Holiday Inn opened in 1994. Small casino, indoor pool and health club, coffee shop, and RV park.

⊞ **Jailhouse Motel & Casino.** 211 Fifth St.; 775-289-3033 or 800-841-5430 $-$$
This motel is located at the main downtown intersection. It has a slots-only casino, a coffee shop, a dining room and a curious "jailhouse" theme: The rooms are known as "cells."

⊞ **Hotel Nevada.** 501 Aultman St.; 775-289-6665 or 800-406-3055 $-$$
One of the oldest hotels in the state, The Hotel Nevada was built in 1908 at the main intersection downtown. All 65

rooms in this six-story building were renovated in 1997.

**Motel 6.** 770 Ave. O; 775-289-6671 or 800/466-8356 $
The largest lodging in Ely, this typical Motel 6 has 122 rooms. It's conveniently situated on the east end of town near the fast food stands.

**Ramada Inn Copper Queen.** 701 Avenue I; 775-289-4884 or 800-851-9526. $-$$
The Ramada Inn is attractive to travelers for its reservation system and uniformity of rooms and prices. It's the only hotel-casino in Nevada where slots surround an indoor pool. (I call it the Chlorine Queen.)

**Steptoe Valley Inn.** 220 E. 11th St.; 775-289-8687. $$
The building dates back to 1907, when it was a grocery store; it was fully renovated in 1990. All five guest rooms have private baths; there are also a library, lounge, and verandah. Open March to December.

X **Hotel Nevada Coffee Shop.** 501 Aultman St.; 775-289-6665 or 800-406-3055 $
The coffee shop here is the place in Ely for bargain casino meal deals. The steak and eggs special would be a Top Ten value in Las Vegas.

X **Jailhouse Cell Block.** 211 5th St.; 775-289-3033 $$
The Jailhouse has a decent coffee shop and a steakhouse, the best themed fine-dining room in town (it ought to be: It's the only steakhouse in town, themed or not). The booths are behind bars; the featured meal is called the Inmate Special. The menu lists prime rib, ribs, steaks, chicken, and seafood.

X **Silver State.** 1204 Aultman St.; 775-289-2712 $
This isn't a retro '50s diner; it's the real thing, with orange vinyl seating. The menu consists of road food with some Mexican meals and a big T-bone steak.

## Eureka *map C-2*

**Best Western Eureka Inn.** 251 N. Main St.; 775-237-5247 $$
The newest lodging in Eureka is also the largest; the 42 rooms are sparkling clean and the exterior is a pleasing brick, to go with the rest of downtown.

**Jackson House.** Main St. and Ruby Hill; 775-237-5518 $-$$
Built in 1880, this venerable downtown landmark was restored in 1994; heavy wood decor, heavy quilts, and funky floors give it as much character as any lodging in the state. The nine rooms are all individual; the accessible balcony overlooks downtown. Register at the Best Western.

**Sundown Lodge.** Main St.; 775-237-5334 $
This is a standard motel right downtown. Eureka is a popular destination; make reservations as far in advance as possible.

⚔ **Eureka Cafe.** 90 N. Main St.; 775-237-7165 $-$$
This classic Chinese-American eatery has been around just short of forever; it's rumored that there's an extensive underground temple under the cafe, built by early Eureka Chinese for security. The menu consists of Mandarin and Szechuan dishes, along with American breakfasts and steaks.

⚔ **Jackson House Cafe.** Main St. and Ruby Hill; 775-237-5518 $$
There's no telling what might turn up on the menu at this fantastic restaurant, run by a graduate of New York's French Culinary Institute.

### Fallon *map A-2*

⚏ **Bonanza Inn and Casino.** 855 W. Williams Ave.; 775-423-6031 $-$$
The main action right in the heart of downtown Fallon. The casino can get crowded and rooms can get noisy on the weekends. The coffee shop is open 24 hours.

⚏ **Best Inn & Suites.** 1830 W. Williams Ave.; 775-423-5554 or 888-691-6388 $$
The largest lodging in Fallon, the Comfort Inn is modern looking with classy gray brick. Among the 84 rooms are some suites with Jacuzzis. A complimentary continental breakfast is served.

⚏ **Holiday Inn Express.** 55 Commercial Way; 775-428-2588 or 800-HOLIDAY $$
The 60-room Holiday Inn is the newest lodging in Fallon, opened in 1997. There are two pools (indoor and out) and Stockmen's Casino is next door.

⚔ **Angelica's Steakhouse.** 1560 W. Williams Ave.; 775-423-2117 $$
This is the big-city gourmet room at Stockman's Casino, serving steaks, seafood, chicken, and more.

⚔ **La Cocina.** 125 S. Maine St.; 775-423-6166 $-$$
One of the great Mexican restaurants in Nevada, the tostadas are the biggest you'll ever see: impossible to finish in one sitting.

⚔ **Waterhole.** 111 S. Allen Rd.; 775-423-3051 $$
A good homegrown restaurant sits unobtrusively behind Raley's, serving steak, seafood, and Italian and Mexican entrees.

### Gardnerville *map A-3*

⚏ **Jansen Mansion Bed and Breakfast.** 1431 Ezell St.; 775-782-7644 $$-$$$
Built in 1910 in the Southern Colonial style, the Nenzel has 12-foot ceilings, a huge Great Room, and four rooms up a 25-step staircase.

⚔ **Overland.** 691 Main St.; 775-782-2138 $$
The Overland is one of the most authentic Basque restaurants in an area full of authentic Basque restaurants. The soup, salad, french fries, appetizers, lamb, chicken, and steak entrees, and desserts are served family-style.

X **Sharkey's Nugget.** 1440 US 395; 775-782-3133 $-$$
The restaurant here is one of the largest coffee shops in Nevada, with an extensive menu and circus and Indian memorabilia covering every inch of wall space. The prime rib is "world famous"; there's also steaks, ribs, veal cutlet, homemade ravioli, breakfasts and burgers, and a prime rib sandwich with fries.

### Genoa *map A-3*

⊞ **Genoa House Inn Bed and Breakfast.** 180 Nixon St., 775-782-7075 $$$
This 130-year-old house is on the list of National Historic. Lovingly restored, it's as cute as it gets in Nevada; three rooms.

### Gold Hill *map A-2/3*

⊞ **Gold Hill Hotel.** 1540 Main St.; 775-847-0111 -$ $$$
The oldest lodging house, and the second oldest building, in the state, the Gold Hill is down the hill from Virginia City. The four rooms in the original wing are authentic (two share a bath); the new-wing rooms are luxurious; four suites have fireplaces. Some of the rooms are *very* inexpensive... but splurge on the pricier ones (6–10); they're worth it.

X **Crown Point.** Gold Hill Hotel. 1540 Main St.; 775-847-0111 $$-$$$
Serving lunch and dinner, the Crown Point is a fine-dining room in a 1980s addition to the venerable Gold Hill Hotel. Creative gourmet menu.

### Hawthorne *map A-3*

⊞ **El Capitan Lodge & Casino.** 540 F St.; 775-945-3321 $
The El Capitan is the casino and 103-room motel in the center of town; the rooms are standard, though the location is convenient to everything. There's also a heated pool and a 24-hour coffee shop.

⊞ **Sand 'n' Sage Lodge.** 1301 E. Fifth St., 775-945-3352 $
One of the nicer motels in Hawthorne, some refrigerators are available and some rooms have balconies.

X **El Capitan.** 540 F St.; 775-945-3321 $
The 24-hour casino coffee shop serves typical road food—bacon and eggs, burgers, sandwiches, prime rib, T-bone, liver and onions, and graveyard specials.

X **Maggie's Bakery.** 758 E. Main St.; 775-945-3908 $-$$
Maggie serves three meals, with nearly everything made from scratch. The salad bar is always reliable.

### Jackpot *map D-1*

⊞ **Barton's Club 93.** US 93; 775-755-2341 or 800-258-2937 $-$$
The old "Hillside" wing rooms are the bargain; the newer "Sandstone" wing rooms are larger and more luxurious.

⊞ **Cactus Petes Hotel-Casino.** 1385 US 93; 775-755-2321 or 800-821-1103 $-$$$$
This is the highest-rise hotel within several hundred miles in every direction.

The casino has every amenity imaginable, including a gourmet restaurant and showroom.

✕ **Plateau Room at Cactus Petes.** 1385 US 93; 775-775-2321 or 800-821-1103 $$-$$$
You'll think you're in Las Vegas when you dine in this gourmet room. Cactus Petes also has a snack bar, 24-hour coffee shop, and buffet. If you're lucky enough to be here on a Wednesday, the food in every restaurant is 50% off.

### Jean *map A-3*

▦ **Gold Strike.** 1 Main St.; 702-477-5000 or 800-634-1359 $-$$
This hotel-casino on I-15 20 miles from Las Vegas is well-known for 800 rooms, one of which is almost always available (even during the largest conventions) at an outrageously low rate.

▦ **Nevada Landing.** 2 Goodsprings Rd.; 702-387-5000 or 800-628-6682 $-$$
Same as the Gold Strike across the highway, one of the great bargain venues in Nevada.

### Incline Village *map A-2*

▦ **Hyatt Regency Lake Tahoe.** 111 Country Club Dr.; 775-832-1234 or 800-233-1234 $$$-$$$$
This Hyatt has a strange exterior (though a total renovation is planned) and luxurious on the inside. A half-block from the lake, with its own private beach and cabin-cruiser. It has a fancy casino,

three restaurants, heated pool and spa, massage, tennis, and game room.

▦ **Inn at Incline.** 1003 Tahoe Blvd.; 775-831-1052 or 800-824-6391 $$-$$$
This is the only motel in Incline Village. It has an indoor pool and spa and serves a complimentry continental breakfast.

✕ **Azzara's.** 930 Tahoe Blvd.; 775-831-0346 $-$$
A typical Italian trattoria with light, inviting decor, Azzara's serves a dozen pasta dishes and many pizzas, as well as chicken, lamb, veal, shrimp, and beef.

✕ **Las Panchitas.** 930 Tahoe Blvd.; 775-831-4048 $-$$
A long-time high-quality Mexican restaurant in the Raley's shopping center, Las Panchitas is popular for a pronto lunch and a leisurely dinner.

✕ **Stanley's.** 941 Tahoe Blvd.; 775-831-9944 $-$$
This local favorite is a good bet any time for straightforward American fare on the hearty side. Lighter bites, such as seafood Cobb salad, are also available, along with ample breakfasts. There's a deck for outdoor dining in summer.

✕ **Wildflower Cafe.** 869 Tahoe Blvd.; 775-831-8072 $
A little unreconstructed flower power is alive and well at this cozy breakfast and brunch nook in the middle of town. The breakfast burrito, house potatoes, pancakes, or homemade pastries will fill you up at least until you're ready for burgers, sandwiches, or chili for lunch.

## Las Vegas *map D-5*

⌂ **Alexis Park Resort.** 375 E. Harmon Ave.; 702-796-3300 or 800-582-2228 $$-$$$$
One of the only full-scale resorts in Las Vegas without a casino, Alexis Park is a sprawling low-rise business hotel minutes from the airport and convention center and across the street from the Hard Rock. All the rooms are suites, some mini, some maxi.

⌂ **Arizona Charlie's.** 740 S. Decatur Blvd.; 702-258-5200 or 800-342-2695 $-$$
The rates at this popular locals casino on the west side are especially attractive to out-of-towners in the know. The Meadows Tower is original (1990), with plain rooms, kinda dark. The Klondike Tower is newer (1994); the rooms are the same size as the Meadows, but a little brighter and more colorful. Bargain food abounds.

⌂ **Bally's.** 3645 Las Vegas Blvd. S.; 702-739-4111 or 800-634-3434 $$-$$$
Built in 1973, Bally's rooms have been renovated in the past few years. The parking garage is some distance from room the tower elevators (shuttles run between them), but the location at center Strip can't be beat. Good buffet.

⌂ **Bellagio.** 3600 Las Vegas Blvd. S.; 702-693-7111 or 800-627-6667 $$$-$$$$
Bellagio is the most expensive hotel ever built, and one of the most expensive Las Vegas hotels to stay at. It has a huge casino, 11 restaurants, rainforest-style pool, barber and beauty shops, and health club. *Not* kid-friendly.

⌂ **Binion's Horseshoe.** 128 E. Fremont St.; 702-382-1600 or 800-237-6537 $-$$
The old wing of this quintessential old-time downtown Las Vegas gambling hall built in 1950; the rooms are tiny but serviceable. The new wing was built in 1965, with standard hotel rooms. The pool is on the 22nd floor; a glass elevator takes you to the top.

⌂ **Caesars Palace.** 3570 Las Vegas Blvd. S.; 702-731-7110 or 800-634-6001 $$$-$$$$
One of the most famous hotels in the world, Caesars has 2,500 rooms in four towers, the newest completed in 1997; many rooms have Roman tubs. Caesars has everything, including 19 restaurants, the most country's most successful shopping mall, one of the few headliner showrooms in town, and a decent pool area.

⌂ **California.** 12 Ogden Ave. 702-385-1222 or 800-634-6255 $-$$$
An inexpensive downtown hotel-casino, the California caters primarily to a Hawaiian package-tour clientele.

⌂ **Circus Circus.** 2880 Las Vegas Blvd. S.; 702-734-0410 or 800-634-3450.
This is the original Las Vegas family resort, now 3,800 rooms. The latest expansion (1996) added 1,000 tasteful rooms, as opposed to the original wings, including the "garden motel rooms," which are utilitarian at best. The casino, buffet, and most restaurants are straight out of *Alice in Wonderland.*

**Courtyard by Marriott.** 3275 Paradise Rd.; 702-791-3600 or 800-321-2211 $$-$$$$
This is a limited-service and lower-priced Marriott that's directly across the street from the Convention Center. The grounds are lush and the king-size beds are plush. Some rooms have balconies and refrigerators.

**Desert Inn.** 3145 Las Vegas Blvd. S.; 702-733-4444 or 800-634-6906 $$$-$$$$
The smallest and most exclusive resort-casino on the Strip, the "DI" has a distinct country-club atmosphere-to go with the 18-hole backyard golf course. The rooms were renovated in the late '90s and are spacious and luxurious.

**El Cortez.** 600 E. Fremont St.; 702-385-5200 or 800-634-6703 $
The El Cortez is as different from the Desert Inn as my house and Bill Gates's. The 300-room tower was built in 1983; the digs are downscale but livable, especially for less than $40.

**Excalibur.** 3850 Las Vegas Blvd. S.; 702-597-7777 or 800-937-7777
This Renaissance fair cum medieval theme park has 4,000 rooms and a giant casino attached, a great location, and family values that would warm Tipper Gore's heart.

**Fitzgeralds.** 301 Fremont St.; 702-388-2400 or 800-274-LUCK $-$$
The rooms at the Fitz are managed by Holiday Inn. They're a little rough around the edges, but one is usually available when the town is crowded, and a bargain when it's not.

**Flamingo Hilton.** 3555 Las Vegas Blvd. S.; 702-733-3111 or 800-732-2111 $$-$$$$
The house that Bugsy built in 1946 would be unrecognizable to him today: It's been expanded a dozen times in the past 53 years, with 3,600 rooms in six towers (a bit of a maze). The Flamingo has the best water park in town, complete with African penguins.

**Fun City.** 2233 Las Vegas Blvd. S.; 702-731-3155 $-$$
This typical motel (painted an atypical pink) just north of Sahara Ave. is a good weekly room play. Most rooms have a kitchenette.

**Golden Gate.** 1 E. Fremont St.; 702-385-1906 or 800-426-1906 $
This is the location of the first lodging in Las Vegas (1906), and the rooms are original, the only ones in town with a historic downtown-hotel feel (they were renovated and upgraded in the early '90s). They're small but very comfortable, and excellent value.

**Golden Nugget.** 129 E. Fremont St.; 702-385-7111 or 800-634-3454 $-$$$$
The classiest and largest hotel-casino downtown, the 1,900 rooms are standard size (the North Tower rooms are larger), but luxuriously appointed. The Nugget is one of the few downtown joints with a pool.

**Hard Rock.** 4455 Paradise Rd.; 702-693-5000 or 800-473-7625 $$-$$$ Though the Hard Rock room inventory doubled in 1999, there are only 680 of them, and they're still difficult to come by. French windows let in fresh air.

**Hops.** 3412 Paradise Rd.; 702-732-2494 $$ A two-minute walk from the Convention Center, Hops is a great place for a weekly stay. Most rooms are two-room suites with a kitchenette.

**Imperial Palace.** 3535 Las Vegas Blvd. S.; 702-731-3311 or 800-634-6441 $-$$$$ Busloads descend on the IP every afternoon of the year, which caters heavily to package travelers. If you don't mind fighting the hordes at check-in, a maze of a resort, and rooms a bit worn, you can't beat the location.

**King Albert.** 185 Albert Ave.; 702-732-1555 or 800-553-7753 $ A standard motel on a side street a half-block from the Flamingo Hilton, the Albert is one of the best motels in town for weekly rooms. All have kitchenettes with full refrigerators.

**Lady Luck.** 206 N. 3rd St.; 702-477-3000 or 800-523-9582 $-$$$ This popular downtown casino is slightly off the beaten gulch. The rooms are in two towers (you have to take two elevators to get to the newer West Tower rooms); they're clean and quiet and a mini-fridge is standard.

**Hilton.** 3000 Paradise Rd.; 702-732-5111 or 800-732-7117 $$-$$$$ This 3,200-room megaresort is right next door to the Convention Center (a 10-15 minute walk from the Strip), catering mostly to business clientele (and trekkies, thanks to the Star Trek Experience attraction). The rooms are standard, though they've been remodeled recently.

**Luxor.** 3900 Las Vegas Blvd. S.; 702-262-4000 or 800-288-1000 $$-$$$$ The 2,500 original rooms (1993) are in the pyramid, standard except for the sloped floor-to-ceiling windows and the Egyptian decor; the 2,000 added rooms (1996) are a little nicer.

**Mandalay Bay.** 3950 Las Vegas Blvd. S.; 702-632-7000 or 800-632-7000 $$-$$$$ The 3,200 rooms at MBay are no less nice than those at Bellagio and Paris, but they're much more reasonable. They're slightly larger than standard, roomy and uncluttered, with a separate tub and shower and the toilet in its own room with phone.

**MGM Grand.** 3799 Las Vegas Blvd. S.; 702-891-1111 or 800-929-1111 $$-$$$$ Though there are lots of rooms here (5,035 in all), they're not that easy to get: MGM runs at more than 90% occupancy year-round. Checking in and out of the world's largest hotel for a weekend can cause the world's largest headache. The rooms are standard (nice marble tubs), though a bit pricey.

🛏 **Mirage.** 3400 Las Vegas Blvd. S.; 702-791-7111 or 800-627-6667 $$-$$$$
It's a bit of a hike from the front desk to the rooms, but once there, you'll like all the marble, 25-inch TVs, and personalized service that Mirage resorts are known for.

🛏 **New York–New York.** 3790 Las Vegas Blvd. S.; 702-740-6969 or 800-693-6763. $$-$$$$
This place is a helluva maze; finding the right elevator to the right tower to the right room can be daunting. Reportedly, there are dozens of different styles of rooms, all heavy into Art Deco, many of them dinky in size. The Strip-facing rooms are disturbingly noisy due to the roller coaster right outside the windows.

🛏 **Orleans.** 4500 W. Tropicana Ave.; 702-365-7111 or 800-675-3267 $-$$$
A locals casino with a huge following (including myself), the Orleans has 800 oversized rooms, half facing the Strip, half facing the mountains. There's also swinging lounge entertainment, a giant bowling alley, a 12-plex movie theater, and Kid's Tyme, a child-care facility.

🛏 **Paris.** 3655 Las Vegas Blvd. S.; 877-796-2096 $$-$$$$
It's Paris in the 1930s—supposedly. Detailed replicas of the Eiffel Tower, the Louvre, etc.; attractive "sky" ceiling and French-y restaurants.

🛏 **Plaza.** 1 Main St.; 702-386-2110 or 800-634-6575 $-$$
An inexpensive room here is always available.

🛏 **Rio.** 3700 W. Flamingo Rd.; 702-252-7777 or 800-752-9746 $$-$$$
One of the great resorts in Las Vegas, the Rio boasts 2,500 of the best rooms in town, all one-room suites with big picture windows and sitting areas; a window in the shower looks over the suite and view. Fifteen restaurants and a big pool area don't hurt.

🛏 **Sam's Town.** 5111 Boulder Hwy.; 702-456-7777 or 800-634-6371 $-$$$
Like the Orleans, Sam's Town is a large and popular locals hotel. A 1994 addition gave it a total of 650 rooms. The new 450 rooms are spacious and overlook a park-like indoor atrium and dancing-waters spectacle. There's a major bowling alley here.

🛏 **Stratosphere.** 2000 Las Vegas Blvd. S.; 702-380-7777 or 800-998-6937 $-$$$$
The neighborhood is a little rough around the edges, and an entire wing or rooms stands unfinished, so Stratosphere has to discount its room product a little, making the place a bargain.

🛏 **Travelodge.** 1501 W. Sahara Ave.; 702-733-0001 $-$$
This motel has typical Travelodge rooms, but it's in a great location right next to Circus Circus, with parking right at the room. It's an easy in-and-out, and the price is usually right.

🛏 **Treasure Island.** 3300 Las Vegas Blvd. S.; 702-894-7111 or 800-944-7444 $$-$$$$
The rooms are undersized, but the location, arcade, pool area, pirate battle, and good food recommend the TI.

⊡ **Tropicana.** 3801 Las Vegas Blvd. S.; 702-739-2222 or 800-634-4000 $$-$$$$
This '50s hotel-casino is overshadowed by its bigger and newer neighbors, but the original bungalow rooms have the only balconies on the Strip (great for kids), the pool area is the lushest in town, and the location is fabulous.

⊡ **Venetian.** 3355 Las Vegas Blvd. S.; 702-733-5000 or 800-494-3556 $$$$
These 3,000 suites are the most expensive hotel accommodations in town-and well worth it: they're all 700-square-foot suites, with sunken living room, separate bedroom, two 27-inch TVs, huge bathrooms, mini bar, fax machine/copier/printer, three dual-line telephones, and spare queen-size hide-a-bed.

⊡ **Westward Ho.** 2900 Las Vegas Blvd. S.; 702-731-2900or 800-634-6803
The Ho claims to be the largest motel in the world. You'll find good deals on large suites (some sleep six), and four pools.

✕ **Aureole.** Mandalay Bay. 3950 Las Vegas Blvd. S.; 702-632-7401 $$$$
The signature restaurant at Mandalay Bay, Aureole is a creation of New York celebrity-chef Charlie Palmer. The food is contemporary eclectic, the setting is subterranean (some seats overlook a patio), and the one-of-a-kind "wine tower" holds upwards of 12,000 bottles.

✕ **Bacchanal.** Caesars Palace, 3570 Las Vegas Blvd. S.; 702-731-7731 $$$$
Here you gorge on a set seven-course Roman feast while toga-clad wine god-

desses fill your bottomless goblet and massage your aching (upper) body. You do the Bacchanal for the experience, not the cuisine.

✕ **Baja Fresh.** Texas Station. 2101 Texas Star Ln.; 702-307-1717 $
The best Mexican fast food in town, Baja Fresh boasts "no can openers, no microwaves, no lard, and no MSG." There's often a line out the door at lunch for the burritos. Four locations around town.

✕ **Bamboo Garden.** 4850 W. Flamingo Ave.; 702-871-3262 $-$$
Though this restaurant is modestly located in a storefront in a W. Flamingo strip shopping center, it's one of the best Chinese restaurants in town. Try the Szechuan green beans or the Hunan eggplant.

✕ **Boston Pizza.** 1507 Las Vegas Blvd. S.; 702-385-2595 $
If you're a fan of the ubiquitous Greek Houses of Pizza in Boston, you'll be right at home at Boston Pizza, the only one of its kind in Las Vegas.

✕ **Buffet at Bellagio.** 3600 Las Vegas Blvd. S.; 702-693-7111 $$
If price is no object, the upscale superbuffet at the upscale megaresort is the best place to shovel home all-you-can-eat gourmet offerings. The seafood alone will send you back to the serving lines time after time, as will gourmet salads, six different kinds of potatoes, ethnic entrees, fresh bread, and desserts galore.

✗ **Center Stage.** Plaza. 1 Main St.; 702-386-2110 $-$$
This is the quintessential Las Vegas "bargain gourmet" restaurant, serving steakhouse fare at coffee shop prices. With a window table, you're looking directly down Fremont Street at the neon signs and the singing canopy.

✗ **China Grill Cafe.** Mandalay Bay. 3950 Las Vegas Blvd. S.; 702-632-7777 $-$$
The place touts itself as serving "world" cuisine, which is trendy Pacific Rim, such as Phuket chicken wings, pad Thai and curry noodles, shrimp spring rolls, stir-fried duck, and lettuce tacos, along wokked dishes, Oriental pizzas, and California rolls. The centerpiece bar is circled by a conveyor belt, carrying plates of appetizers, primarily sushi.

✗ **Deli.** Golden Gate. 1 E. Fremont St.; 702-385-1906 $
If you eat one thing while you're in Las Vegas, it ought to be the 99-cent shrimp cocktail at the Golden Gate. More than thirty million of these six-ounce crunchy crustacean cocktails have been served right here since 1959.

✗ **Deli.** Binion's Horseshoe. 128 Fremont St.; 702-382-1600 $
Towering pastrami, corned beef, and turkey sandwiches, lox and bagels, and matzoh ball soup are served at this deli counter, which faces the sports book. Grab a corned beef on rye and hang with the wise guys.

✗ **El Sombrero.** 807 S. Main Street; 702-382-9234 $
The squat adobe building looks like a Juarez jailhouse, but this is the oldest Mexican cantina in Las Vegas. Only two cooks have been putting out the food since El Sombrero opened in 1950; you can't argue with the consistency or authenticity. The house special is a burrito "smothered" enchilada-style. For dessert there's natillas, Mexican vanilla pudding with raisins.

✗ **Emeril's New Orleans Fish House.** MGM Grand, 3799 Las Vegas Blvd. S.; 702-891-7374 $$$-$$$$
That's Emeril *Lagasse*, the flamboyant New Orleans celebrity chef who runs this oyster bar and seafood restaurant (when he's in town). Some of the most unusual preparations of salmon, tuna, shrimp, and meats are on parade here.

✗ **Hound Doggie's.** Riviera. 2901 Las Vegas Blvd. S.; 702-734-5110 $
This is the best-value casino snack bar in town: $1 hot dogs, $2 hamburgers, $3 steak sandwiches, and best of all, 50-cent draft beer.

✗ **Main Street Station Buffet.** 200 N. Main St.; 702-387-1896 $
The best buffet downtown occupies the most decorative room and charges some of the cheapest prices in town. This buffet, which caters to a Hawaiian clientele, has a distinct Japanese and Polynesian flair.

FOOD & LODGING

✕ **Mayflower Cuisinier.** 4750 W. Sahara Ave.; 702-870-8432 $$-$$$
A popular, expensive, unusual Chinese restaurant, fusing elements of French, Italian, Californian, and Pan-Asian cuisines, such as an Asian mushroom burrito, Mongolian lamb chops, and Chinese pasta.

✕ **Nobu.** Hard Rock. 4455 Paradise Rd.; 702-693-5000 $$$-$$$$
Yet another Las Vegas branch of a world-class eatery (Nobu in Manhattan), this restaurant sports bamboo pillars, a wall of seaweed, and birch decor. The cuisine is contemporary Japanese, full of sashimi, miso, mochi, and green tea.

✕ **Picasso.** Bellagio. 3600 Las Vegas Blvd. S.; 702-693-7111 $$$$
You sit among the works of art of the 20th century's most famous artist and eat ol' Pablo's native Miditerranean cuisine. Jacket and tie aren't required, buy you'll feel dumb without them.

✕ **Roxy's Pizzeria.** Fiesta. 2400 N. Rancho Dr.; 702-631-7000 $-$$
The pizza is from Regina's, Boston's oldest pizzeria (1926), with a crust that will immediately dissolve all your crustiness. Meanwhile, the entire three-story back wall of the barn-like restaurant is covered with the 16-ton 1927 organ from New York's Roxy's Theater, complete with 3,000 pipes, horns, and fluted tubes, played live nightly by renowned organists.

✕ **Second Street Grille.** Fremont. 200 E. Fremont St.; 702-385-6277 $$-$$$
Tucked away in an obscure corner of the obscure Fremont, Second Street Grille is the place for fine dining Hawaiian style. The seafood is flown in fresh from around the Pacific Rim and there's always a bargain special.

✕ **Spago.** Forum Shops at Caesars. 3500 Las Vegas Blvd. S.; 702-369-6300 $$-$$$$
Wolfgang Puck's original Las Vegas eatery kicked off the whole celebrity-chef contemporary-cuisine movement here. Spago remains one of the best restaurants in town. The cafe out front is casual, while the dining room is more formal. Both are bustling and noisy.

✕ **Sourdough Cafe.** Arizona Charlie's. 740 S. Decatur Ave.; 702-258-5200 $-$$
This is one of the best casino coffee shops around, evidenced by the long lines usually waiting to get in; for immediate seating, try the counter. The $2.49 steak-and-eggs is a classic Vegas meal deal. The hot roast beef sandwich is not low-fat.

✕ **Thai Spice.** 4433 W. Flamingo Ave.; 702-362-5308 $-$$
This classy storefront restaurant perennially wins the Best Thai Food ranking in local polls. The tom kha kai soup is nectar and ambrosia; the blackjack noodles are fat and sassy.

✕ **Top of the World.** 2000 Las Vegas Blvd. S.; 702-380-7711 or 800-99 TOWER $$$-$$$$
The food's good enough, but the room sits at 850 feet above the valley and revolves once every hour or so (pay attention if you have to go to the restroom: Your table will be in a different place when you return). Very romantic.

✕ **Wild Oats.** 6720 W. Sahara Ave.; 702-253-7050 $-$$
This natural-foods grocery store has a cafe, with an excellent salad bar, soups, smoothies, sandwiches, juices, and gourmet coffees. There's a solarium so you can sit and eat in splendid natural light.

### Laughlin *map D-5*

⊞ **Colorado Belle.** 2100 Casino Dr.; 702-298-4000 or 800-477-4837 $-$$
An anomaly in Nevada, this Mandalay Resort Group resort is a riverboat casino actually on a river. The 1,200 rooms frequently go for less than $20 a night.

⊞ **Flamingo Hilton.** 1900 S. Casino Dr.; 702-298-5111 or 800-352-6464 $-$$$$
This is the newest and largest hotel-casino in Laughlin, opened in 1990 with 1,900 good-size rooms.

⊞ **Harrah's.** 2900 S. Casino Dr.; 702-298-4600 or 800-427-7247 $-$$
A 1,600-room Harrah's, with standard hotel rooms at low low rack rates and the only Laughlin hotel-casino with a public beach on the river. Boat rentals are available too.

⊞ **Pioneer.** 2200 S. Casino Dr.; 702-298-2442 or 800-634-3469 $
This motel-like low-rise 400-room low-roller joint right on the river has frequent bargain room specials; they're nearly given away. Some rooms are on the riverfront.

⊞ **Ramada Express.** 2121 Casino Dr.; 702-298-4200 or 800-AGENT-46 $
This 1,500-room resort is so heavily railroad-themed that even th pool is shaped like a cartoon train engine. Ramada Express, the only hotel-casino on the non-river side of Casino Drive, often boasts the least expensive rooms in a town full of inexpensive rooms.

⊞ **River Palms.** 2700 S. Casino Dr.; 702-298-2242or 800-835-7903 $-$$$
Hippest hotel-casino in Laughlin, the River Palms is undergoing a major renovation, in which all the tower rooms will be remodeled and the garden rooms will be completely replaced-completing is slated for 2002.

⊞ **Riverside.** 1650 Casino Dr.; 702-298-2535 or 800-227-3849 $-$$$
Owned by town founder and namesake, Don Laughlin, the Riverside is the oldest resort in town, though the latest expansion added a 1,000-room tower

✕ **Beef Baron.** Flamingo Hilton. 1900 S. Casino Dr.; 702-298-5111 $$-$$$
Hilton's steakhouse brand offers good value for decent food, such as steaks, blackened prime rib, hickory smoked salmon, ribs, catfish, and chicken.

✕ **Boarding House.** Pioneer. 2200 S. Casino Dr.; 702-298-2442 $-$$
This coffee shop, which doubles as the buffet, always has a line out the door, evidence of the good food-eggs, burgers, sandwiches, steaks, crab legs-at excellent prices.

✕ **Fresh Market Square Buffet.** Harrah's. 2900 S. Casino Dr.; 702-298-4600 $-$$
Harrah's brand superbuffet is the largest and most diverse in Laughlin (where the buffets are very cheap and the quality reflects it).

✕ **Granny's.** Pioneer. 2200 S. Casino Dr.; 702-298-2442 $$$-$$$$
A sleeper gourmet restaurant occupies an old-fashioned room on the second floor of the low-roller Pioneer, serving the likes of lamb chops and rack of lamb, veal, sea bass, pheasant, chateaubriand, and salmon.

✕ **Jane's Grill.** Golden Nugget. 2300 S. Casino Dr.; 702-298-7111 $-$$
Similar to the California Pizza Kitchens at the Mirage and Las Vegas Golden Nugget, this restaurant serves soup, salads, appetizers, pizzas, calzone, pasta, chicken, and salmon, all under $10.

✕ **Passagio's.** Ramada Express. 2121 Casino Dr.; 702-298-4200 $-$$
Red-checked tablecloths give this Italian restaurant a classic feel, as do the big bowls of pasta, thin-crust pizza, eggplant parmesan, vegetarian lasagna, veal, and beef.

✕ **Prime Rib Room.** Riverside. 1650 Casino Dr.; 702-298-2535 $
Interesting idea for a restaurant: Generous portions of prime rib are carved at the tables; you can also opt for chicken cordon bleu. There's a salad and potato bar, and fresh-baked pies and cakes for dessert. Drinks are included. All for about eight bucks.

## Lovelock *map B-2*

⌂ **Lovelock Inn.** 55 Cornell Ave.; 775-273-2937 $-$$
Modern motel off the I-80 west exit, next to the museum and chamber of commerce.

⌂ **Sturgeon's Ramada Inn.** 1420 Cornell Ave.; 775-273-2971 or 888/234-6835 $-$$
This is the largest lodging in Lovelock, with 75 remodeled motel rooms at the east I-80 exit, along with a big casino (for Lovelock) and coffee shop.

✕ **Sturgeon's Coffee Shop.** 1420 Cornell Ave.; 775-273-2971 $-$$
The 24-hour diner at Sturgeon's serves typical road food in massive quantities, especially the daily specials, at bargain prices.

## Minden *map A-3*

⌂ **Carson Valley Inn.** 1627 US 395, 775-782-9711 or 800-321-6983 $-$$$$
The 150 rooms at the Inn are standard

hotel rooms; there's luggage, valet, child-care, and room service.

🛏 **Carson Valley Motor Lodge.** 1643 US 395 N.; 775-782-9711 or 800-321-6983 $-$$$
The Motor Lodge and Inn are the main accommodations in downtown Minden. The Motor Lodge is a 76-room motel where standard rooms are significantly less expensive.

✕ **Fiona's.** 1627 US 395, 775-782-4347 $$-$$$
The tropical decor is a pleasant surprise at Fiona's, the Carson Valley Inn steakhouse, serving steaks, seafood, a variety of chicken dishes, and pasta. The salad bar is awesome.

### Primm  *map D-5*

🛏 **Buffalo Bill's.** I-15 at the Stateline; 702-382-1111 or 800-FUNSTOP $
Newest of the Primm trio, Buffalo Bill's has 1,300 standard hotel rooms, which rarely go below $39 and can often go as low as $18. Desperado roller coaster runs around the property.

🛏 **Primm Valley.** I-15 at the Stateline; 702-382-1212 or 800-FUNSTOP $
Primm Valley has 681 rooms at Primm's renowned low rates; this one's attached to the Factory Outlet Stores.

🛏 **Whiskey Pete's.** I-15 at the Stateline; 702-382-4388 or 800-FUNSTOP $
The original Primm resort, the 830 rooms are a little older but no less comfortable and inexpensive.

### Rachel  *map C-4*

🛏 **Little A-Le-Inn.** NV 375; 775-729-2515 $
✕
The seven-room motel in the famous UFO town fills up fast; make your reservations as far ahead as possible. The diner serves typical road food at the combo bar-counter.

### Reno  *map A-3*

🛏 **Adventure Inn.** 3575 S. Virginia St.; 775-828-9000 or 800-937-1436 $-$$$
Staying here is an adventure, with its highly themed rooms and suites: Jungle, Bridal, Roman, Adam and Eve, Tropical, Bordello, Cave, and Space. All come with round or heart-shaped beds, "rainforest" showers, free limo rides within 10 miles, complimentary champagne, and more. Wedding chapel, too.

🛏 **Atlantis.** 3800 S. Virginia St.; 775-825-4700 or 800-723-6500 $-$$$
This full-scale Caribbean-themed resort-casino outside of the downtown core has been continually expanded from a 1960s motel. The latest expansion added 600 rooms (1999). The original garden rooms often a good deal.

🛏 **Best Western Airport Plaza.** 1981 Terminal Way; 775-348-6370 or 800-648-3525 $$-$$$$
A low-rise 270-room casino-motel directly across from the entrance to the airport, it's a seven-minute walk from the terminal building.

FOOD & LODGING

▣ **Boomtown.** I-80 at Garson Rd.; 775-345-6000 or 800-648-3790 $-$$
The major resort-casino on the CA-NV state line has 200 rooms, a big casino, a big kid's amusement center (motion theater, merry-go-round, Ferris wheel, indoor miniature golf, arcade games), and a good cheap buffet.

▣ **Castaway Inn.** 525 W. 2nd St.; 775-329-2555 $-$$$
One of the best weekly plays in Reno, the Castaway's clean rooms, though on the small side, have full kitchenettes. It's in a good location too: far enough from the main action downtown to be quiet, but close enough to walk to it.

▣ **Circus Circus.** 500 N. Sierra St.; 775-329-0711 or 800-648-5010 $-$$$
A 100-foot clown licks a giant lollipop out front and pandemonium reigns inside. It can be tough to book a room in Reno's most popular tourist attraction, but unless you have kids in tow, you might as well stay at Silver Legacy or Eldorado, which are connected by skywalk.

▣ **Eldorado.** 345 N. Virginia St.; 775-786-5700 or 800-648-5966 $-$$$$
Rooms in the new tower are luxurious, but everything you see at the Eldorado is classy, tasteful, and reasonable.

▣ **El Cortez.** 239 W. Second St.; 775-322-9161 $-$$
If your taste (like mine) runs toward funky old downtown hotels with the bath down the hall with bargain-basement rates, this is the place.

▣ **Executive Inn.** 205 S. Sierra St., 775-786-4050 $$-$$$$
The 87 rooms here are all oversized and uncluttered, and come with a microwave and full refrigerator. Good for weekly or long-term stays.

▣ **Flamingo Hilton.** 255 N. Sierra St.; 775-322-1111 or 800-648-4882 $$-$$$$
The roughest around the edges of the Hilton Nevada hotel-casinos, at press time the 600-room Flamingo Hilton is for sale for a bargain basement $26 million. Plenty of better deals can be found downtown.

▣ **Harrah's.** 210 N. Center St.; 775-786-3232 or 800-427-7247 $$-$$$$
Opened in 1937, the oldest casino in Reno and one of the oldest in the state is a snazzy joint, covering nearly two blocks with three casinos and two hotel towers. Many of the rooms have oversized tubs.

▣ **La Quinta.** 4001 Market St.; 775-348-6100 or 800 531-5900 $$-$$$
This is a standard motel, but its size (130 rooms) and location (across the freeway from the airport) make it convenient for travelers.

▣ **Miner's Inn.** 1651 N. Virginia St.; 775-329-3464 or 800-823-1762 $-$$
This is a clean and comfortable 70-room motel directly across the street from the University.

▣ **Peppermill.** 2707 S. Virginia St.; 775-826-2121 or 800-282-2224 $-$$$
The Peppermill has been expanded and

remodeled many times over the decades, most recently in 1997. The rooms here run the gamut: Penthouse, Royal, and Luxury suites, Jacuzzi king, and Tower queen (photos of the various rooms are posted in the lobby).

🏨 **Reno Hilton.** 2500 E. 2nd St.; 775-789-2000 or 800-648-5080 $-$$$
The big boy on the block is the largest hotel-casino in the state outside of Vegas. The 2,001 rooms have all been renovated (since Hilton bought the joint from Bally's in 1992). With six restaurants, a hip new bar and lounge entertainment, a 2,000-seat showroom, retail area, movie theater, barber and beauty shop, lighted indoor and outdoor tennis, golf driving range, spa, bowling alley, and arcade, you never have to leave.

🏨 **Residence Inn by Marriott.** 9845 Gateway Dr.; 775-853-8800 or 800-331-3131 $$-$$$
A 120-room business-travelers low-rise eight miles south of downtown, right off the freeway, in the Double Diamond business park neighborhood.

🏨 **Silver Legacy.** 407 N. Virginia St.; 775-329-4777 or 800-687-8733 $$-$$$$
New kid on the block, the Legacy opened in 1995, with 1,700 rooms, third largest in Reno. The lobby is classy, the rooms standard size, tasteful, and comfortable.

🏨 **Vagabond Inn.** 3131 S. Virginia St.; 775-825-7134 $-$$
This is a newer standard 130-room motel at the south end of South Virginia Street near the Convention Center. A Continental breakfast is complimentary.

✕ **Baldini's Buffet.** 865 S. Rock Blvd.; 775-358-0116 $
One of the great bargains in Reno, this is a mini-superbuffet at a favorite locals casino. Pile your plate high with Mexican, Chinese, Italian, and American; there's even a Mongolian grill (where you can also get a grilled burger). Kids are half price and you get a 25% discount in perpetuity just for joining the slot club.

✕ **Bavarian World.** 595 Valley Rd.; 775-323-7646 $-$$
Germany in Reno, the Bavarian is an old-world German grocery, deli, and restaurant. Fill up on shnitzel, sauerbraten, potato pancakes, and beef, then take out some rye bread and Swiss chocolate. The place to be in October.

✕ **Bertha Miranda's.** 336 Mill St.; 775/786-9697 $-$$
The Miranda family is locally renowned for its authentic Mexican cooking, excellent salsa, and generous portions. Bertha's wins the Best of Reno poll consistently.

✕ **Blue Heron.** 1091 S. Virginia St.; 775-786-4110 $
This is one of the few natural foods restaurants you'll find in this meat-and-potatoes state, and it's great for grains, veggies, tofu, tempeh, and macrobiotic meals. Much of the produce is grown on the owner's farm in California's Central Valley.

✕ **Cafe de Thai.** 3314 S. McCarran Ave. (Mira Loma Shopping Center); 775-829-8424 $$
What this glorified hole-in-the-wall in a strip mall lacks in atmosphere, it more than makes up for in food. The creative menu includes satay and papaya salad appetizers, tom kha gai, Oriental sausage salad, pad Thai, and spicy curries.

✕ **Harrah's Steak House.** 219 N. Center St.; 775-786-3232 $$-$$$
In the basement of the busy Harrah's casino, this dark, romantic restaurant has no view of slot machines to disrupt the warm ambience of the luxurious red booths and candlelight. Burgers, BLTs, and chicken sandwiches are available for lunch; veal steaks, chops, chicken, and fish are offered at dinner.

✕ **Johnny Rocket's.** Reno Hilton. 2500 E. 2nd St.; 775-789-2000 $-$$
The coolest '50s diner in town, Johnny's is straight out of *American Grafitti*, with a black-and-white floor, red naugehyde booths, and juke boxes. The straw holders are a trip. The diner food is expensive, but the portions are small.

✕ **La Strada.** Eldorado. 345 N. Virginia St.; 775-786-5700 $-$$
This exceptional Italian restaurant has a special wood-fired brick oven imported from Italy and an Italian chef who knows his stuff. His wild-mushroom ravioli is especially good, all the pastas are handmade, and the pizza is perfect.

✕ **Louis' Basque Corner.** 301 E. 4th St.; 775-323-7203 $$
At Louis', you'll probably be seated with people you don't know, but they won't be strangers for long, as you all face huge portions of soup, salad, Basque beans, french fries, a choice of beef, lamb, or seafood entrees, along wine, and dessert. The potent Basque cocktail, Picon Punch, will quickly put you in the lively spirit of this place.

✕ **Palais de Jade.** 960 W. Moana Lane; 775-827-5233 $$-$$$
The ritziest Chinese restaurant in Reno is in a tasteful black-and-white room, understated and elegant. The dishes tend toward fancy Cantonese, with the moo shu, cashew, and kung pao you've come to know, along with some scallop and lobster preparations and Szechuan specials.

✕ **Peppermill Buffet.** 2707 S. Virginia St.; 775-826-2121 $$-$$$
The Peppermill completed a $65 million expansion in late 1999, which included an entirely new buffet. It's expensive, but the food is so good (and the room is so theatrical) that it would compete for top honors in the tough buffet competition in Las Vegas.

✕ **Rapscallion Seafood House & Bar.** 1555 S. Wells Ave.; 775-323-1211 $$-$$$
Steaks and pastas are available at this clubby restaurant, but the specialty here is fish: Up to 30 varieties of fresh seafood

appear on the menu daily. Salads, burgers, fish, and steak sandwiches are served at lunch.

X **The Ridge.** 1200 Razorback Rd.; 775-825-1250 $$$
The setting-right on the Lakeridge Golf Course overlooking Truckee Meadows-is as outstanding as the well-prepared fare. The lunch menu consists of sandwiches, seafood, steaks, and chicken.

X **Top Deck.** Cal-Neva. 140 N. Virginia Ave.; 775-323-1046 $$
This is the place for the most venerable and popular 99-cent breakfast in Nevada: two eggs, ham, sausage, or bacon, hash browns, toast, and coffee, served 24/7. There's also a big menu of the usual coffee shop fare, but the prices are so low that the Top Deck is a madhouse all day (sit at the counter if you're in a hurry.

X **Top of the Hilton.** Flamingo Hilton. 255 N. Sierra St.; 775-785-7010 $$-$$$
On the 21st floor of the Flamingo tower, this exquisite dining room serves exquisite gourmet fare: steaks, prime rib, salmon, sea bass, and the like. The appetizers have a Pan-Asian flair.

### Sparks *map A-3*

🏨 **John Ascuaga's Nugget.** 1100 Nugget Ave.; 775-356-3300 or 800-648-1177 $-$$$$
Opened in 1956 and continually expanded ever since, "John A's" has a wide variety of motel and hotel rooms in several different buildings, as well as the nicest indoor pool in the state and great food.

🏨 **Silver Club.** 1040 Victorian Ave.; 775-358-4771 or 800-905-7774 $-$$
This is a 200-room hotel-casino directly across the street from John Ascuaga's Nugget; the rooms tower is a block off the main drag in a quiet location.

X **John's Oyster Bar.** John Ascuaga's Nugget. 1100 Nugget Ave., 775-356-3300 $$
Sit down at the counter or a table for some of the freshest crustacean cocktails, chowders, louies, steamers, pan roasts, and stews this side of San Francisco's Fisherman's Wharf. The seafood is of a consistent high quality and served piping hot in generous portions, straight out of the steam pots. You might see John A himself in an apron—he often cooks here to relax!

X **Victoria's. Silver Club.** 1040 Victorian Ave.; 775-358-4771 $$
This steakhouse on the mezzanine level of the Silver Club is locally popular for its big portions and reasonable prices. There's always a bargain play here too.

### Tahoe *map A-3*

🏨 **Caesars Tahoe.** 55 US 50; 775-588-3515 or 800-648-3353 $$$-$$$$
Most of the rooms and suites here (across Hwy. 50 from the lake) have Roman tubs, king-size beds, two telephones, and a view of the lake or mountains.

FOOD & LODGING

▣ **Harrah's Lake Tahoe.** US 50; 775-588-6611 or 800-427-7247 $$$-$$$$
The opulent guest rooms here have private bars and two full bathrooms, each with a television and telephone. There's also an indoor pool, big arcade, and butler service in the suites.

▣ **Harvey's.** US 50, 775-588-2411 or 800-427-8397 $$$-$$$$
The oldest casino on the lake, Harvey's has expanded and remodeled continually through the early '90s. Rooms have custom furnishings, oversize marble baths, and minibars.

▣ **Lakeside Inn.** US 50 at Kingsbury Grade; 775-588-7777 or 800-624-7980 $$
The Lakeside, located a mile north of the main high-rise action, is the only low-rise resort among them. Here you'll find 125 standard motel rooms, the least expensive at Stateline.

✕ **Bill's Roadhouse Cafe.** Bill's Casino. US 50; 775-588-2455 $-$$
This trendy coffee shop has some of the more reasonably priced food at a Stateline casino: wings, sweet potato skins, burgers, chicken breast sandwiches, ribs, meat loaf, prime rib, steaks, and pizza—all for 10 bucks or less.

✕ **Chart House.** 329 Kingsbury Grade; 775-588-6276 $$-$$$
It's worth the drive up the steep grade to see the view from here. Try to arrive for sunset. The American menu of steak and seafood is complemented by an abundant salad bar. The restaurant has a children's menu.

✕ **El Vaquero.** Harvey's. US 50, 775-588-2411 $-$$.
You'll find this decent Tex-Mex beanery in the basement of Harvey's, directly across from the tunnel under US 50 to Harrah's. The menu consists of the usual burritos, tostadas, fajitas, and a few fancier entrees.

✕ **Empress Court.** Caesars Tahoe. 55 US 50; 775-588-3515 $$-$$$
Caesars brand-name Oriental restaurant serves fine Chinese food at fancy prices. Try the seafood chow mein, Singapore rice noodles, or steak and lobster.

✕ **Llewellyn's Restaurant.** Harvey's Resort. U.S. 50; 775-588-2411 $$-$$$
Almost every table at the restaurant atop Harvey's casino has superb views of Lake Tahoe. Dinner entrees-seafood, meat, and poultry-are served with unusual accompaniments, such as sturgeon in potato crust with saffron sauce or veal with polenta, herbs, and pancetta. Lunches are reasonably priced, with gourmet selections as well as hamburgers.

✕ **North Beach Deli.** Harrah's Lake Tahoe. US 50; 775-588-6611 $
The many varieties of sandwiches at this great deli are huge and inexpensive. They also dish up good soups, salads, and desserts.

✗ **Summit.** Harrah's Lake Tahoe. US 50; 775-588-6611 $$$$
On the 16th floor, the Summit is one of the most exclusive and exquisite restaurants in the state. Start with some caviar, then try the escargot or frog-legs appetizers, then go for a venison, rack of lamb, or wild-game mixed grill entree, and finish up with a Grand Marnier soufflé dessert. Bring two credit cards.

### Tonopah *map B-3*

🛏 **Best Western High Desert Inn.** 320 S. Main St.; 775-482-3511 or 800-528-1234 $-$$
This is the most modern and expensive motel in town, one of the few with a pool.

🛏 **Jim Butler.** 100 S. Main St.; 775-482-3577 or 800-635-9455 $-$$
Named after the founder of Tonopah, this 25-room motel is in the heart of downtown.

🛏 **Mizpah.** 100 Main St., 775-482-6202 $-$$
The six-story 50-room brick Mizpah, built in 1906, has some of the finest restored old hotel rooms in Nevada, with brass beds, mock kerosene lamps, water-closet-type toilets with pull chains, and solid brass sink and tub fixtures. This is the place to stay in Tonopah-if it's open (hit or miss over the past few years).

🛏 **Station House.** 1100 Erie Main St.; 775-482-9777 $-$$
The 78 rooms at the Station House, the most extensive hotel-casino in Tonopah, are oversized and quiet. There's a snack bar and coffee shop here, and a supermarket next door.

✗ **El Marques.** 348 Main St.; 775-482-3885 $-$$
Mexican restaurants (actually, all restaurants) come and go with regularity in Tonopah, but this one's been around for as long as I have. It's open for lunch and dinner, serving good Tex-Mex.

✗ **Mary's Kitchen.** Station House. 1100 Erie Main St.; 775-482-9777 $
Tonopah is primarily a coffee shop kind of town, and this is the best of the bunch. Get your fill of road food at typical prices; graveyard specials include $1.49 breakfasts and $6.95 steaks.

### Virginia City *map A-2*

🛏 **Comstock Lodge.** 875 S. C. St.; 775-847-0233 $-$$
This whole motel has been recently remodeled; its 13 rooms are half the total inventory in Virginia City.

🛏 **Sugar Loaf.** 430 S. C St.; 775-847-7705 $-$$
Motel rooms are precious in Virginia City and the Sugar Loaf's 12 of them are the most likely to be open and available.

FOOD & LODGING

✗ **Palace Restaurant and Saloon.** 51 S. C St.; 775-847-4441 $
Virginia City is a diner food kind of town and the Palace is typical, serving bacon and eggs, huevos rancheros, burgers, club sandwiches and fried shrimp, all for less than $8.

✗ **Sawdust Corner.** Delta Saloon. 18 S. C St.; 775-847-0919 $
The largest diner in Virginia City, the Sawdust is attached to the Delta Saloon, serving breakfast, lunch, and dinner during the summer, some combination thereof during the winter.

✗ **Solid Muldoon.** 65 N. C St.; 775-847-9181 $-$$
This is one of the few places in town serving more than diner food: steak or Italian sausage and eggs for breakfast, gourmet burgers and spaghetti for lunch, yes, but also blackened prime rib, blackened catfish, steak and shrimp, and a petite filet for dinner.

✗ **Wagon Wheel.** 171 S. C St.; 775-847-0500 $
The only stand-alone restaurant in Virginia City, on the south edge of town, the Wagon Wheel's breakfasts include steak (fried or broiled) and eggs and huevos rancheros; lunches: "famous" chili, Chinese chicken salad, Reuben, and club; dinners: spaghetti and meatballs, steak, chicken picatta, and bratwurst.

**Wendover** *map D-1/2*

⌧ **State Line/Silver Smith.** 100 Wendover Blvd.; 775-664-2221 or 800-848-7300 $-$$$$
The oldest continuously operating casino in Nevada (1931), the State Line and Silver Smith are Siamese facilities on either side of Wendover Blvd., connected by a skywalk. Both have classy casinos, restaurants, and rooms; the Silver Smith has a small showroom.

⌧ **Super 8.** 1325 Wendover Blvd.; 775-664-2888 or 800-800-8000 $-$$
The only motel among the several hotel-casinos in Wendover.

**Winnemucca** *map B-1*

⌧ **Best Western Gold Country Inn.** 921 W. Winnemucca Blvd.; 775-623-6999 or 800-346-5306 $$-$$$
This is the fanciest, and most expensive, motel in Winnemucca.

⌧ **Days Inn.** 511 W. Winnemucca Blvd.; 775-623-3661 or 800-DAYSINN $-$$
Standard chain motel rooms, close to downtown.

⌧ **Parker's Model T.** 1130 Winnemucca Blvd.; 775-623-0222 or 800-645-5658 $-$$
This is a truck-stop casino at the west end of town, with a standard 75-room motel attached. If you were allowed, you could jump out the back-room windows into the pool.

⌂ **Red Lion.** 741 W. Winnemucca Blvd.; 775-623-2565 or 800-633-6435
This is the largest lodging in Winnemucca, with 106 rooms, a mini-casino, and a 24-hour coffee shop.

⌂ **Scott Shady Court.** 400 First St.; 775-623-3646 $-$$
These accommodations date back to 1928, and the Shady Court is one of only two motels off Winnemucca Boulevard, so it's a little quieter than most. The 70 rooms are standard, but the indoor pool in a separate building is a treat.

✗ **Griddle.** 460 W. Winnemucca Blvd.; 775-623-2977 $
A breakfast and lunch place, the Griddle hops from 5 A.M. till 1 P.M., sending bountiful plates of eggs, potatoes, and pastries from a tiny kitchen into the cozy old dining room and a warm log-cabin addition.

✗ **Martin's.** Railroad and Melarkey Sts.; 775-623-3197 $$
Another old Winnemucca Basque landmark, Martin's is a bar and dinner house, serving Basque food, where there's always something intensely local going on.

✗ **Winnemucca Hotel.** 95 Bridge St.; 775-623-2908 $$
The second-oldest still-operating hotel in the state is an old-time boarding house that serves Basque breakfasts, lunches, and dinners family style daily.

## Yerington *map A-3*

✗ **Casino West.** 11 N. Main St.; 775-463-2481 or 800-227-4661 $-$$
This is the big motel (79 rooms) in the heart of quaint Yerington. There's a pool, bowling alley, and complimentary Continental breakfast.

✗ **Giuseppe's.** Dini's Lucky Club. 45 N. Main St.; 775-463-2868 $$-$$$
This steakhouse puts out an amazing amount of food at reasonable prices: king crab, steaks, raviolis and the like are served with an antipasto plate, soup or salad, potato or spaghetti, vegetable, sourdough bread, and mint or kahlua parfait.

# TRAVELERS INFORMATION

## WEATHER IN NEVADA TOWNS

| WEATHER STATION | AVG. TEMPERATURES (°F) | | | | RECORDS | | PRECIPITATION (IN) | | | | ANNUAL | |
|---|---|---|---|---|---|---|---|---|---|---|---|---|
| | JAN | APR | JUL | OCT | H | L | JAN | APR | JUL | OCT | R | S |
| Austin | 41/17 | 63/30 | 90/52 | 68/31 | 105 | -25 | 0.8 | 0.7 | 0.2 | 0.4 | 6 | 33 |
| Elko | 37/13 | 59/29 | 90/50 | 66/29 | 108 | -43 | 1.1 | 0.8 | 0.3 | 0.6 | 9 | 38 |
| Ely | 39/9 | 58/26 | 86/48 | 64/28 | 100 | -30 | 0.7 | 0.9 | 0.7 | 0.7 | 9 | 51 |
| Lake Tahoe | 37/17 | 50/26 | 79/43 | 58/31 | 94 | -15 | 6.1 | 2.2 | 0.3 | 0.4 | 31 | 213 |
| Las Vegas | 56/33 | 79/50 | 105/76 | 80/55 | 118 | 8 | 0.5 | 0.2 | 0.4 | 0.2 | 4 | 1 |
| Laughlin | 60/38 | 80/55 | 107/76 | 80/56 | 124 | 12 | 0.9 | 0.5 | 0.9 | 0.5 | 7 | 0 |
| Reno | 45/20 | 63/30 | 91/48 | 70/31 | 106 | -19 | 1.0 | 0.5 | 0.3 | 0.4 | 7 | 25 |
| Tonopah | 43/18 | 66/33 | 92/53 | 70/30 | 98 | -15 | 0.5 | 0.5 | 0.4 | 0.4 | 5 | 17 |
| Winnemucca | 42/17 | 65/29 | 93/51 | 72/30 | 108 | -36 | 1.0 | 0.9 | 0.2 | 0.6 | 8 | 24 |

## METRIC CONVERSIONS

To convert feet (ft) to meters (m), multiply feet by .305. To convert meters to feet, multiply meters by 3.28.

| | |
|---|---|
| 1 ft = .30 m | 1 m = 3.3 ft |
| 2 ft = .61 m | 2 m = 6.6 ft |
| 3 ft = .91 m | 3 m = 9.8 ft |
| 4 ft = 1.2 m | 4 m =13.1 ft |
| 5 ft = 1.5 m | 5 m =16.4 ft |

To convert miles (mi) to kilometers (km), multiply miles by .62. To convert kilometers to miles, multiply kilometers by 1.61.

| | |
|---|---|
| 1 mi = 1.6 km | 1 km =.62 mi |
| 2 mi = 3.2 km | 2 km = 1.2 mi |
| 3 mi = 4.8 km | 3 km =1.9 mi |
| 4 mi = 6.4 km | 4 km =2.5 mi |
| 5 mi = 8.1 km | 5 km =3.1 mi |

To convert pounds (lb) to kilograms (kg), multiply pounds by .46. To convert kilograms to pounds, multiply pounds by 2.2.

| | |
|---|---|
| 1 lb = .45 kg | 1 kg = 2.2 lbs |
| 2 lbs = .91 kg | 2 kg = 4.4 lbs |
| 3 lbs = 1.4 kg | 3 kg = 6.6 lbs |
| 4 lbs = 1.8 kg | 4 kg = 8.8 lbs |

To convert degrees Fahrenheit (°F) to Celsius (°C), subtract 32 from degrees F and multiply by .56. To convert degrees C to degrees F, multiply degrees C by 1.8 and add 32.

| | |
|---|---|
| 0°F = -17.8°C | 60°F = 15.5°C |
| 10°F = -12.2°C | 70°F = 21.1°C |
| 32°F = 0°C | 80°F = 26.7°C |
| 40°F = +4.4°C | 90°F = 32.2°C |
| 50°F = +10.0°C | 98.6°F = 37.0°C |

# I N D E X

PHOTO BY CHRIS BURT

## ■ ABOUT THE AUTHOR

Nevada has been **Deke Castleman's** beat since 1988, when he wrote the first edition of the epic *Nevada Handbook.* He's the author of the Compass guide *Las Vegas,* now in its sixth edition. He's also the senior editor of Huntington Press, the largest mainstream book-publishing company in Nevada, which produces regional and gambling titles.

He has lived in Nevada since 1989, first in east Sparks, then in west Las Vegas, and now in south Reno, with his wife and sons.

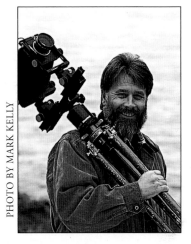

PHOTO BY MARK KELLY

## ■ ABOUT THE PHOTOGRAPHERS

**Jeff Gnass** travels extensively to photograph scenic and wilderness places, and to document the natural history and heritage lands he visits. Since first picking up a large format camera in 1979, his images have illustrated thousands of pages in books, calendars, and magazines throughout the world. The rugged and varied landscape of the American West, especially Nevada, is still his favorite subject. He makes his home in southeastern Alaska.

**Kerrick James,** who photographed the Las Vegas chapter in this book, is based in Mesa, Arizona, and specializes in landscapes of the Southwest and Mexico. He is a frequent contributor to many periodicals, and he is also the photographer for Compass American Guides' *San Francisco, Las Vegas,* and *The American Southwest.*